# Hands-on MuleSoft Anypoint Platform Volume-I

*Designing and Implementing RAML APIs with MuleSoft Anypoint Platform*

**Nanda Nachimuthu**

www.bpbonline.com

**FIRST EDITION 2021**

**REPRINT 2023**



**ISBN: 978-93-89898-231**



## LIMITS OF LIABILITY AND DISCLAIMER OF WARRANTY



## Distributors:

**BPB PUBLICATIONS**
20, Ansari Road, Darya Ganj
New Delhi-110002
Ph: 23254990/23254991

**MICRO MEDIA**
Shop No. 5, Mahendra Chambers,
150 DN Rd. Next to Capital Cinema,
V.T. (C.S.T.) Station, MUMBAI-400 001
Ph: 22078296/22078297

**DECCAN AGENCIES**
4-3-329, Bank Street,
Hyderabad-500195
Ph: 24756967/24756400

**BPB BOOK CENTRE**
376 Old Lajpat Rai Market,
Delhi-110006
Ph: 23861747



Published by Manish Jain for BPB Publications, 20 Ansari Road, Darya Ganj, New Delhi-110002 and Printed by him at Manipal Technologies Limited, Manipal

# Dedicated to

*Rathi Shravanti Shashank*

# About the Author

**Nanda Nachimuthu** is an engineering graduate from the Tamilnadu Agricultural University, Coimbatore, Tamilnadu. He has done an advanced diploma from Indian Institute of Technology, Kharagpur in the field of Java and Internet Computing. He has also completed an advanced diploma from Indian Institute of International Trading, Delhi which specializes in Strategies for International Business.

His 25 years of experience comes from various domains like banking, healthcare, government, and airlines. He is into technologies like Java, Big Data, Cloud, ESB, Security and IoT. He played various roles of a technical architect, solutions architect, cloud architect, and enterprise integration architect and always wanted to be in an individual contributor role with hands-on coding experience.

He is passionate about social entrepreneurship and pro bono consultations in multiple fields like information technology, manufacturing, trading, agriculture and Internet of Things.

He is the founder of some social platforms, and he owns few trademarks under his kitty.

Presently, he is focusing on integration technology platforms like MuleSoft, as he thinks that there is a lot of scope in future for digital marketing and machine-to-machine communication.

# Acknowledgement

Even though I came from a rich technical background and was with MuleSoft since its inception, when the API-led connectivity paradigm shift started, it was difficult for me to cope up with the mission and vision of the entire platform architecture. I too have struggled to understand the futuristic implementation approaches of the MuleSoft team.

Then, I started taking a deep dive into the entire MuleSoft ecosystem to find out some of the key technical aspects of MuleSoft. I realized that the MuleSoft integration platform would become the most sought after integration approach after thoroughly studying the Centre for Enablement, machine-to-machine communication, IoT implementation, and so on for 2-3 years.

When I started following the MuleSoft updates provided in the form of Meetups or LinkedIn tutorials, I felt that there must be a book available for the audiences who were not aware of the enterprise integration practices. Still, they can become API designers or business analysts provided they have some basic rudimentary knowledge.

Before I begin with the Mastering MuleSoft Series, I would like to thank the active MuleSoft community, be it Meetups, blogs, LinkedIn materials, independent tutorial providers, and many other MuleSoft activists.

Without their contributions and web presence, it was very difficult for me to design and write this Mastering MuleSoft series.

Thanks again, Muleys!

# Preface

In my view, it is not so easy for an upcoming technical or business candidate to get a chance to work with advanced system integration scenarios. Imagine a financial integration scenario where the information like the sales invoice is flowing across the SaaS systems like SAP and Financial Force. It is difficult or practically not possible for many freshers to get a chance to get a chance to work on these applications. Especially, when most of the cloud-based SaaS applications are securely deployed, licensed, and community-based.

So, system integration and enterprise architecture are still new to many fresh and averagely experienced candidates.

The exposure to many of these SaaS applications and understanding their API models will play an important role in future if you want to get into roles like API designers and API developers.

It is important to get to know the concepts like web services before trying to read about the APIs exposed by SaaS systems. We need to have a strong understanding of web services like REST and SOAP because we will be defining the specifications for web services in the future as an API designer. Moreover, the API specifications developed by our team will be for handshaking with SaaS applications, legacy applications, mobile devices, machine-to-machine communication, etc.

So, the audiences of this book need to understand that they will become an integral part of a larger enterprise architecture instead of working on a particular project, product, or service layer.

*Over the nine chapters in this book, you will learn the following:*

**Chapter 1** introduces, MuleSoft ecosystem, resources, solutions, products, and blogs. It also talks about ESB and API-led connectivity.

**Chapter 2** demonstrates the MuleSoft Anypoint Platform features. It explains the RAML basics and talks about basic RAML API creation and execution.

**Chapter 3** covers how to design and develop the basic RAML API using Design Center. It also explains how to import the same into Anypoint Studio, build the project using the Anypoint Studio APIKit, and execute the RAML API endpoints in the local system.

**Chapter 4** talks about the various types of endpoints in RAML API, and designs and executes the same.

**Chapter 5** discusses MuleSoft Exchange, MuleSoft connectors, and how to download examples provided by MuleSoft Exchange into the local file system. It also discusses how to open the examples in Anypoint Studio and how to explore the provided examples.

**Chapter 6** talks about exploring dummy RESTful services available over the Internet, how to understand them, how to reuse their input and output data in our RAML design. It also talks about the PostMan installation and invoking RESTful and SOAP web services.

**Chapter 7** gives you a complete idea about how to develop a RESTful API using RAML specification for various operations like create, retrieve, update, and delete of a business entity.

**Chapter 8** focuses on the internals of RAML specification like exploring RAML examples, understanding QueryParams, data types, nested data types, traits, and resource types.

**Chapter 9** focuses on how to design, develop, test and document a BOOKAPI RESTful web service step by step with reusable working code by explaining you the topics like public fake APIs, commercial APIs, reusing examples from the Internet, etc.

# Downloading the code bundle and coloured images:

Please follow the link to download the
*Code Bundle* and the *Coloured Images* of the book:

## https://rebrand.ly/ebtndb0

## Errata

We take immense pride in our work at BPB Publications and follow best practices to ensure the accuracy of our content to provide with an indulging reading experience to our subscribers. Our readers are our mirrors, and we use their inputs to reflect and improve upon human errors if any, occurred during the publishing processes involved. To let us maintain the quality and help us reach out to any readers who might be having difficulties due to any unforeseen errors, please write to us at :

**errata@bpbonline.com**

Your support, suggestions and feedbacks are highly appreciated by the BPB Publications' Family.

## BPB is searching for authors like you

If you're interested in becoming an author for BPB, please visit **www.bpbonline.com** and apply today. We have worked with thousands of developers and tech professionals, just like you, to help them share their insight with the global tech community. You can make a general application, apply for a specific hot topic that we are recruiting an author for, or submit your own idea.

The code bundle for the book is also hosted on GitHub at **https://github.com/bpbpublications/Hands-on-MuleSoft-Anypoint-Platform---Volume-I**. In case there's an update to the code, it will be updated on the existing GitHub repository.

We also have other code bundles from our rich catalog of books and videos available at **https://github.com/bpbpublications**. Check them out!

## PIRACY

If you come across any illegal copies of our works in any form on the internet, we would be grateful if you would provide us with the location address or website name. Please contact us at :

**business@bpbonline.com** with a link to the material.

## If you are interested in becoming an author

If there is a topic that you have expertise in, and you are interested in either writing or contributing to a book, please visit **www.bpbonline.com**.

## REVIEWS

Please leave a review. Once you have read and used this book, why not leave a review on the site that you purchased it from? Potential readers can then see and use your unbiased opinion to make purchase decisions, we at BPB can understand what you think about our products, and our authors can see your feedback on their book. Thank you!

For more information about BPB, please visit **www.bpbonline.com.**

# Table of Contents

# CHAPTER 1
# MuleSoft Fundamentals

In this chapter we will discuss the following topics:

- What is MuleSoft?
  - History of MuleSoft
  - MuleSoft as open-source ESB
  - MuleSoft as API Led Connectivity
- Explore MuleSoft Website and Materials

## Objectives

After studying this unit, you should be able to:

- Have a clear vision about MuleSoft ecosystem
- Access various MuleSoft materials
- Interact with MuleSoft community

## About target audience

The target audience of the book series may be ranging from fresher, non-IT members, the business community, technology aspirants, and

C-Suite members. This book will talk about MuleSoft technology in-depth, how to design and implement larger enterprise integration where the enterprise will have 1000 plus branches across global and the enterprise may not have modern architecture like API Led Connectivity and connectivity to niche applications like Salesforce, FinancialForce, Workday, Coupa, etc.

# About the book design

This book is designed to address the upcoming common Information Technology audience who wish to become an integral part of a niche technology that will be playing a predominant position in the coming 20 years of Information technology history.

We planned to release 10 + volumes of books which will cover most of the MuleSoft technology features from basics to advanced concepts. The first 8 volumes will cover topics as given below:

- **volume 1:** Mastering MuleSoft – RAML, API Design
- **volume 2:** Mastering MuleSoft - Anypoint Studio - Components and Flows
- **volume 3:** Mastering MuleSoft – Core Connectors like DB, FILE, JMS, ObjectStore, etc.
- **volume 4:** Mastering MuleSoft – SaaS Connectors like Box, Slack, Stripe, etc
- **volume 5:** Mastering MuleSoft – Data Weave Language and Transformations
- **volume 6:** Mastering MuleSoft – DevOps for MuleSoft (Maven, Jenkins, Docker, Kubernetes, etc)
- **volume 7:** Mastering MuleSoft – WorkDay Integrations
- **volume 8:** Mastering MuleSoft – Internet of Things

We are not sure about the forthcoming volumes other than the titles listed above but may cover topics like Integrating with SAP, Collibra, Concur, Salesforce, ServiceNow, Coupa, FinancialForce, RPA, etc. in future.

# Before starting

It is nice to know a few aspects of software evolution in the past 20 years; this is a must to know facts especially for the fresher and non-

IT audience. Java started as a strongly typed internet programming language before 2000 and so many programming paradigms got added like Applets, JDBC, JSP, Beans, RMI, Corba, EJB, Struts, Spring, Web Services, SOA, ESB, etc. in the next 20 years.

It is strongly recommended for you to explore concepts like System Integration, Cloud Computing, DevOps, BigData, Docker, Kubernetes, SaaS, IaaS, PaaS, Puppet, Robotics, Internet of Things, etc. Also, try to understand the scenarios for Enterprise Service Bus space; anyways we will be explaining these concepts throughout this series.

Another important nice to have knowledge is about corporate companies, which means, you must explore case studies about larger enterprises like McDonalds, Mckesson who will have a global presence and they will be using advanced software suites like SAP and Salesforce for different business domains. This is important for you to understand how data will be exchanged between different systems in different formats and protocols.

Even if you are coming under, functional, non-IT, or non-development team, you will be able to design and manage multiple **Application Programming Interfaces (API)** without bothering much about how the APIs will be developed and implemented.

# MuleSoft-background

As we mentioned earlier when concepts like SOA and System Integrations evolved, we got another interesting area called **Enterprise Service Bus (ESB).** ESB is architecture to integrate different systems using a centralized messaging system, meaning; different systems can post and receive data through a central message bus. The data may come in a different format, maybe a text file, CSV, Email, XML, or the data may be in a corporate format like SWIFT, IATA, HIPPA, etc. Also, the protocols may vary like SMTP, FTP, SFTP, etc.

The ESB developers will be receiving these data from the source systems messaging queue and they will do transformations and will give it back to the destination systems. MuleSoft started as an open-source ESB server and later enhanced its capabilities to address the API Led connectivity architecture. Let us start exploring the latest MuleSoft technology, API Led model, API Management, API design, and other concepts throughout this book.

# ESB (Enterprise Service Bus)

For an enterprise, the enterprise service bus act as a central spine where different systems in different departments can exchange data. Those systems may be developed by different software companies across the globe using different technologies like Java, .NET, or PHP. These systems will be having different databases like Oracle, MySQL, etc. Now, if a sales team wants to send the opportunities or the deals won by the sales team to a finance team where billing and invoicing will be handled by them. These two systems that are customer relationship application and billing and invoicing application may have different databases application and different ways of sharing data for example customer relationship application may share the data in CSV file as CSV file, billing, and invoicing application may share the data as an XML file. Different ways of sharing data, for example, customer relationships. These two systems may share the data through different protocols, that means the sales application will share the CSV file through e-mail protocol, whereas the finance application may prefer to use secured file transfer protocol, meaning the finance application wants to store the XML files in a secured file folder so that the authorized other departments' applications can access that. If an enterprise having multiple departments then has multiple applications and those applications need to exchange data for various workflows then those enterprises should implement an ESB platform and that enterprise service bus platform is the MuleSoft ESB platform.

MuleSoft ESB platform has been developed as an open-source project by Mike Ross on say December 2006. MuleSoft ESB developers can developer MuleSoft flow components for various data transactions between applications of different departments that means the MuleSoft flow will be having the access privileges to get the files from a secured file system or an email or through some web services like RESTful and SOAP, or by accessing particular Message queues. Now we can understand MuleSoft has been designed to access various protocols like email, SFTP, database, etc. The ESB developers are responsible for data transformation also data transmission means read the sales information from sales application via email as CSV format and convert those data into XML format and save these XML files inside the secured file system of the finance publications. Also, data transformation will be used for extracting the information need by the finance system, meaning the sales application may expose 50 fields to the MuleSoft flow component but the finance application requires only 35 fields. So MuleSoft developers have to understand the finance application and they have to develop XML file content based on the CSV file contents.

The next complex scenario will be the ESB developers will be interacting with multiple source systems they may have to merge all system data and they may have to distribute the merged file to multiple destination systems. As I already mentioned please explore different industry-standard data formats like data, swift, hippa, peci, picof which are used for various business domains.

In a nutshell, the enterprise service bus MuleSoft flow will be responsible for accessing multiple protocols, getting data I different formats, transforming the data like merging, filtering then routing the data to a destination system so this data transaction can happen when we are adding a record in the database or when a messaging queue receives a new message or when an email inbox receives a new message or a scheduled job can invoke the mule flow on a particular time everyday or a scheduled batch update can happen between a source and a destination system.

# API LED connectivity

There is a phenomenal transformation for MuleSoft in recent days which are called API LED connectivity. In the last paragraph, you would have understood that the enterprise service bus will be talking to various applications based on their preferred protocol data format.

After the introduction of service-oriented architecture, all these applications started exposing their data through web services that are restful and soap so that every application can maintain a web service catalog, meaning a finance application can expose their finance data by creating a restful web service so that the MuleSoft developer no need to directly accessing the source systems file folder, database, etc. Instead, they can talk to the API's if the source systems and destination systems. It doesn't mean the developers shouldn't access the endpoints of the source and destination systems like database, secured folders, etc. so the current scenario of API led connectivity will be a combination of botbbsystem API and other endpoints like DB, secured file folders, message queues, etc. in the future it is expected that 80 to 90 percent of pure API led connectivity architecture implementation can be achieved this is possible only if the source and destination systems API's have been completed utilized my MuleSoft developers. To add more fuel to this topic if h revisit the MuleSoft.com u can understand this API led connectivity architecture is very appropriate for the upcoming advanced technologies like the **Internet of Things (IoT),** robotic process automation, machine learning, artificial intelligence, etc. Also, API led connectivity architecture is a combination of microservices architecture, cloud architecture, and domain-driven architecture, so that the API design, the API development, the API management, the API deployment, designing the API as a domain asset are possible and can be handled by various teams.

# Achieving API Led connectivity

Let us see the *tentative process* to be in place to achieve MuleSoft API led connectivity:

- An enterprise architect or the C-Suite members must understand the concept of having a center for the enablement team.
- Center for enablement team is responsible for understanding the enterprise-wide API application between various applications, devices censors' robots, drones, GPS trackers, machine learning tools, artificial intelligence tools, reporting tools, forecasting tools, management dashboards, etc.
- Any devices like Biomedical instruments, agricultural machinery, logistics devices, airline devices, security devices, and any devices used in any industry can have a MuleSoft API flow running in it.
- So that the center for the enablement team is responsible for structuring the entire MuleSoft force for an enterprise they must identify who is responsible for API design and how they are going to maintain it.
- After the API design team designed an API it is supposed to be shared to the API development team and API testing team also, so eventually the API design specification will be having information like how to request an API what input must be given to an API and what response an API will be giving back in what format and the API will be having a sample response data also.

- Other than this the API design specification will contain details like what is the error message, response code, etc.
- The developers cannot modify the API design specifications for example the API design team is developing an API design without an option to insert, update and delete the data meaning that particular API design is having only one option just to retrieve the data from the source system.
- Now if the API development team want to add one additional feature to delete some records also this particular modifications will not affect the central API server after development is completed the enterprise may have a deployment platform which will be controlled by develops team and the deployments of the MuleSoft flow into the cloud or on prim MuleSoft servers. Once t deployment is done, the MuleSoft flow API went live, the center for enablement team can ask the API management team to monitor the live API's performance, traffic, security, etc.
- Finally, the API design team will be using RAML, API design center, and exchange to achieve their API designing and exchanging. The development team will be using the exchange and API tool kit to retrieve the RAML specification from the design center. The deployment team will be using ten enterprises develops platforms. The API management team will be using the API manager which will have all the controls to monitor track and taking reports of a live API.

# MuleSoft resources – MuleSoft.com

We need to understand the available resources and how to access those before taking a deep dive into the MuleSoft fraternity. The first step is to understand the MuleSoft website and the contents available there. Please do visit MuleSoft.com and get to know the following details:

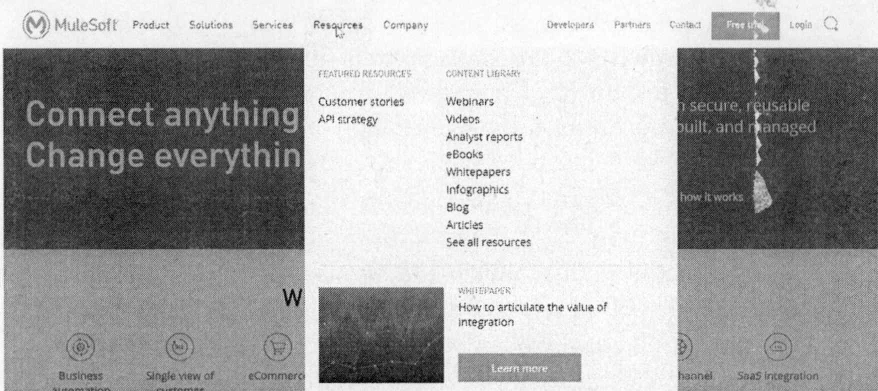


*Figure 1.1: MuleSoft resources*

The resources section will make you access various customer stories and case studies. Get to know the leaders who have a global presence and niche software suites like SAP, Concur, Salesforce for their business needs, and how MuleSoft makes it possible to integrate these software suites so that the data transfer and transformation is seamless across the globe and systems. You can also access the blogs, webinars, and whitepapers to get more details about MuleSoft capabilities, future road maps, etc.:

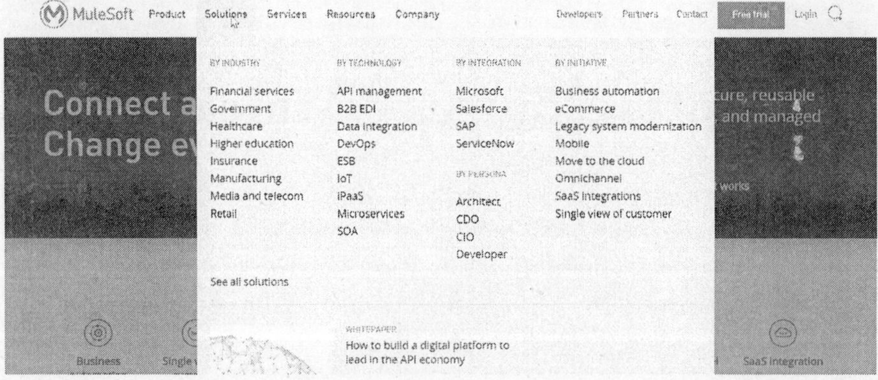


*Figure 1.2: MuleSoft solutions*

Visit the solutions section and you can understand the vast coverage of business domains MuleSoft is working on. You will have good insight into the industry, technology, integration techniques, various roles of MuleSoft technocrats in an organization, and the initiatives of

MuleSoft futuristically in the areas like legacy system modernization. For example, you can explore the initiative called legacy system modernization to understand what is meant by *legacy system modernization*, is it a mainframe system migration, then what is the alternate for mainframes, so that what is the business opportunities we are expecting, then which technology we may have to focus and so on:

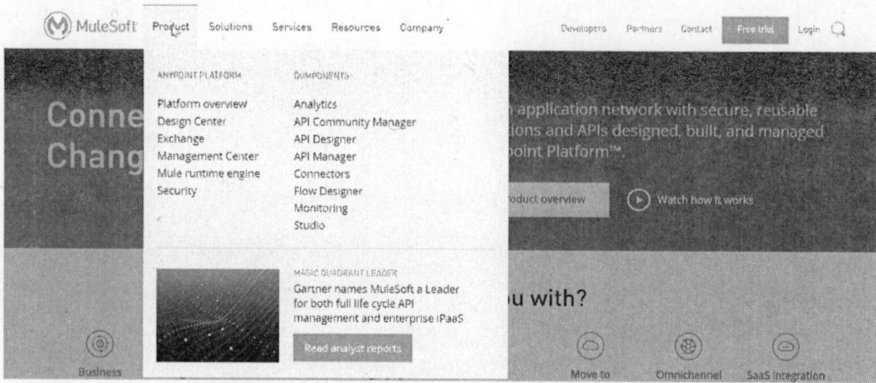


*Figure 1.3: MuleSoft product*

The product section will provide you the details of various products MuleSoft providing to us like API designer, API manager, flow designer, studio, etc. It is important for you to understand, invariably if you are technical or functional, about all the products offering from MuleSoft, so that when you start working with a MuleSoft team, you can have a clear picture about inside the team, who plays what role and what product they will be using:

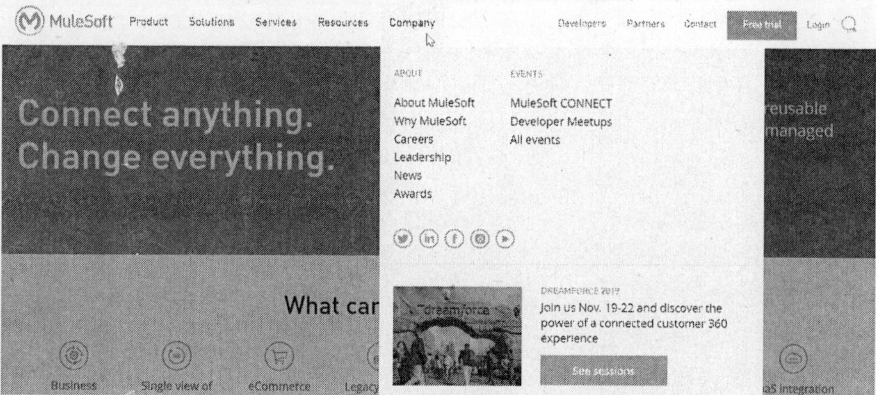


*Figure 1.4: MuleSoft about company*

From the about company page you can get to know the foundation details of the company, what is MuleSoft, why MuleSoft, etc. Apart from what kind of Developer MeetUps happening, what topics were discussed, what's the significance of MuleSoft connect, etc.:

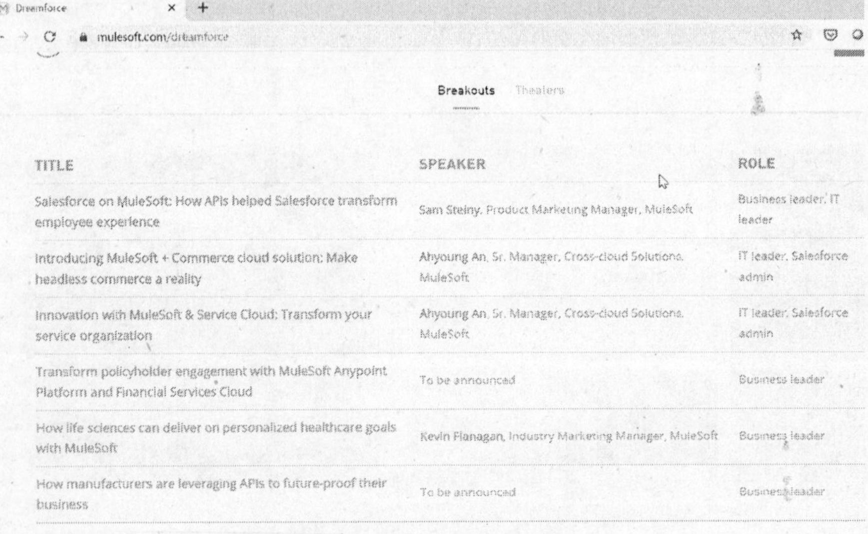


| TITLE | SPEAKER | ROLE |
|---|---|---|
| Salesforce on MuleSoft: How APIs helped Salesforce transform employee experience | Sam Steiny, Product Marketing Manager, MuleSoft | Business leader, IT leader |
| Introducing MuleSoft + Commerce cloud solution: Make headless commerce a reality | Ahyoung An, Sr. Manager, Cross-cloud Solutions, MuleSoft | IT leader, Salesforce admin |
| Innovation with MuleSoft & Service Cloud: Transform your service organization | Ahyoung An, Sr. Manager, Cross-cloud Solutions, MuleSoft | IT leader, Salesforce admin |
| Transform policyholder engagement with MuleSoft Anypoint Platform and Financial Services Cloud | To be announced | Business leader |
| How life sciences can deliver on personalized healthcare goals with MuleSoft | Kevin Flanagan, Industry Marketing Manager, MuleSoft | Business leader |
| How manufacturers are leveraging APIs to future-proof their business | To be announced | Business leader |

***Figure 1.5:*** *MuleSoft DreamForce*

Visit the MuleSoft DreamForce page to access all the present and future seminars conducted by industry experts. You can get very good insights about what's happening in the industry and this information will not be available anywhere other than DreamForce.

# MuleSoft resources – social media

Let us see some of the MuleSoft resources readily available for you to get some good insights about the MuleSoft technology:

***Figure 1.6:*** *MuleSoft partners*

In LinkedIn, try to follow the MuleSoft partner companies like **APISERO** so that you can understand the contributions from those partners. In the above screenshot I am trying to explain to you that the Marketing Director of APISERO has shared a post which is talking about the key benefits of MuleSoft 4 Caching Mechanism:

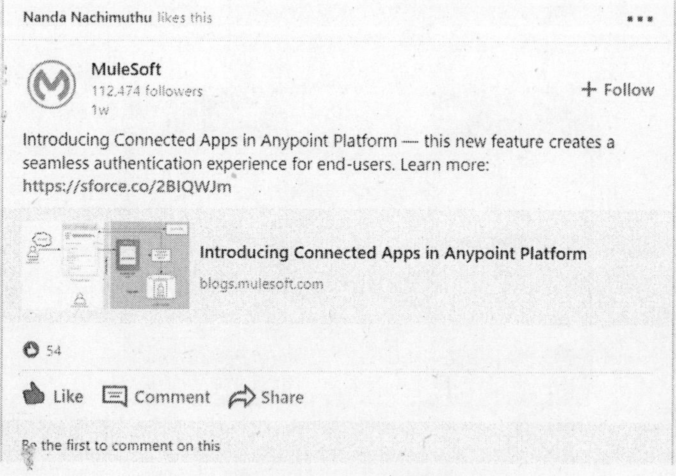


***Figure 1.7:*** *MuleSoft Blog*

Follow the official MuleSoft on LinkedIn to get updates about the articles posted at **blogs.MuleSoft.com**. There is a huge MuleSoft community to post so many articles about various MuleSoft techniques:

***Figure 1.8:** MuleSoft handy guides*

The Partner sites will be updating the latest guides and the links to access them; you can follow these partner sites to get these updates:

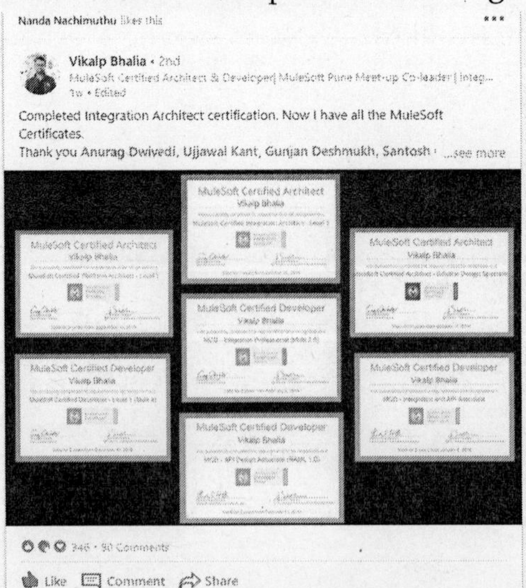


***Figure 1.9:** MuleSoft Certifications First Look*

Get to know the MuleSoft Champions, their activities like MeetUps, conference speaking, etc. You can understand what kind of certifications they have done and interact with them to get more insights into these niche topics:

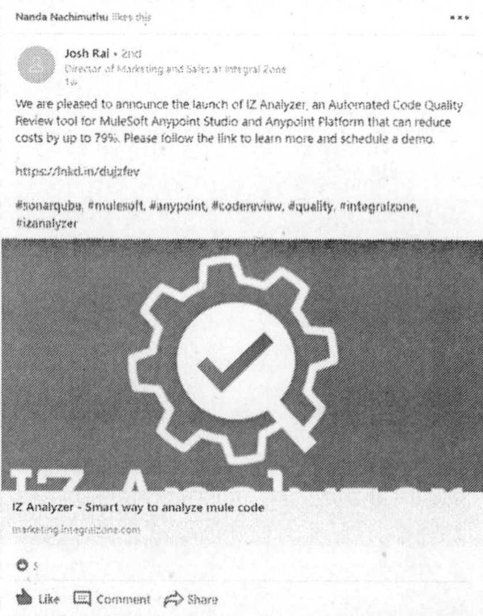


***Figure 1.10:** MuleSoft Plugins – Tools*

You will get a chance to get updates on what kind of third-party tools and plugins available for MuleSoft and which company is developing that, how to get a demo on those tools and plugins. As we already insisted you may from the technical or functional team, but it is important to update yourself about the latest additions to MuleSoft ecosystem:

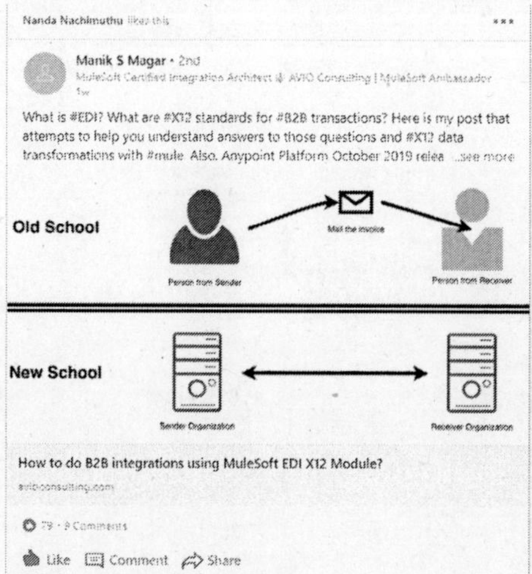


***Figure 1.11:** MuleSoft consultants resources*

From the above screenshot, you can understand how the third party independent consultants are creating a technical article and sharing in social media. You can instantly get to know the keywords like EDI, X12, B2B, etc. from the above article; you can directly interact with them to understand this kind of technical article:

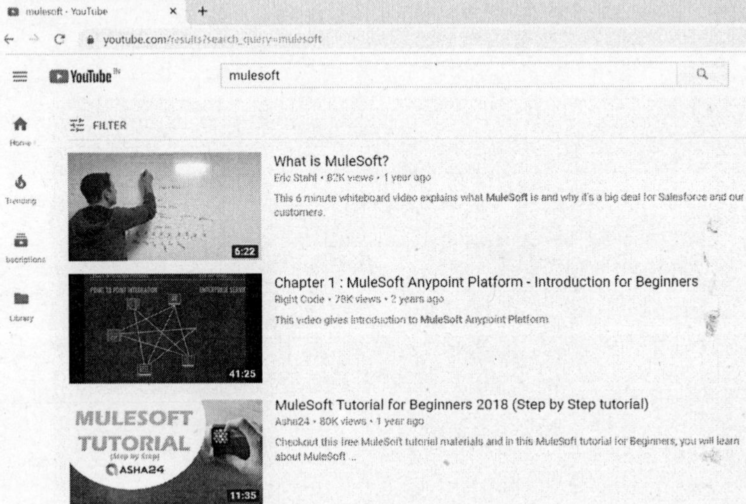


*Figure 1.12: MuleSoft YouTube*

Needless to mention, the above screenshot is self-explanatory:

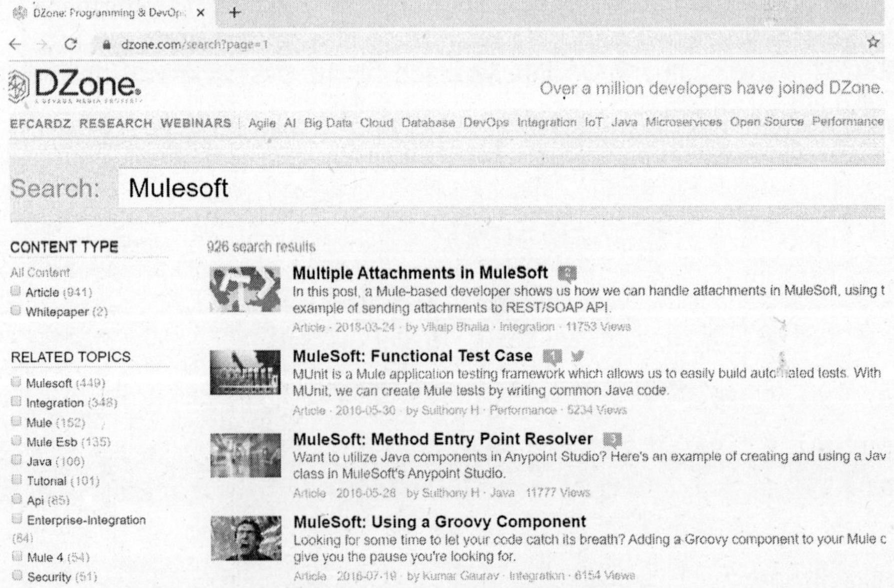


*Figure 1.13: MuleSoft DZone*

I appreciate this site DZone which is having unlimited MuleSoft tutorials.

# DIY

Try to find and watch various webinars available in the internet:

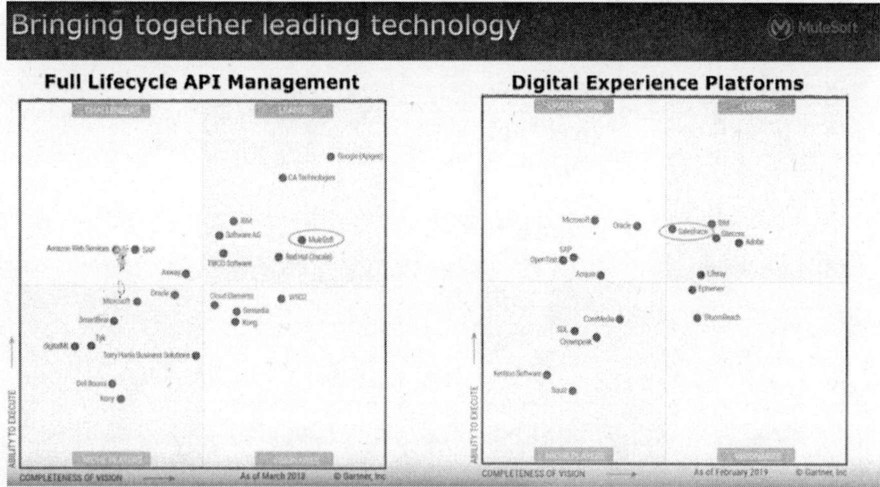


*Figure 1.14: Gartner Reports*

Access this link **https://www.MuleSoft.com/ty/webinar/developer-portal-community-manager** and start watching this webinar.

# Conclusion

In this chapter, we get to know the key concepts of MuleSoft like how it started the background and the resources available to make you take a deep dive. We covered the concepts like ESB and system integrations as well. The next chapter will explain to you the internals of MuleSoft like how it has been designed to address various technical segments and audiences. Cheers.

# Points to remember

- Start exploring the available resources, don't restrict yourself.
- You may be from any background, say technical or functional, please keep in mind that MuleSoft is designed for any

category of the audience and it became easy to understand the concepts like API designing and Managing APIs.

# Key terms to explore

- **ESB:** Enterprise Service Bus
- **API:** Application Processing Interface
- **SOA:** Service-oriented architecture
- RESTful web services
- SOAP web services and WSDL
- XML, XSD and XSLT
- Legacy System Modernization
- EDI

# CHAPTER 2
# MuleSoft Internals

In this chapter we will discuss the following topics:

- MuleSoft internals
    - MuleSoft building blocks
    - MuleSoft run time
    - MuleSoft Anypoint platform
- Try out the first RAML API

## Objectives

After studying this unit, you should be able to:

- Various components of MuleSoft
- Understand the MuleSoft Anypoint platform
- RAML specification

## MuleSoft building blocks

To understand the different components involved in designing a MuleSoft Flow, you must get into the MuleSoft Anypoint platform by visiting **https://anypoint.mulesoft.com/**

Let us take a tour to look inside the MuleSoft Anypoint platform. Follow these screenshots to get an insight into this:

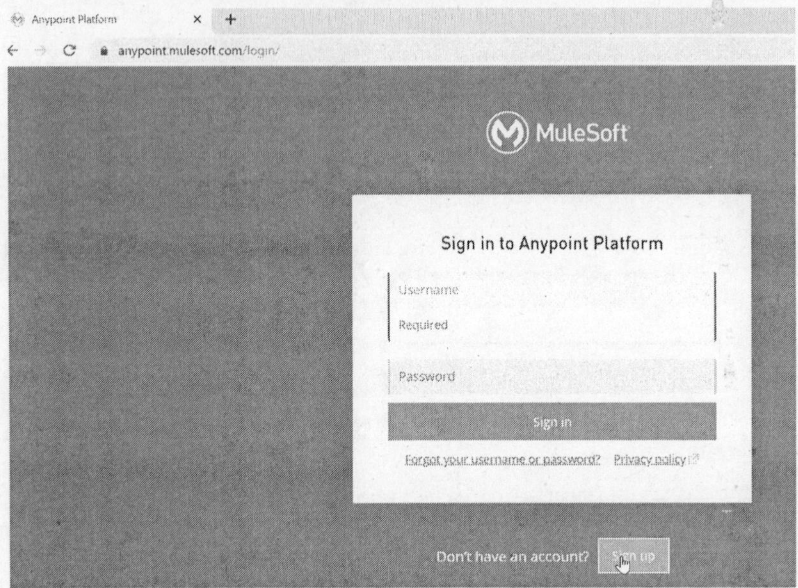


***Figure 2.1:*** *MuleSoft Anypoint Platform Sign In*

Visit **anypoint.mulesoft.com** and sign up for a one-month free trial:

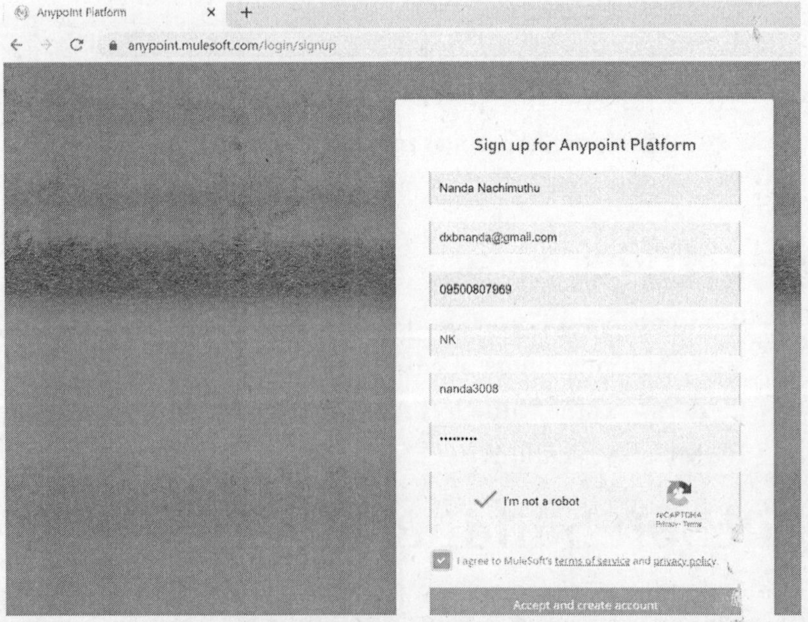


***Figure 2.2:*** *MuleSoft Anypoint Platform Sign Up Form*

Fill the details as shown above and create your Anypoint Account, please make a note that this account is valid for 30 days and make sure you are backing up all your work:

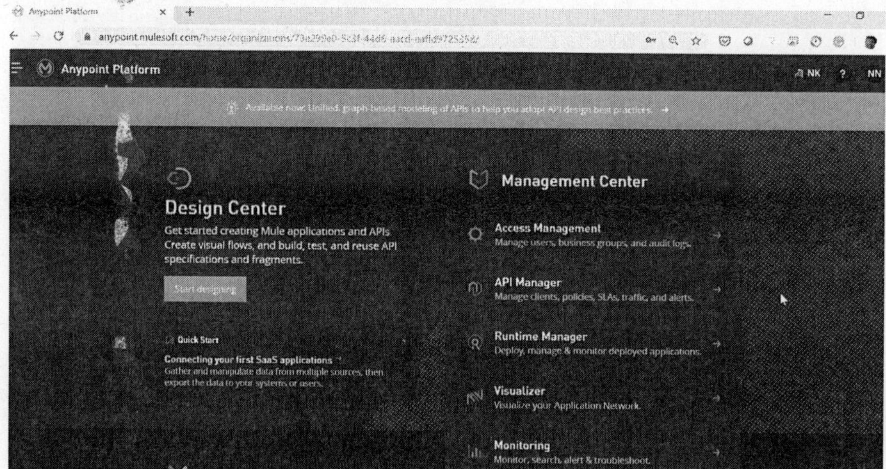


*Figure 2.3: MuleSoft Anypoint platform*

On successful registration, you will be re-directed to the MuleSoft Anypoint platform as shown above. You can see the building blocks of Anypoint platform like Design Center, Management Center, etc. Let us try to design our first RAML API using the design center:

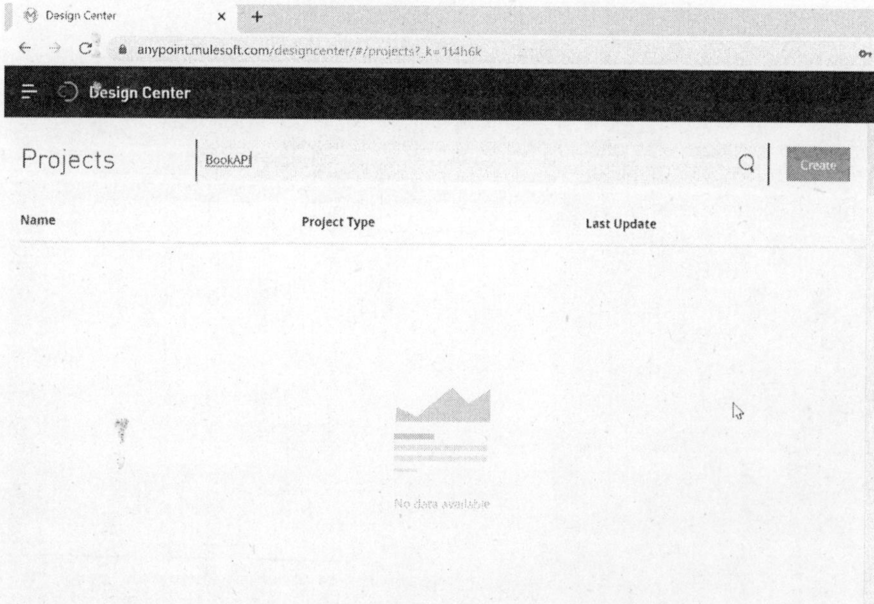


**Figure 2.4:** *MuleSoft Design Center*

Click the start designing button and create a project as shown above:

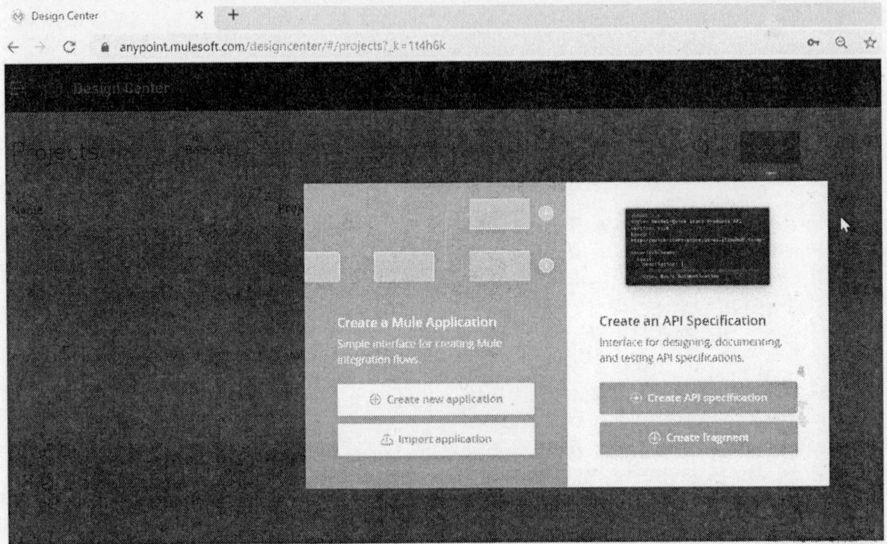


*Figure 2.5: MuleSoft Design Options*

Now you can see the different options like **`Create new application`**, **`Import application`**, **`Create API specification`**, and **`Create fragment`**. We can see these options in detail in our forthcoming chapters. To get an idea about how MuleSoft has been designed to choose the option **`Create API specification`**:

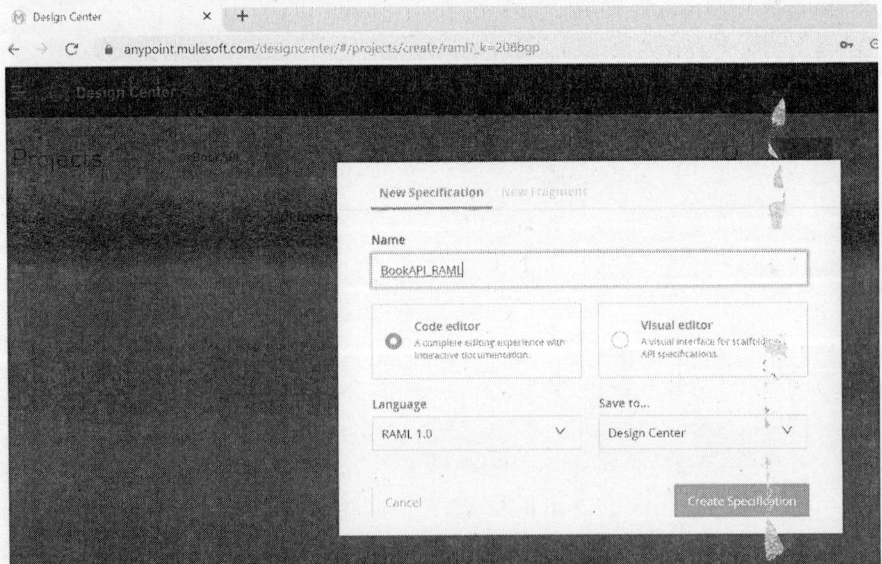


*Figure 2.6: MuleSoft New Specification*

The specification creation dialogue will have options like **`New Specification, New Fragment`**, then how do you wish to create the specification like using **`Code editor`** or using **`Visual editor`**, and you have options to choose in which **`Language`** you would like to create the specification:

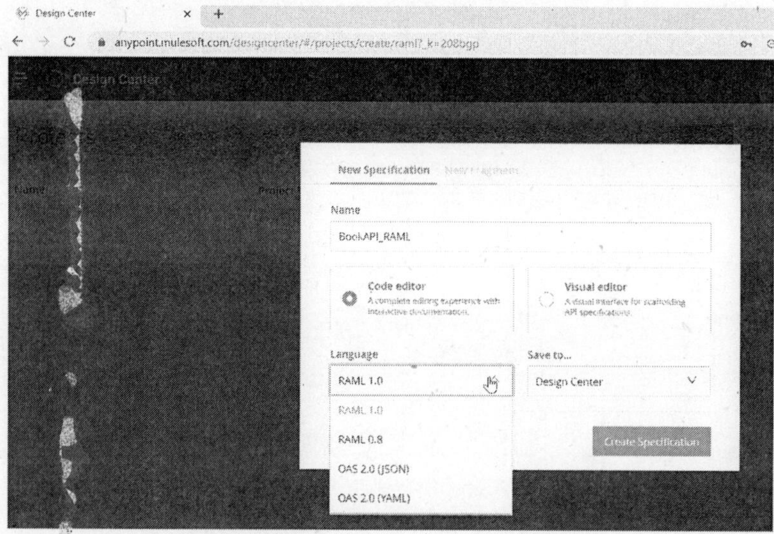


***Figure 2.7:** MuleSoft RAML and OAS*

Choose the first option RAML 1.0 and you may have only one option in the save to drop down so, click the **`Create specification`** button. Let's see the type of languages like RAML and OAS and their version details later:

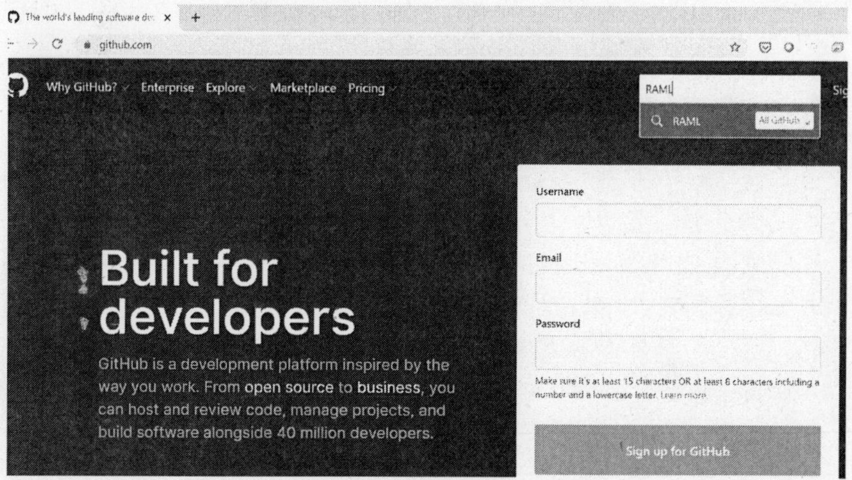


***Figure 2.8:** Search RAML in GitHub*

Before getting into the RAML Specification, try to get available RAML samples from **github.com**. Visit their site and search for RAML as shown above:

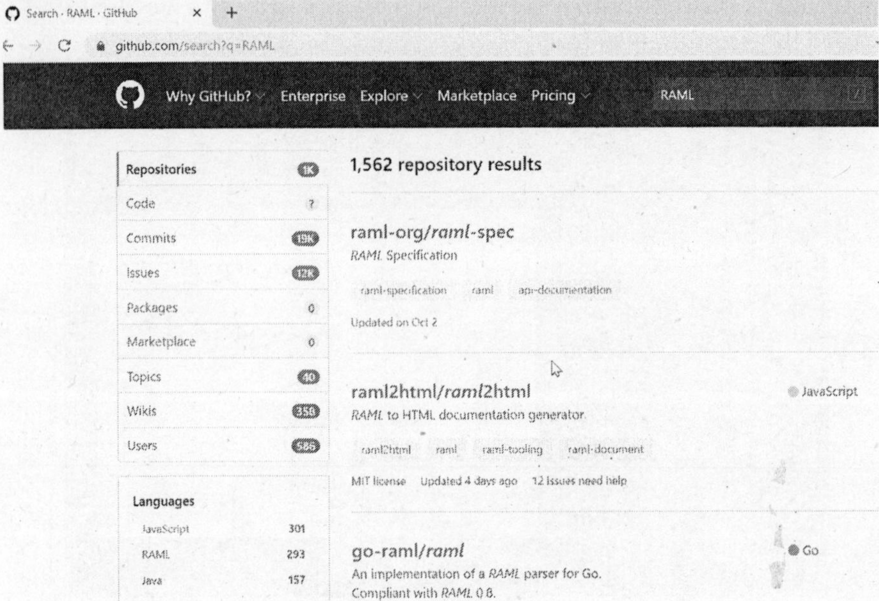


***Figure 2.9:*** *RAML repository*

You can see the various RAML source codes available:

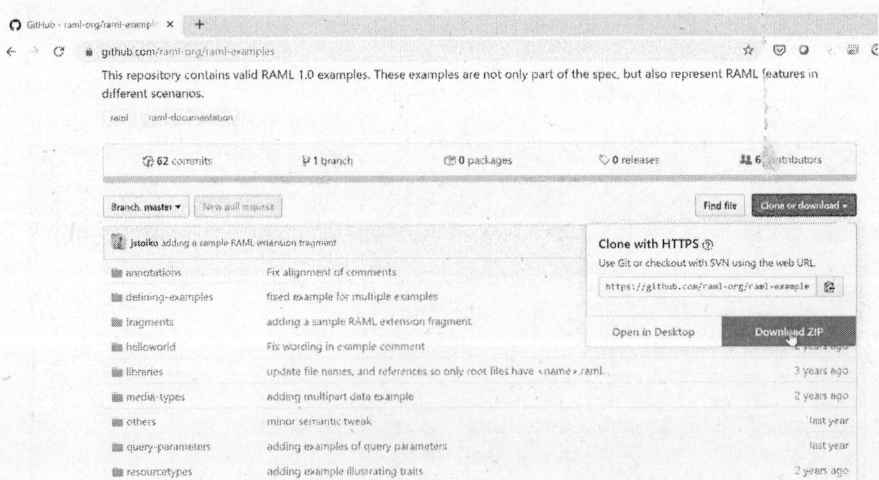


***Figure 2.10:*** *RAML examples from raml.org*

Choose the **http://github.com/raml-org/raml-examples** link and download the `raml-examples-master.zip` file to your local folder and unzip the file. After that go to the `\raml-examples-master.zip\raml-examples-master\helloworld` folder and open the `helloworld.raml` file and copy the contents of the file and paste it in the design center editor as shown below:

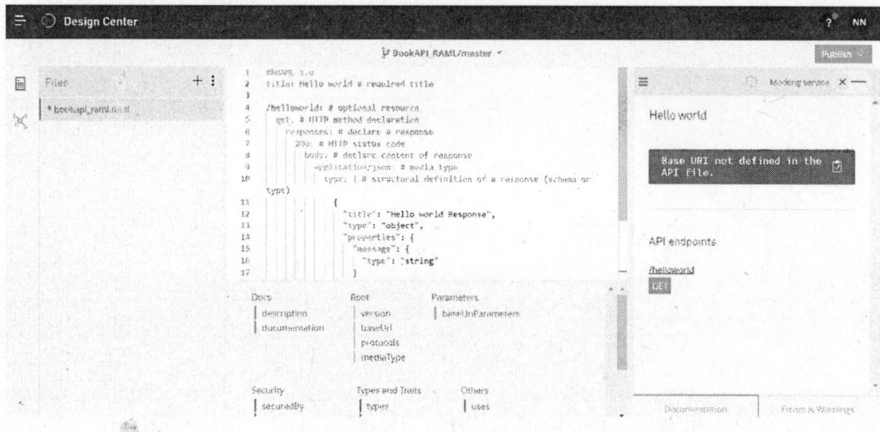

***Figure 2.11:** HelloWorld.raml*

From the above screenshot, you can see the various sections of RAML designers like File dialogue, Editor, Preview Panel, Mocking Service, Documentation, Errors, Warnings, etc. We are not going to take a deep dive into RAML specifications right now. We are trying to understand the internals of MuleSoft. So, click on the **`Mocking Service`** icon to enable it. You can see it got changed to a tick mark as shown below:

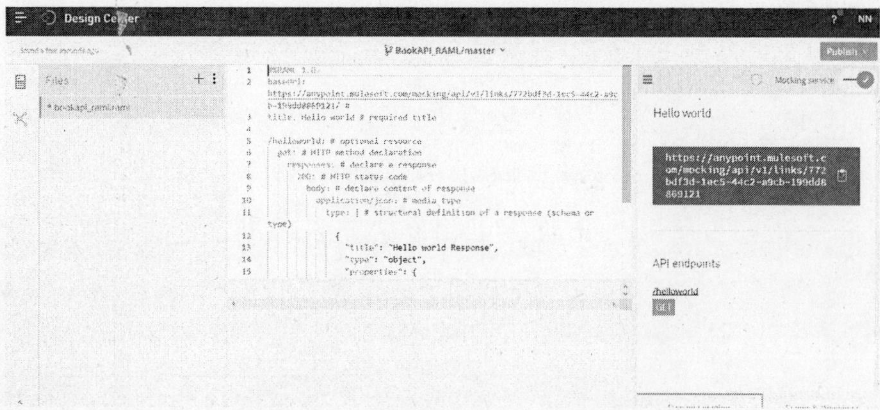

***Figure 2.12:** Mocking Service Invocation*

Now go ahead and click the **GET** button, means you are trying to invoke the get method called `helloworld`:

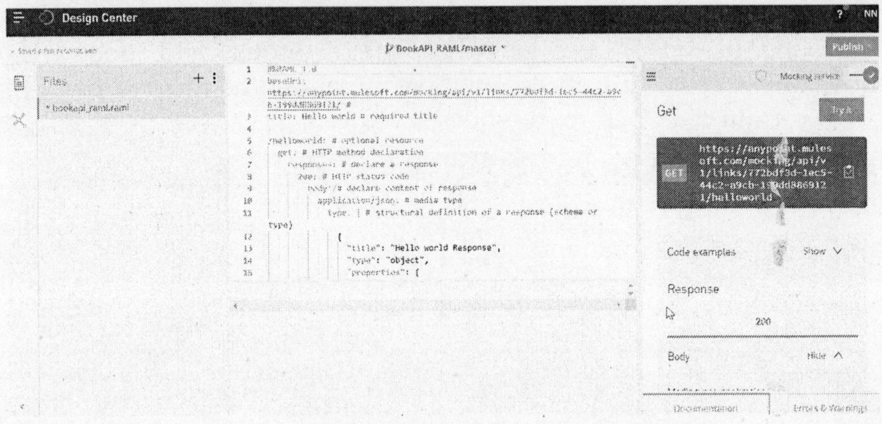


*Figure 2.13: Try invoking the API*

You can see the **https://anypoint.mulesoft.com/mocking/api/v1/links/772bdf3d-1ec5-44c2-a9cb-199dd8869121/helloworld** link enabled and deployed and now you can click the `Try It` button:

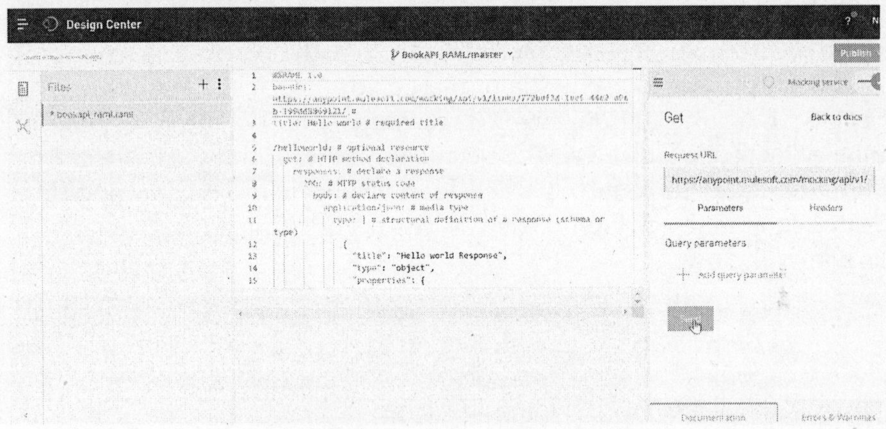


*Figure 2.14: Send the details to API*

You can see different details like **`Parameters`**, **`Headers`**, **`Add query parameter`**, etc. Let's see these topics in detail later, now click the **`Send`** button to get the results from `HelloWorld` API:

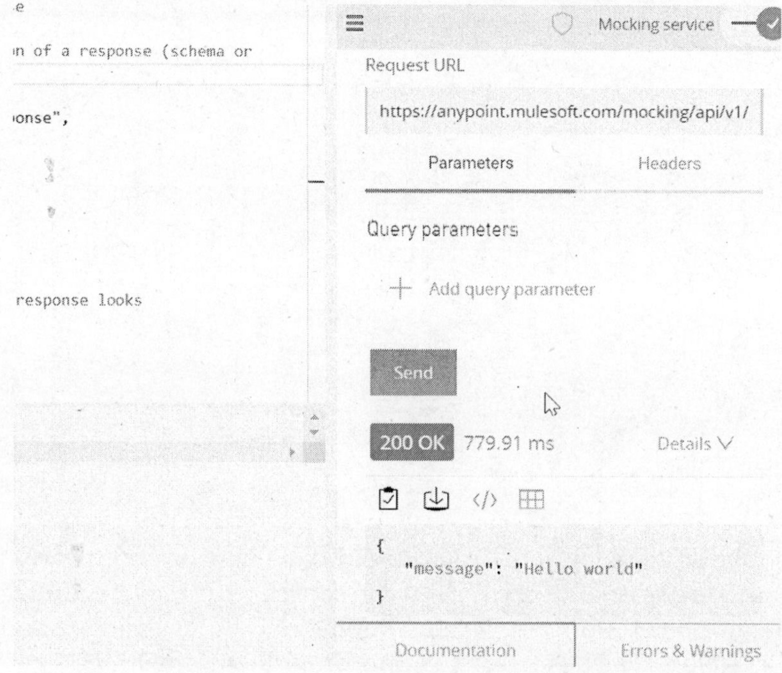


***Figure 2.15:*** *MuleSoft HelloWorld API response*

Congrats, you got your first `HelloWorld` MuleSoft API result with a response code `200` successfully on your screen. Welcome to the MuleSoft world now you become a MULEY:

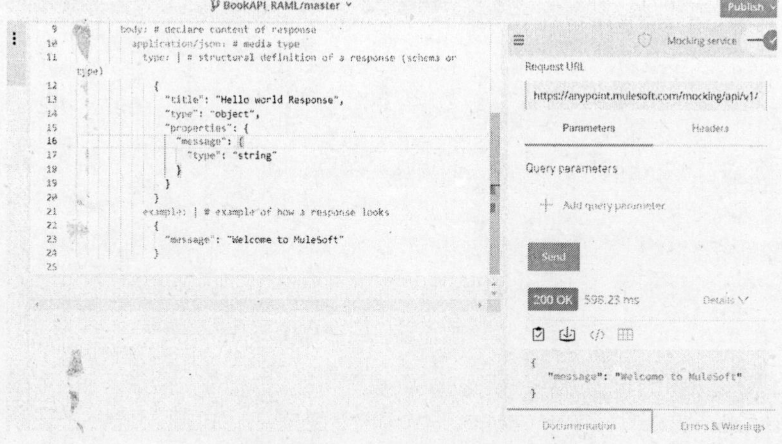


***Figure 2.16:*** *Modified response*

Now try to modify the `Hello World` message in the editor, use *Ctrl + S* to save it, and recall the API to achieve the result given above:

Design Center

BookAPI_RAML/master

kapi_raml.raml

```
      }
      example: | # example of how a response looks
        {
          "message": "Welcome to MuleSoft"
        }


/helloworld: # optional resource
  get: # HTTP method declaration
    responses: # declare a response
      200: # HTTP status code
        body: # declare content of response
          application/json: # media type
            type: | # structural definition of a response (schema or type)
              {
                "title": "Hello world Response",
                "type": "object",
                "properties": {
                  "message": {
                    "type": "string"
                  }
                }
              }
            example: | # example of how a response looks
              {
                "message": "Welcome to MuleSoft"
              }
```

***Figure 2.17:*** *Adding additional API calls*

Try copying the complete `HelloWorld` code and paste it below the original code, as shown above, you can see the warnings since already you have a `helloworld` API call. To remove these warnings, modify the `helloworld` as `helloworld1` and provide different message like the response from `helloworld1`, refer the following screenshot, run these 2 API calls and see different results:

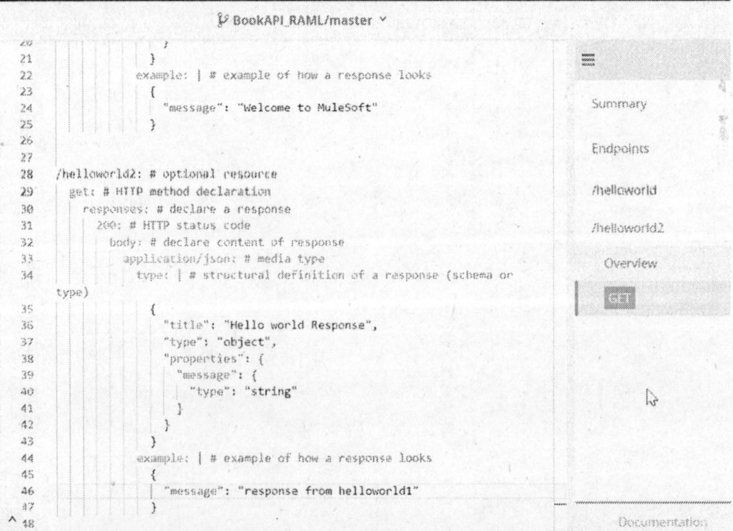


***Figure 2.18:*** *Adding additional API calls and running*

Try to add more endpoints and invoke the same.

# DIY

Try Googling muley `mulesoft` and explore the results:

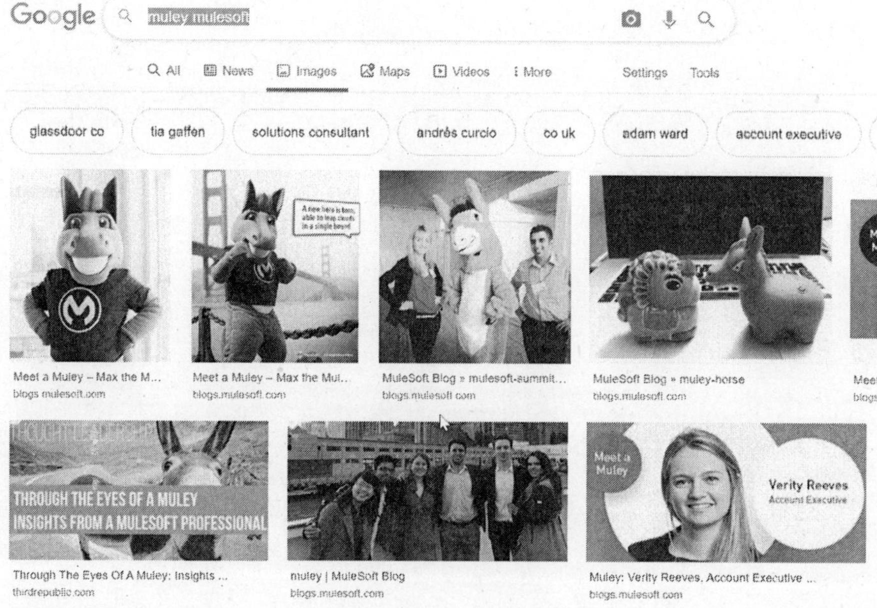


***Figure 2.19:** muley mulesoft*

# Conclusion

In this chapter, we get to know the Internals of MuleSoft like Design Center and RAML basics. In our next chapter, we will have more details about Mule Run Time, Mule Flow, how it is been designed, etc. The next chapter will deal with how to integrate these specifications, API toolkit concepts as well. Cheers.

# Points to remember

- MuleSoft is designed for all categories of IT professionals.
- You may be from any background, say technical or functional, please keep in mind that MuleSoft is designed for any category of the audience and it became easy to understand the concepts like API designing and Managing APIs.

# Key terms to explore

- RAML
- OAS
- Swagger
- HATEOS
- AOP – Aspect-Oriented Programming
- Annotations
- Mock Service

# CHAPTER 3
# MuleSoft Salient Features

## Introduction

It is important to understand the way MuleSoft ecosystem has been designed using various features like Anypoint Exchange and Anypoint Studio before getting in to the API design and implementation.

## Structure

In this chapter we will discuss the following topics:

- MuleSoft salient features
    - Anypoint Studio
    - Integrating to Anypoint Exchange
    - API tool kit
    - API console

# Objectives

After studying this unit, you should be able to understand:

- Why RAML?
- Why API Kit?
- How the MuleSoft API design team and developer team is positioned?

# Pre-requisites

To understand the internals of MuleSoft you no need to have any additional knowledge, even freshers can start to follow the steps in this chapter and they can understand the internals of MuleSoft.

# MuleSoft salient features

To understand the different components involved in designing a MuleSoft Flow, you must get into the MuleSoft Anypoint platform by visiting **https://anypoint.mulesoft.com/**. Register yourself and you can see the download Anypoint Studio Link, by following that you must be able to download the Anypoint Studio as shown below:

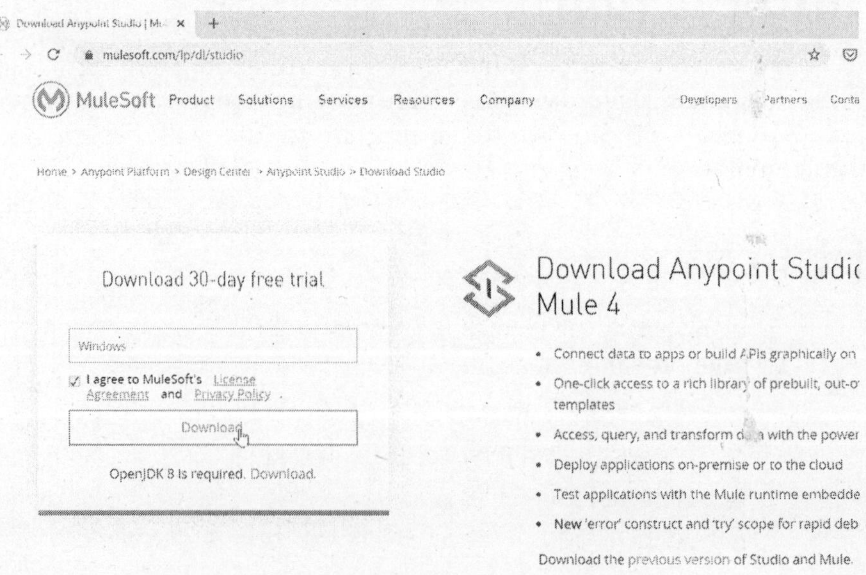


*Figure 3.1: MuleSoft Anypoint Studio Download*

**Note: JDK 8 is mandatory for running Anypoint Studio so please download openJDK8 as well.**

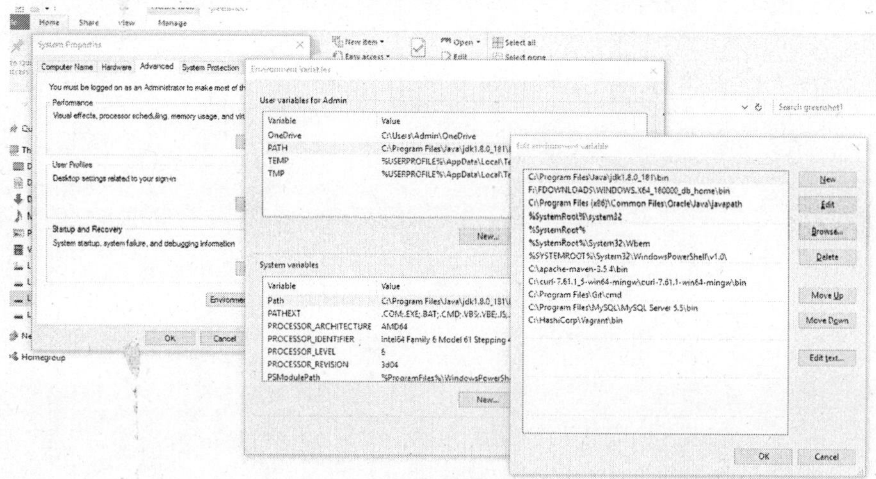


***Figure 3.2:*** *Environment variable set up*

The above screenshot shows the environmental variables setting require to launch the Anypoint Studio after installing JDK, **Yes**, in the path variable values, your JDK installation entry must be the first one:

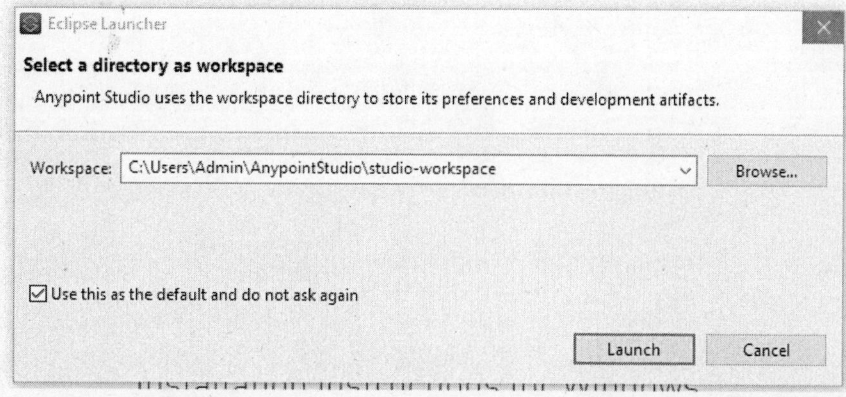


***Figure 3.3:*** *Selecting workspace in Anypoint Studio*

Once the installation completed workspace selection dialogue will appear, choose your local workspace and run Anypoint Studio, go to **`File`** menu click the **`New | Mule Project`** button and you can see a dialog as shown above:

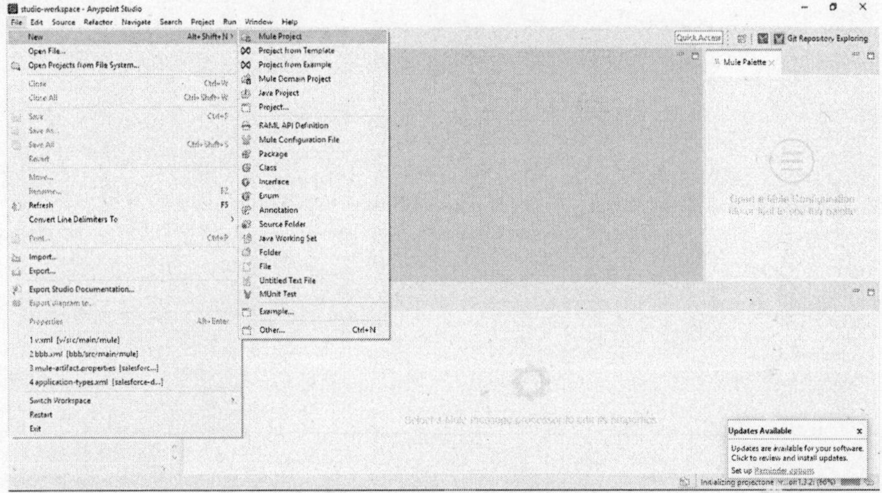


*Figure 3.4: New Mule Project*

Provide your project name, you can see the default runtime version is selected, and then in the API implementation panel select the **`Specify API definition file location or URL`** checkbox. You will be getting the below dialogue when clicking location browsing button as given below:

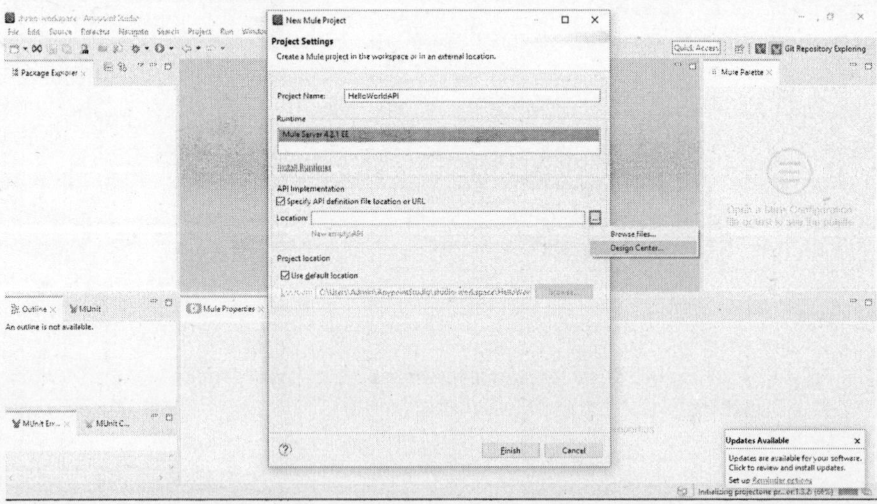


*Figure 3.5: Opening Anypoint Design Center*

In this sign-in dialogue box enter your Anypoint Studio platform credentials and you can log in to your Anypoint account can see all APIs you have created over there:

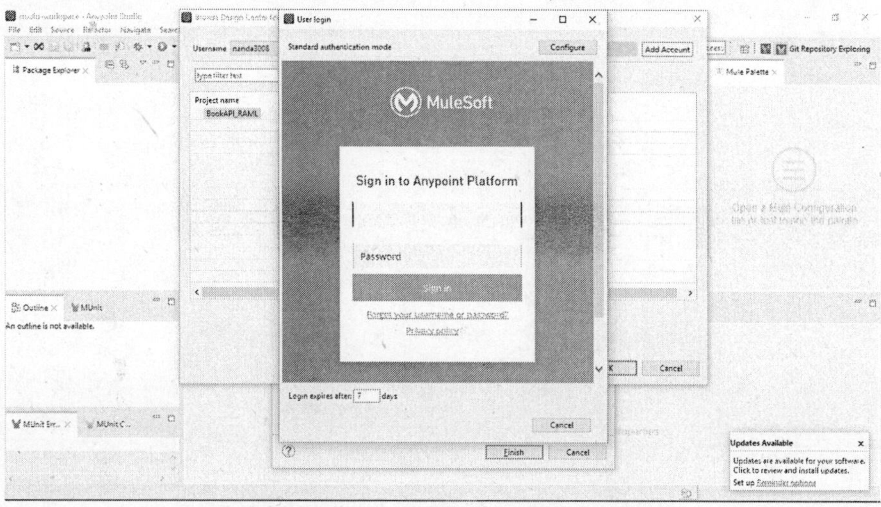


***Figure 3.6:*** *Sign in to Anypoint platform*

Now your Anypoint Studio got integrated with your Anypoint Exchange. You can choose any one of your API and click **`Finish`**:

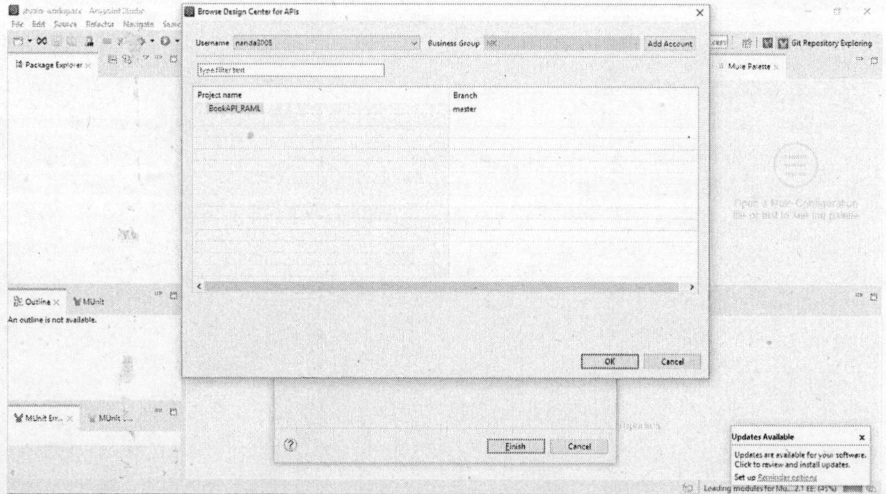


***Figure 3.7:*** *Browse design center for APIs*

You can see the selected API from exchange is reflecting in the API implementation **Location** field in the below screenshot:

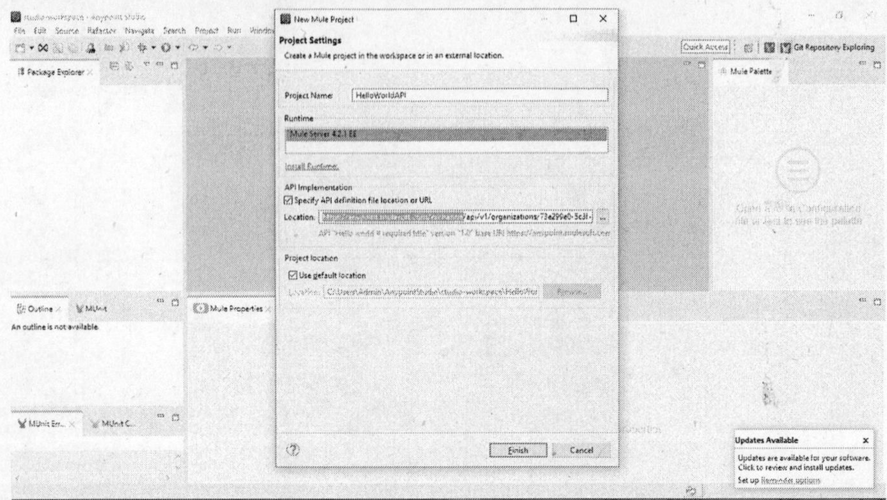

*Figure 3.8: Choose API from the design center*

On finishing the API import into your Anypoint Studio you can see the following result, here you can see your project structure Mule flows, etc.:

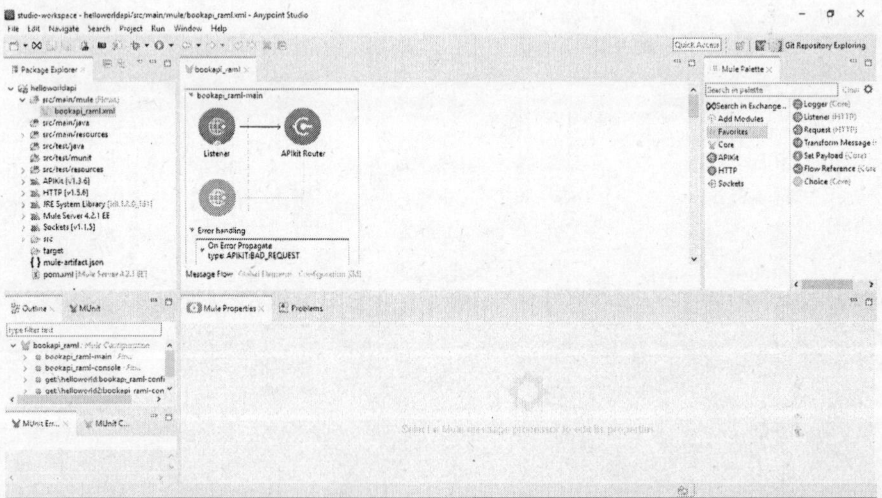

*Figure 3.9: API Imported from Design Center*

After achieving this right-click on the design panel and run the `HelloWorld` API as shown below:

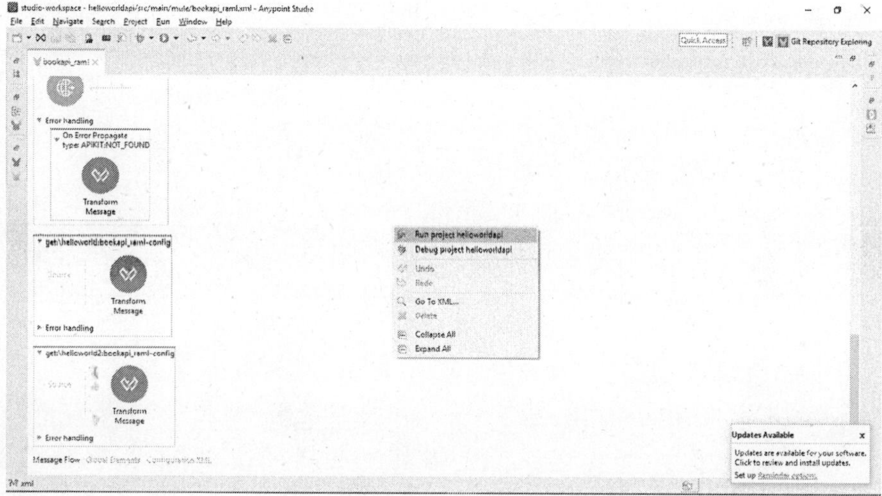


***Figure 3.10:*** *Running the Project*

The following server logs can be found in the server console:

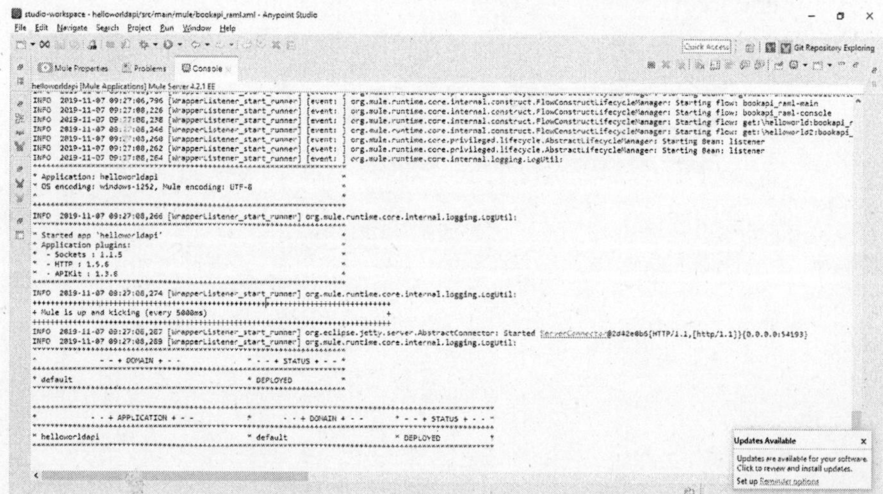


***Figure 3.11:*** *Project Output in Console*

On successful deployment the API Kit Console will appear on the **`APIKit Console`** tab:

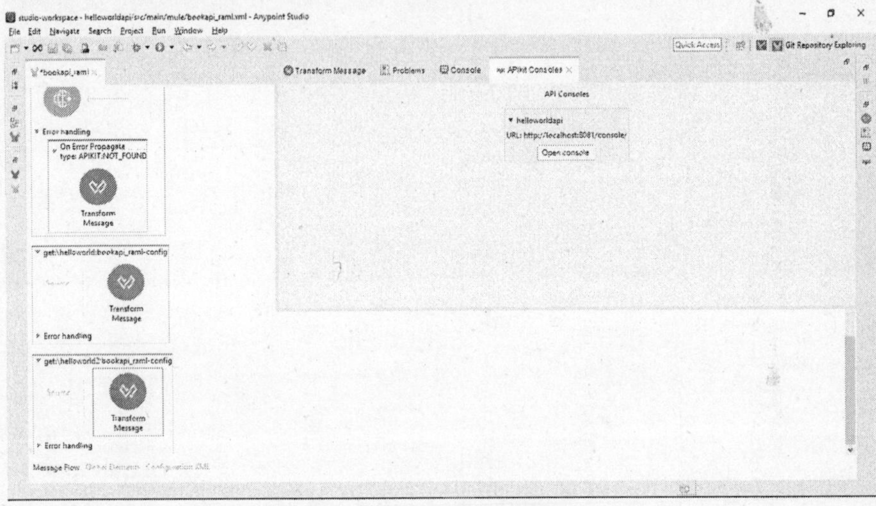


*Figure 3.12: APIKitConsole*

Click the open console button and visit the deployed APIs through a browser console:

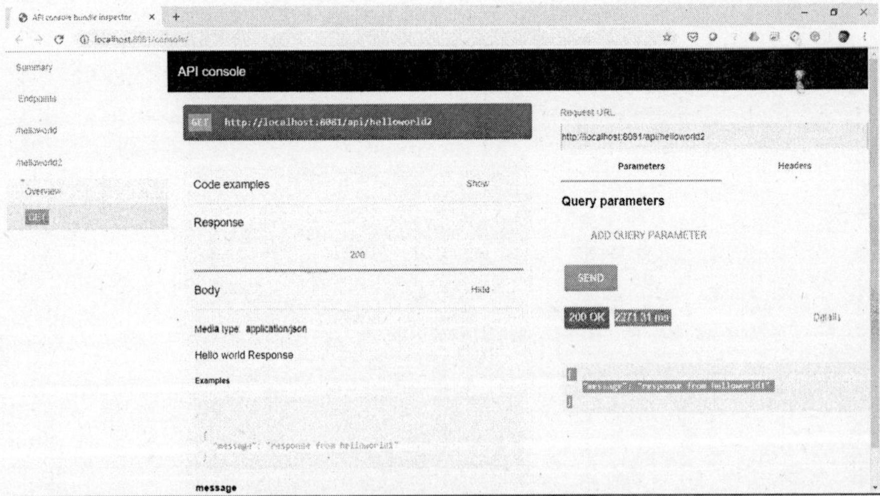


*Figure 3.13: Calling Console Web through a browser*

Check for more APIs and call them in a different flow:

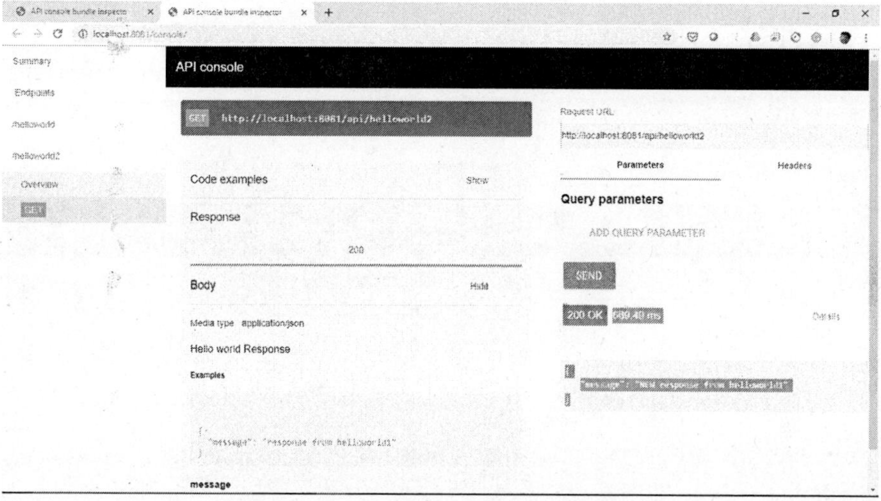

*Figure 3.14: Calling multiple End Points*

At the end of this exercise try to have a look at the MuleSoft Configuration XML file to have a basic understanding of how the XML file is generated and you can set/modify the payload values directly here and save the file. You can notice the auto-deployment of the newly bundled MuleSoft flow and you can see the changes in console outputs:

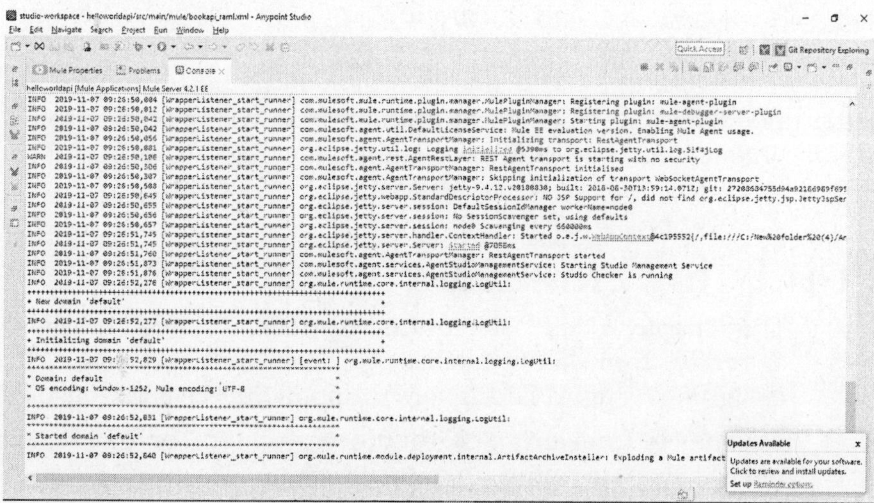

*Figure 3.15: Redeployed Console output*

# DIY

Try to define more API designs in the API designer and integrate the same inside Anypoint Studio. Access them through the console and test it out:

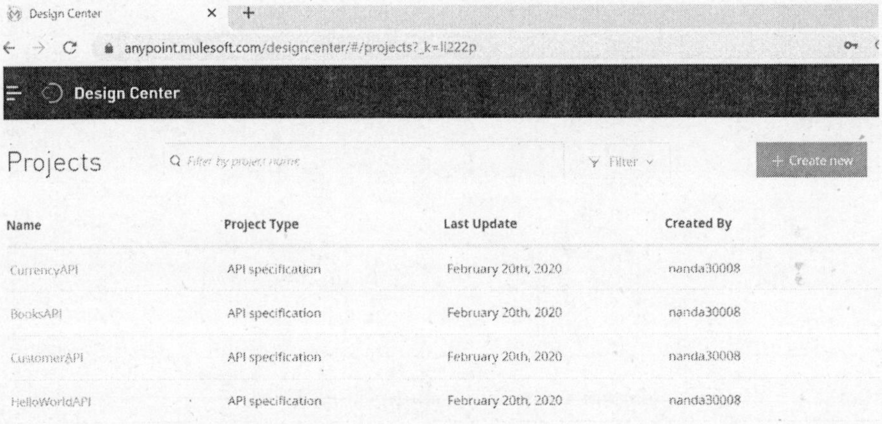

Design Center

anypoint.mulesoft.com/designcenter/#/projects?_k=li222p

Design Center

Projects

| Name | Project Type | Last Update | Created By |
|---|---|---|---|
| CurrencyAPI | API specification | February 20th, 2020 | nanda30008 |
| BooksAPI | API specification | February 20th, 2020 | nanda30008 |
| CustomerAPI | API specification | February 20th, 2020 | nanda30008 |
| HelloWorldAPI | API specification | February 20th, 2020 | nanda30008 |

***Figure 3.16:** Multiple APIs added to the Design Center*

# Conclusion

In this chapter, we explored the Anypoint Studio basics, Console, API Kit fundamentals, and Integrating Anypoint design center and Anypoint Studio. Please practice the given steps extensively so that when we talk about RAML concepts this will be useful to you for better understanding. In our next chapters, we will be having some useful content about MuleSoft's variations as an ESB platform and an API LED connectivity ecosystem. Cheers.

# Points to remember

- This chapter does not require any technical prerequisites, anybody from any business domain can practice API designing using API designer, Anypoint Studio, and Console.
- You may be from any background, say technical or functional, please keep in mind that MuleSoft is designed for any category of the audience and it became easy to understand the concepts like API designing and managing APIs.

# Key terms to explore

- RAML
- Anypoint Studio
- Anypoint Designer
- API Kit
- API Console
- API Deployment

# CHAPTER 4
# From ESB to API LED Connectivity

In this chapter we will discuss the following topics:

- Some more exercises related to the previous chapter
- What are ESB and system integration?
- Why do we need API LED connectivity?
- MuleSoft API LED connectivity paradigms

## Objectives

After studying this unit, you should be able to understand:

- How to design more APIs and play with the payload modifications?
- ESB fundamentals
- How API LED connectivity can be achieved?
- Transformation component
- Config XML file
- Modifying Payloads – basics
- ESB

- API LED connectivity
- Opportunities to become as an API designer

# Pre-requisites

Practice all previous chapter exercises, have some more hands-on with API designer, API Kit, and Console. Try to reiterate that MuleSoft API Designer is meant for Business Team who is responsible for API design specifications.

# Some more exercises related to the previous chapter

Let us quickly do 2 more exercises to understand how to change the payload values using Transformer Component and Configuration XML, This is just to provide you some more insights about the API Designer, API Kit, Transformation Component, and `Config.xml` file:

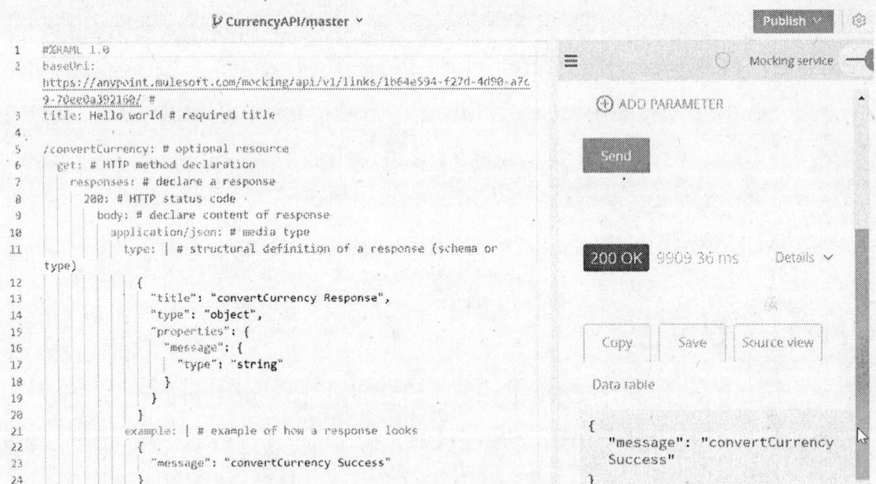


*Figure 4.1: Create a new API called CovertCurrency*

As shown above, try creating a new API in your designer:

New Mule Project
**Project Settings**
Create a Mule project in the workspace or in an external location.
Project Name: ConvertCurrency
Browse Design Center for APIs
Username nanda30008 Business Group Nanda Add A
type filter text

| Project name | Branch |
|---|---|
| BooksAPI | master |
| CurrencyAPI | master |
| CustomerAPI | master |
| HelloWorldAPI | master |

***Figure 4.2:*** *Import ConvertCurrency API*

Import the API as shown above:

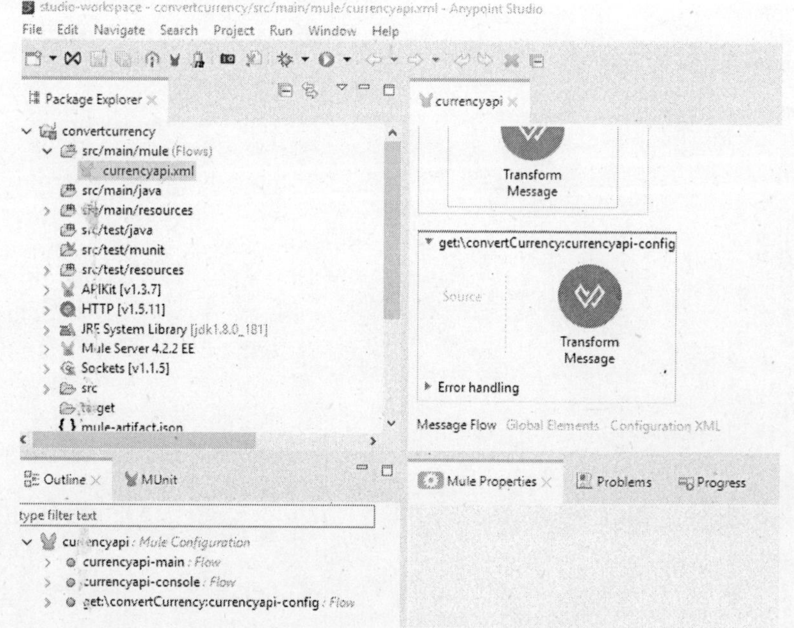


***Figure 4.3:*** *ConvertCurrency API Imported*

You can see the API Kit result as shown in the above screenshot:

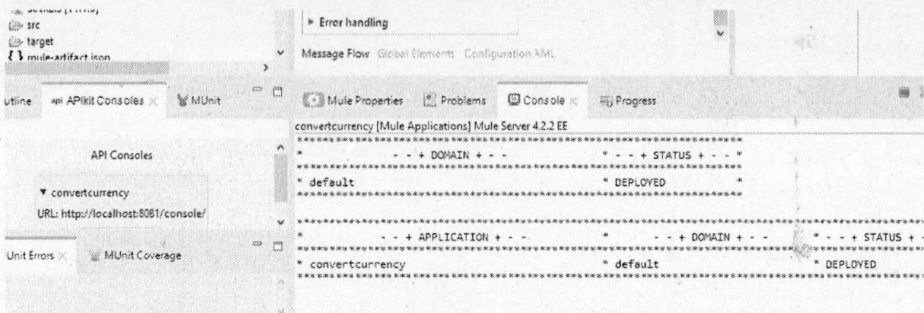


*Figure 4.4: ConvertCurrencyAPI deployed*

Check the complete deployment statements in the console and the API console also up and running:

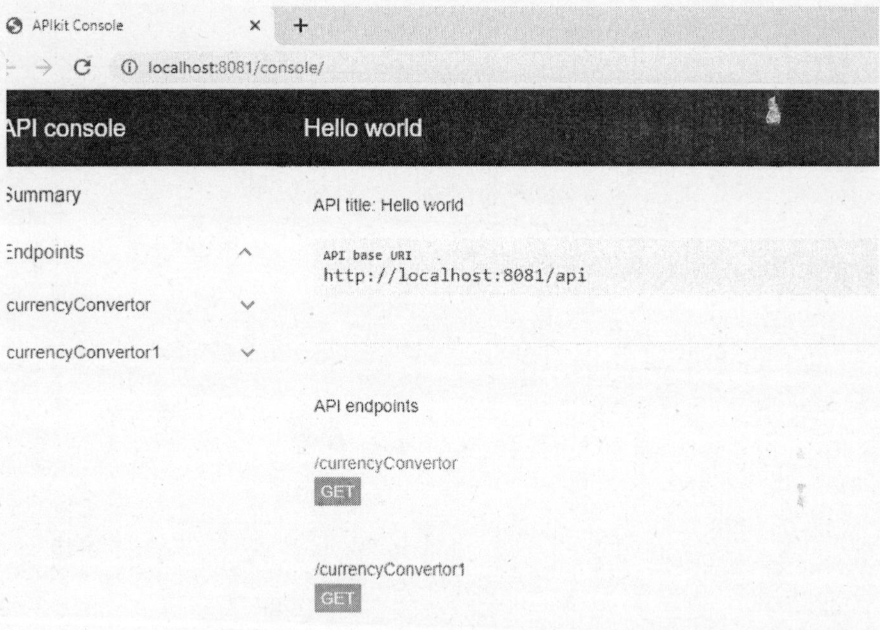


*Figure 4.5: Result of running the web console*

Call the web console and try running the endpoints /`currencyConvertor` and /`currencyConvertor1`:

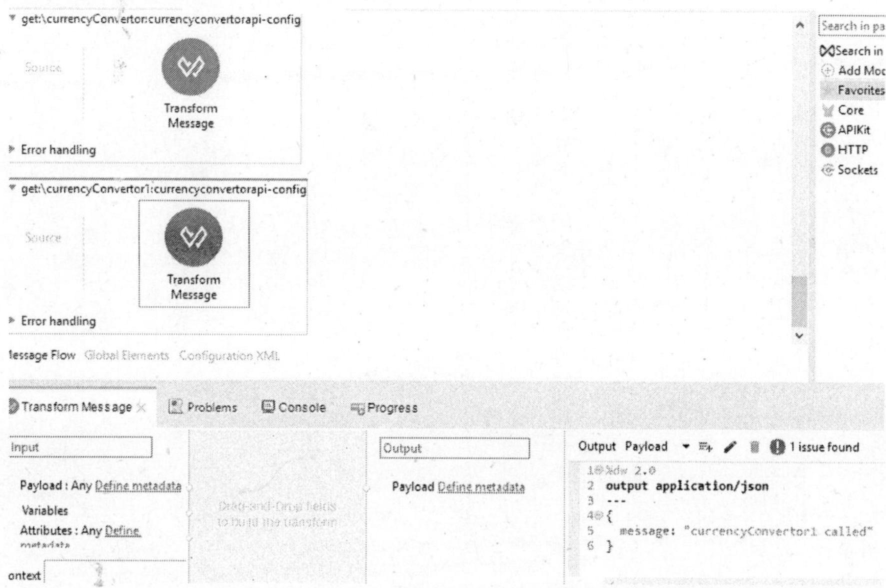


***Figure 4.6:** Selecting Transformation component*

Now go to the **`Message Flow`** tab and select means simply select the **`Transform Message`** component as shown above and you can see the **`Transform Message Properties`** panel in the below tab.:

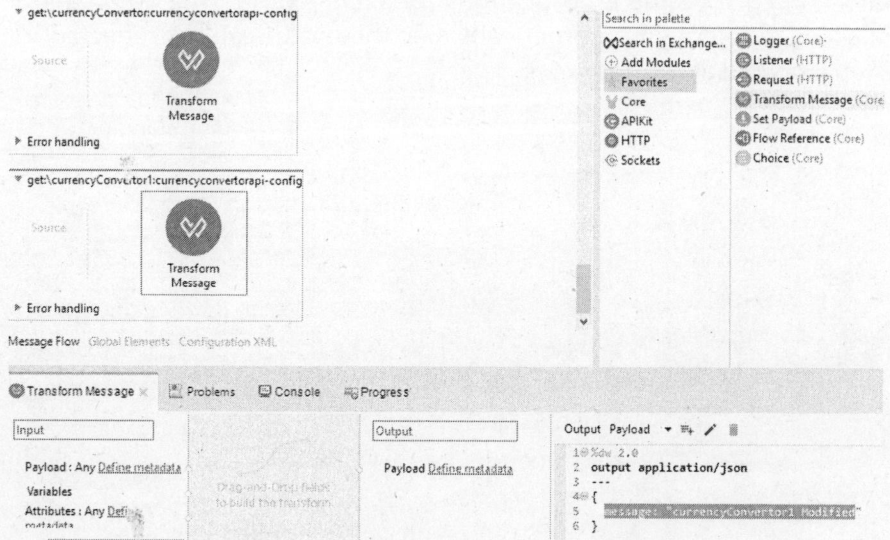


***Figure 4.7:** Modifying Payload directly from Transformation Component*

No need to take a deep dive into the panels like input, output, etc. Instead, focus on the **Output Payload** panel and modify the JSON output as shown above:

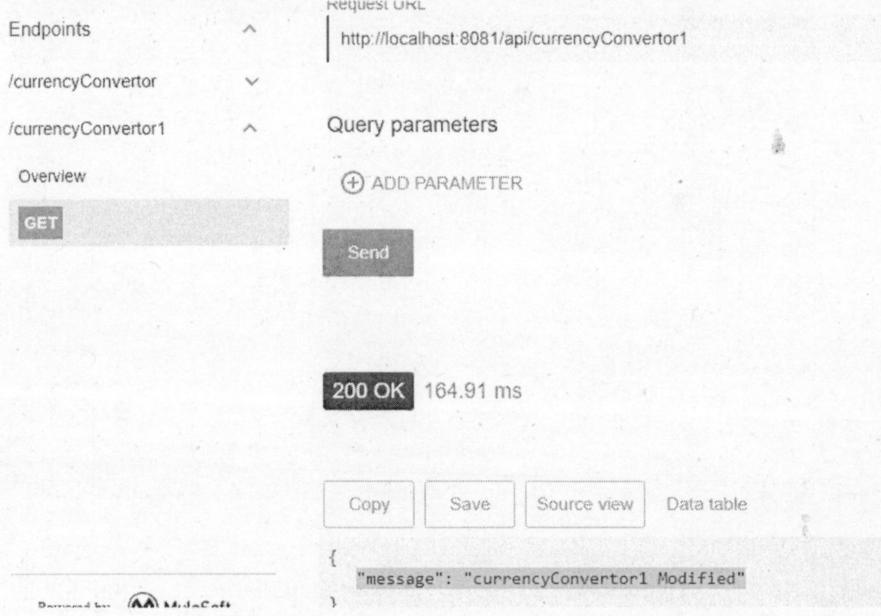


***Figure 4.8:*** *Checking the modifications in the web console*

Once modified simply save the project changes by *Ctrl* + *S* command and you can see the modifications are changed and the application started / redeployed automatically. See the modifications reflected in Web Console as in *Figure 4.8:*

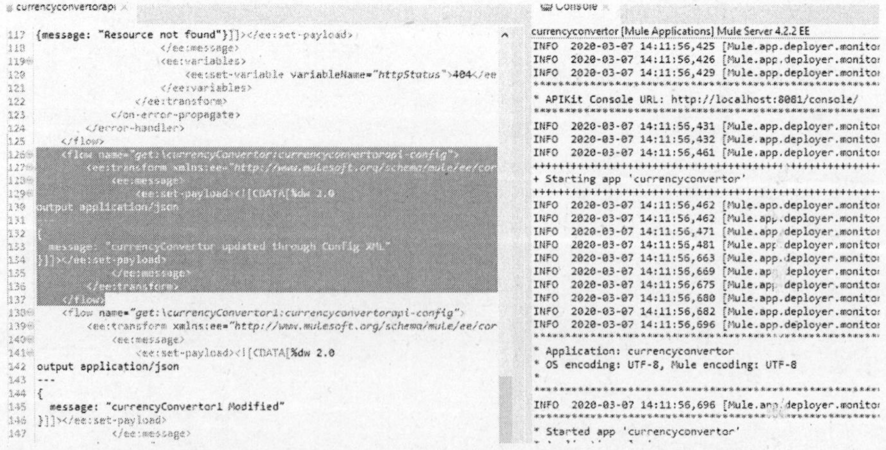


***Figure 4.9:*** *Modifying Payload directly through ConfigXML*

Similarly, in the **`Project`** panel, try to access the **`Configuration XML`** tab which is next to the message flow and global elements tab. Explore the various flow names and configuration details and try modifying the output value as shown above:

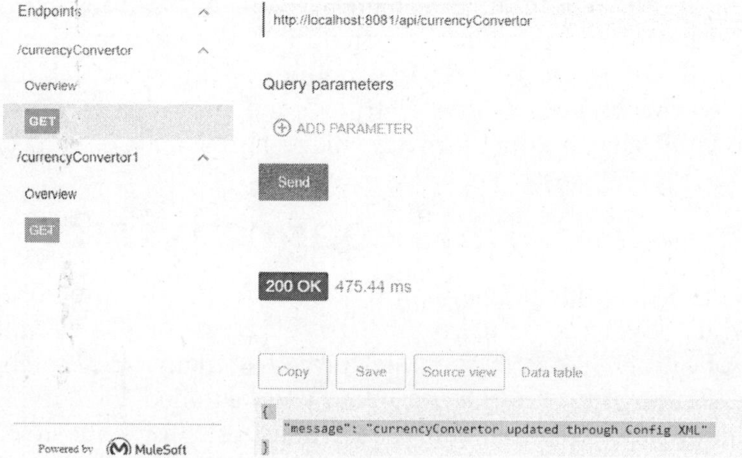


***Figure 4.10:** Checking changes in the web console*

As we mentioned earlier simply save the changes and you can see the application will be redeployed automatically. Needless to say, try checking the web console and invoke the endpoints to confirm the modifications applied.

# What is ESB?

**Enterprise Service Bus (ESB)** and MuleSoft is a famous lightweight ESB platform that facilitates data communication between various systems in a System Integration Project. As per the below diagram, many systems developed using different languages with different protocols can exchange information through a centralized ESB:

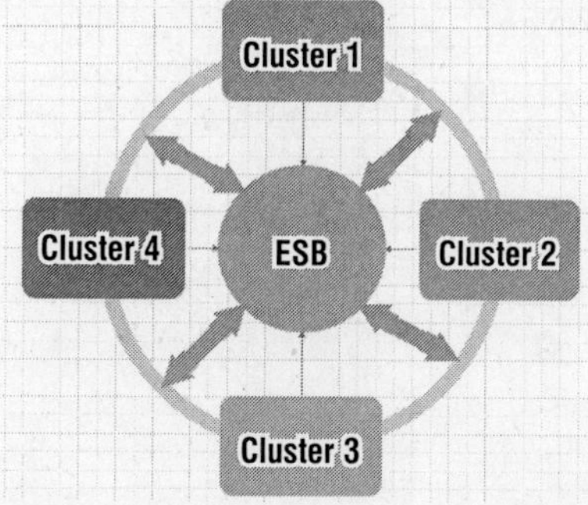


***Figure 4.11:** Enterprise Service Bus*

In the above screenshot, the clusters 1, 2, 3, and 4 will have various groups of Applications developed by different vendors. Those applications may share data in one format and that data must be transformed as per the destination systems format. So these applications will communicate using a centralized message bus and that ESB is responsible for handling the source messages and destination messages. As we mentioned in earlier chapters, technology can be Java, Dotnet PHP, etc. and protocols can be FTP, SMTP, AMQP, etc. and data formats will be JSON, CSV, email, etc.

# What is API LED connectivity?

In the API LED connectivity approach all APIs are differentiated by in which layer they are working. An enterprise will have many SaaS applications like SAP and Salesforce. The main APIs which are responsible for bring out the SaaS data will be called **System APIs.** For example, the `ShipmentsAPI` is responsible for exposing the Shipments data from a particular SaaS application. The next category of API will be `ProcessAPIs`. To process the Shipment data, we may have to develop a `ProcessShipmentAPI` which may use one or more Shipment related System APIs information. Now we need to expose the Shipment Processing Information through a UI, this means there will be a separate Experience API layer where an API will be developed as `ViewShipmentsAPI` and this will be responsible for invoking the Shipment Process API to fetch the shipment information:

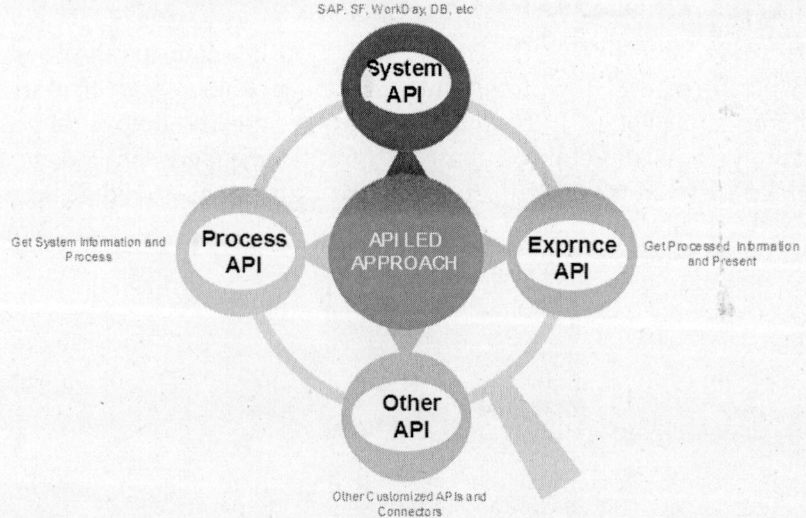


*Figure 4.12: API LED connectivity*

The **System** APIs consists of SaaS application core information, the **Process** APIs will work/process the **System Information** and the **Experience** APIs will consume the information given by the **Process** APIs.

# How API LED connectivity achieved?

Let us see how API LED connectivity achieved in the MuleSoft ecosystem, this means how it is possible for separating the API design team and the implementation team, what kind of API specification security maintained across teams. Let's assume a simple scenario that an API Designer is designing API specification which is having 2 endpoints named `/getShipments` and `/updateShipments`. Let's go ahead and design the API as shown below:

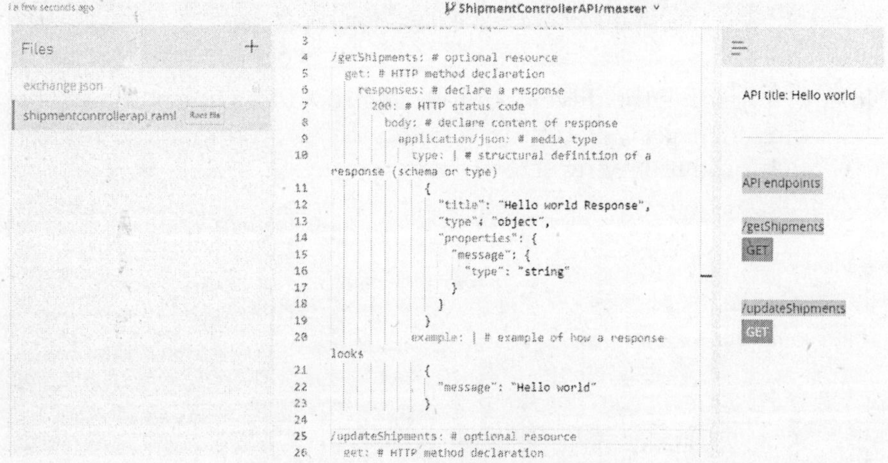


*Figure 4.13: ShipmentControllerAPI*

The next step after designing this API is the API Administrator can give access to this API for developers to implement the business logic to this API. So now the developers can access the design center and the can import these APIs to their Anypoint Studio and they can see the results in the web console. Refer the following screenshot:

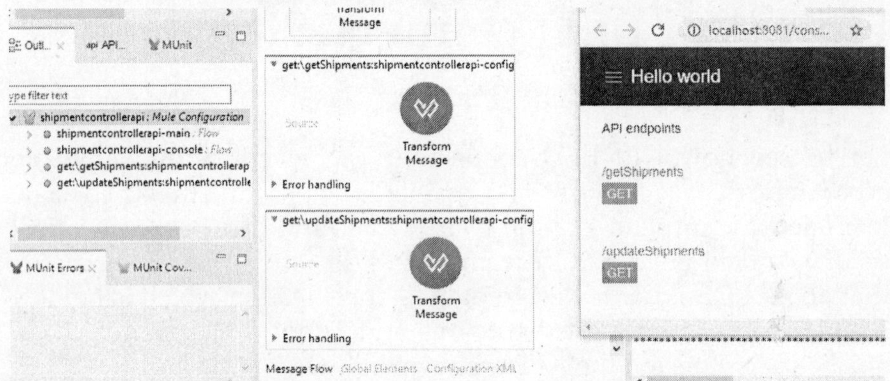

***Figure 4.14:*** *ShipmentControllerAPI Running*

Now, let's assume the developer is trying to add an endpoint for the `ShipmentAPI` say `/deleteShipments` by modifying the `Config.xml`. Refer the following screenshot:

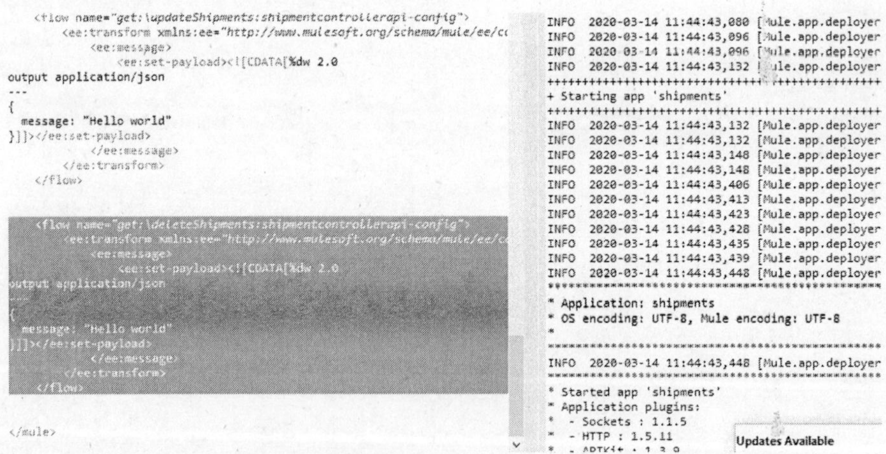

***Figure 4.15:*** *ShipmentControllerAPI added with deleteShipment endpoint*

After adding a new endpoint through `config.xml` save the project by clicking *Ctrl + S* and you can see the project getting auto deployed. Upon running the web console you can see the `APIKit` is referring to the Parent Specification shared by the API Designer and not the local modifications done by the developers. This means the API specifications are registered in the API designer and the developers' local modifications to APIs will not affect the parent specification as shown below:

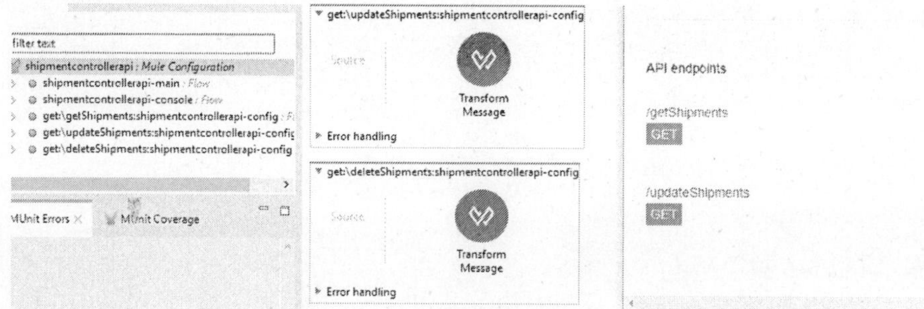


***Figure 4.16:*** *ShipmentControllerAPI Running without deleteShipment*

# How API LED connectivity to bring a new opportunity for API designers?

Now you can understand the concepts of system APIs, process APIs, experience APIs, customized APIs, device and sensor, APIs, etc.

Having said this center for enablement team with the facilities like API Designer, Manager, API Kit, etc. can design and manage numerous API specifications and they will be the sole owner of the entire business process and implementation. In the forthcoming chapters, we are going to explore how best the API designer can utilize the RAML specifications, testing the APIs even before it is shared with developers for implementation, etc.

# DIY

Based on the above API LED connectivity scenarios, try to design your APIs which will be used in a Device or Robot involved in industries.

The sample given below. Try adding endpoints like `getCustomerID`, `getSensorName`, `getCustomerLocation`, etc.:

Design Center

Projects　Filter by project name　Filter　Create new

| Name | Project Type | Last Update | Created By |
|---|---|---|---|
| DroneInspectionAPI | API specification | March 13th, 2020 | nknknk3008 |
| DeliveryRobotAPI | API specification | March 13th, 2020 | nknknk3008 |
| SensorAPI | API specification | March 13th, 2020 | nknknk3008 |
| CurrencyConvertorAPI | API specification | March 8th, 2020 | nknknk3008 |
| FirstAPI | API specification | March 8th, 2020 | nknknk3008 |

***Figure 4.17***

# Conclusion

In this chapter we explore additional use cases for API designing, importing to Anypoint Studio, API Kit, Modifying the payload values through Transformation Component, and Config XML file. Also, we have got a fair idea about what will be a conventional ESB scenario and the new age API LED Connectivity paradigm.

# Points to remember

- This chapter does not require any technical prerequisites, anybody from any business domain can practice API designing using API designer, Anypoint Studio, and Console.
- This chapter demands you to focus more on Designing API Specifications rather than coding some implementations as an API designer.
- We also emphasize that as an API Designer you can take care of the entire ownership of API specifications and developers cannot modify the endpoint point specifications willingly or by mistake.

# Key terms to explore

- Transformation component
- Config XML
- Auto deployment
- ESB
- API LED connectivity

# CHAPTER 5
# Cloud-based SaaS Applications and MuleSoft Connectors

In this chapter we will discuss the following topics

- Cloud-based SaaS applications
- SaaS applications exposing their APIs
- MuleSoft Connectors
- MuleSoft Integration Scope areas
- Popular SaaS applications
- Why Cloud-based SaaS applications?
- How MuleSoft differ from other integration platforms?
- Getting familiarize with SaaS APIs

## Objectives

After studying this unit, you should be able to understand

- What are new-age cloud-based SaaS applications?
- How are the SaaS applications exposing their APIs?
- MuleSoft Connectors for the said SaaS applications
- Exploring MuleSoft Exchange provided Assets

- Internals of MuleSoft Samples and Templates
- Overall view of industry popular SaaS applications

# Pre-requisites

This chapter meant for understanding the MuleSoft Exchange provided Connectors, Sample, and Examples for various businesses process related SaaS applications, you as an API Designer, have to understand how you can design numerous APIs which will take data from SaaS systems, then provide the data to Process APIs and presenting the processed data in Experience layer. So the basic understanding of all the topics covered in the previous chapters is mandatory to go forward, also keep in mind that you not going to implement and develop any of the business logic as a developer.

# Cloud-based SaaS applications

In the beginning, say by 2000, we developed applications using technologies like Java and Dot Net, where you will have screens and components developed and bundled as an archive file and deployed into development, testing, UAT, and Production environments. A single application bundle will be comprised of front end screen programs, middleware business components, DB procedures, property files, etc. So it is difficult for the maintenance team to upgrade the production versions and patches.

So later the concept of web services has been introduced, so that, if a Login service is developed, it can be developed as a separate web service and can be hosted on the server, any programs which need to use the authentication mechanism, can call the Login Service and pass the credentials and get the access token for the web service.

Here come the concepts like SaaS, PaaS, and IaaS where SaaS stands for Software as a Service, PaaS is Platform as a Service and IaaS is Infrastructure as a Service. The SaaS model is purely based on converting all tightly bundled business services into a standalone web service, host the web service on a cloud-based platform, and made it available for multiple customers.

So the pay per use concept, means, a customer can choose the required services hosted by the vendor, and he can pay the usage cost based on the number services used, kind of complexity of the service, traffic on the service, etc. From the vendor point of view, no need to deploy cloud applications for each customer, a concept like multi-tenancy will help the vendor to onboard multiple customers based on a license model.

It is also possible for the vendors to set up a dedicated standalone application set up on the cloud for each of their clients using automated scripts. Some of the industry-standard cloud services are

- Software as a service (SaaS)
- Infrastructure as a service (IaaS),
- Platform as a service (PaaS),
- Desktop as a service (DaaS), [4]
- Managed software as a service (MSaaS),
- Mobile backend as a service (MBaaS),
- Datacenter as a service (DCaaS)
- Information technology management as a service (ITMaaS).

The following business applications scenarios are widely available as a SaaS model

- Payroll Processing software
- Accounting
- Collaboration
- Customer Relationship Management (CRM)
- Management Information Systems (MIS)
- Enterprise Resource Planning (ERP)
- Invoicing
- Human Resource Management (HRM)
- Talent Acquisition
- Learning management systems
- Content management (CM)
- Geographic information systems (GIS)
- Service desk management

# SaaS applications exposing their APIs

The following APIs are mandatory for a successful SaaS application

- Security and Authentication related APIs.
- Transactional APIs
- API management, alerts, reporting APIs

The authentication, license management activities are handled by security, license, and authentication APIs. Transactional APIs will get some inputs and provide the business data for the same. Once the APIs started consumed by the clients we need to manage the traffic, policies, etc. for the particular API for billing and maintenance purposes.

# MuleSoft Connectors

MuleSoft Exchange is the place where all connectors are available for download, the Assets provided by MuleSoft can be accessed, and the developers can publish their assets and share to team and community:

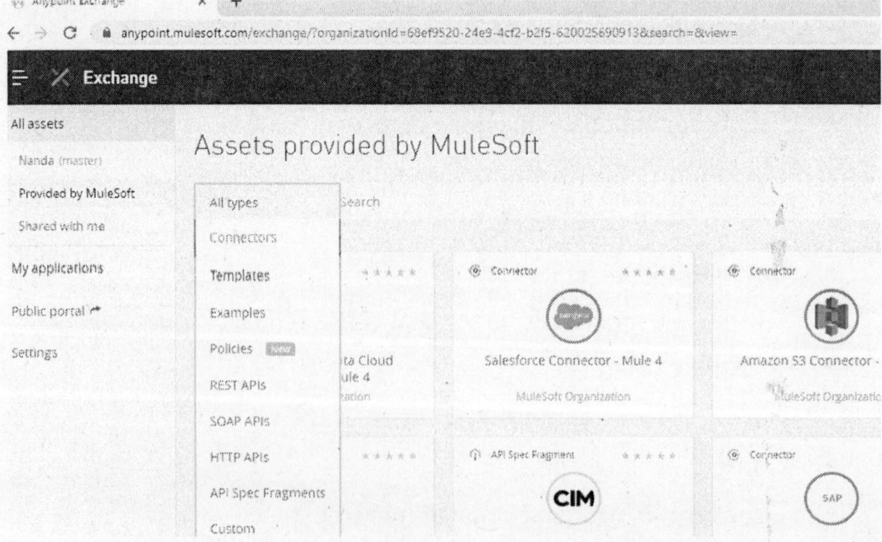


*Figure 5.1: MuleSoft Connectors in MuleSoft Exchange*

MuleSoft is providing connectors for most of the industry's popular SaaS suites. Visit the **https://anypoint.mulesoft.com/home/** and access the Exchange as shown above. You can see a search field where you can search for available **`Connectors`**, **`Templates`**, **`Examples`**, **`Policies`**, **`REST APIs`**, **`SOAP APIs`**, **`HTTP APIs`**, **`API Fragments`** provided by MuleSoft:

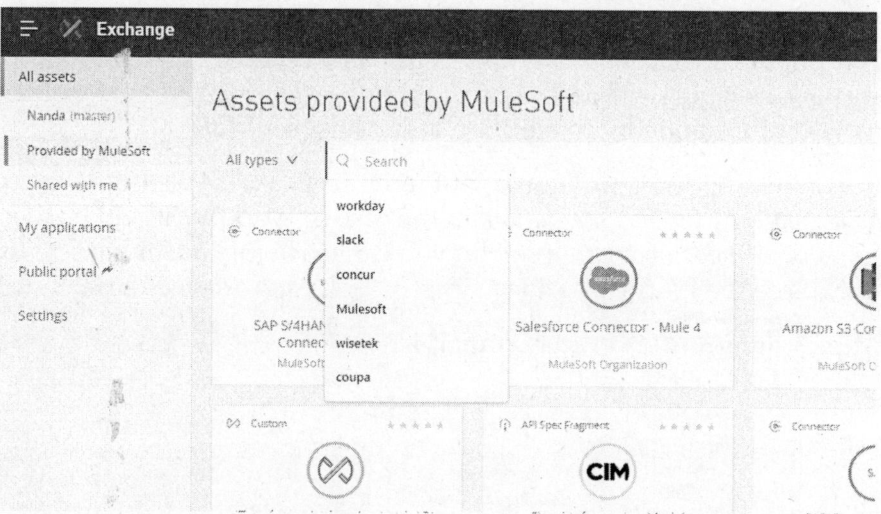


*Figure 5.2: Searching MuleSoft Connectors MuleSoft Exchange*

The above screenshot shows how to search for various connectors by providing the SaaS application names:

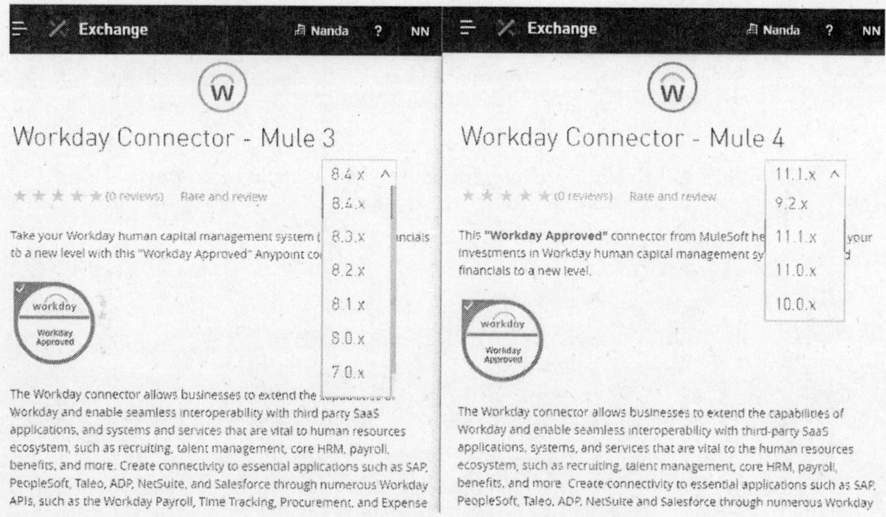


*Figure 5.3: Understanding Workday Connectors for MuleSoft*

We have searched for connectors available for Workday SaaS HR Application and found the results as shown above. You can see the connectors available for MuleSoft Version 3 and 4 and they have mentioned the Workday Connector versions as well.

Here you have to understand the various SaaS applications supported by MuleSoft Connectors, so it is better to do some initial level study about the SaaS applications. For example, Workday is a popular cloud-based HR system, very secured, used by many corporates, and Workday itself providing numerous APIs to access its HR information by Integration Platforms like MuleSoft.

For accessing or studying about any SaaS APIs please Google *SaaSApp + API + documentation*, in the case of Workday it will be like *workday API documentation* so that you can reach the link given below to explore the WorkDay APIs

**https//community.workday.com/api**

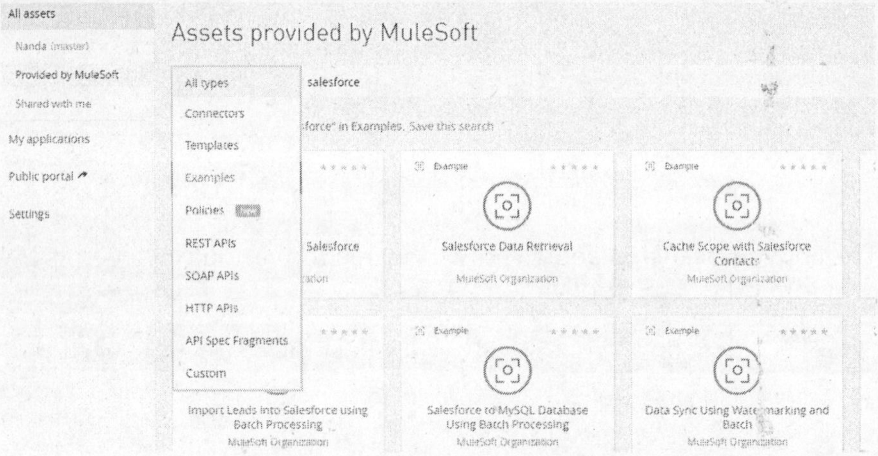

***Figure 5.4:*** *Exploring Examples provided by MuleSoft Exchange*

The examples given by MuleSoft will help you to understand what kind of integrations is common and possible across or within a given SaaS suite. The above screenshot shows how to go to the Examples search screen and how to filter out Salesforce-based examples:

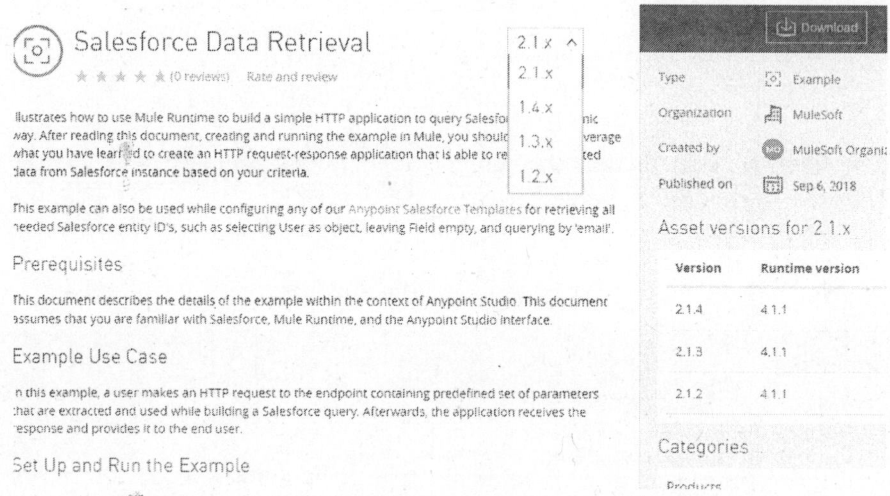


***Figure 5.5:** Downloading Salesforce Data Retrieval Example*

Now we have reached the Example download page for **`Salesforce Data Retrieval`** HTTP application. You can see the description of the example, how to use, asset version details, etc. on this page. On clicking the **`Download`** button if you are in Windows Chrome, you can see a warning like **`This type of file can harm….`** Ignore this warning and go ahead with the clicking keep button so that the JAR file will be saved in your local system.

After downloading the file open Anypoint Studio and right-click the **`Project Explorer`** and click the **`Import`** projects option:

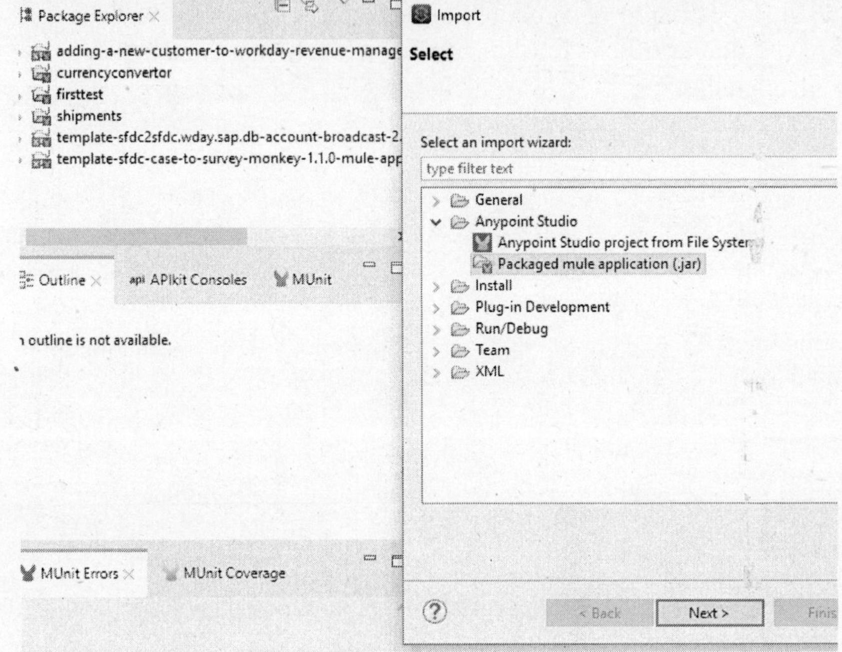


*__Figure 5.6:__ Importing Salesforce Data Retrieval Example to Studio*

In the import wizard choose **`Anypoint Studio | Packaged Mule Application (.jar)`** option and select `salesforce-data-retrieval.jar` file:

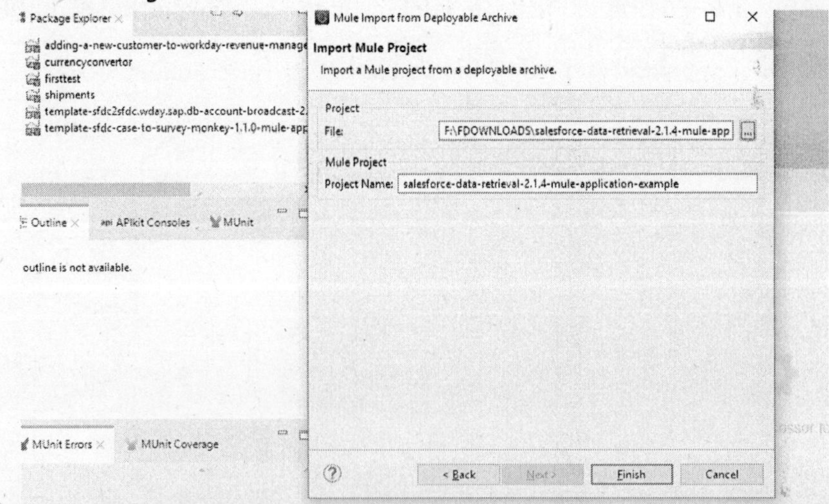


*__Figure 5.7:__ Selecting Salesforce Data Retrieval Example from Downloads*

You can see the project is built with the example JAR file as an input and now you can examine the message flow, global elements, config file, and project structure. Our aim is to understand if the importing of existing is happening rather running them with proper credentials:

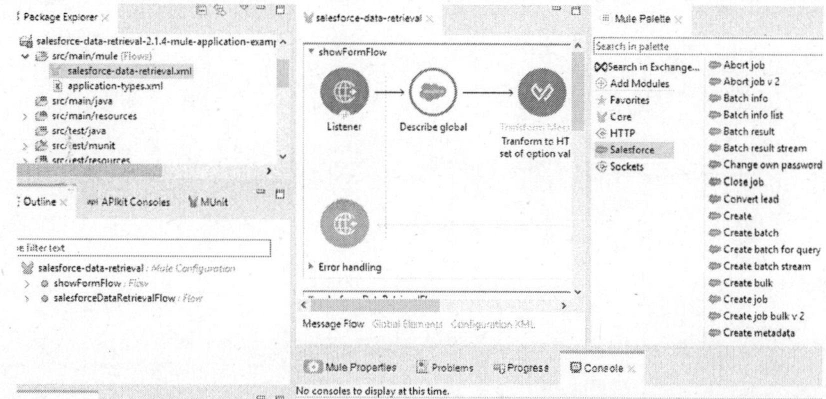


***Figure 5.8:** Imported Salesforce Data Retrieval Example and Pallet first look*

Go to the **`Global Configuration`** and examine the listener configuration, configuration properties, and **`Salesforce Configuration.`** We will the actual connector settings, configurations, and executions in forthcoming chapters. So please give importance to having a look at the examples given by MuleSoft Exchange at this time:

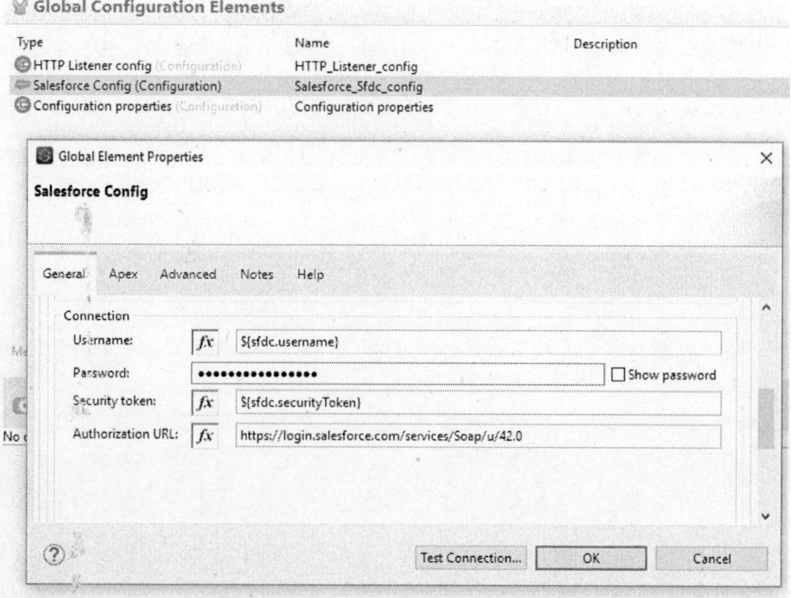


***Figure 5.9:** Exploring Salesforce Data Retrieval Configuration first look*

Here comes the project structure, folders involved, resources involved in a real-time Mule Project:

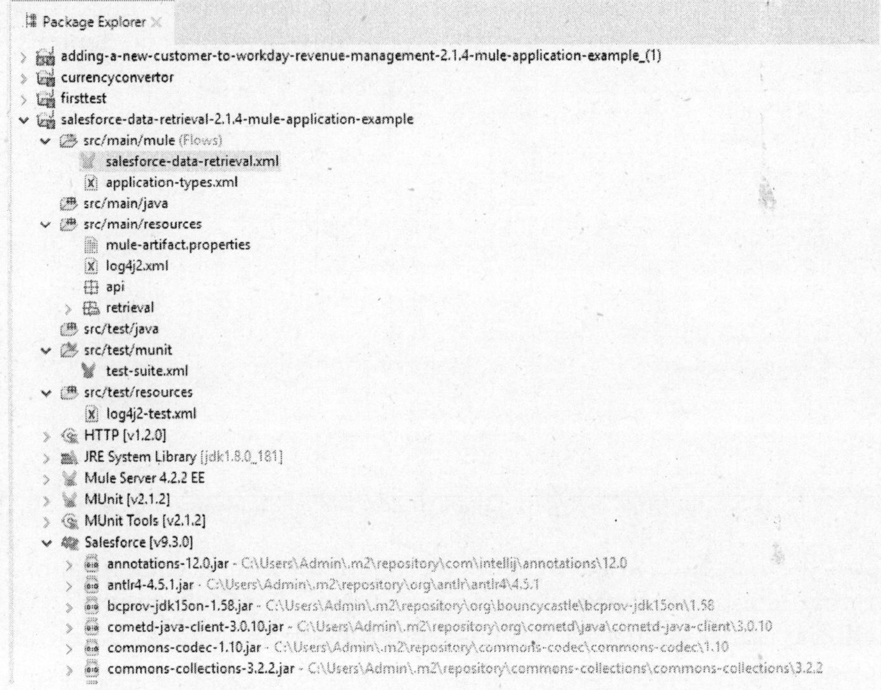


***Figure 5.10:** Exploring Salesforce Data Retrieval Package Explorer first look*

Visit the MuleSoft connectors' page to understand the various connectors supported by MuleSoft:

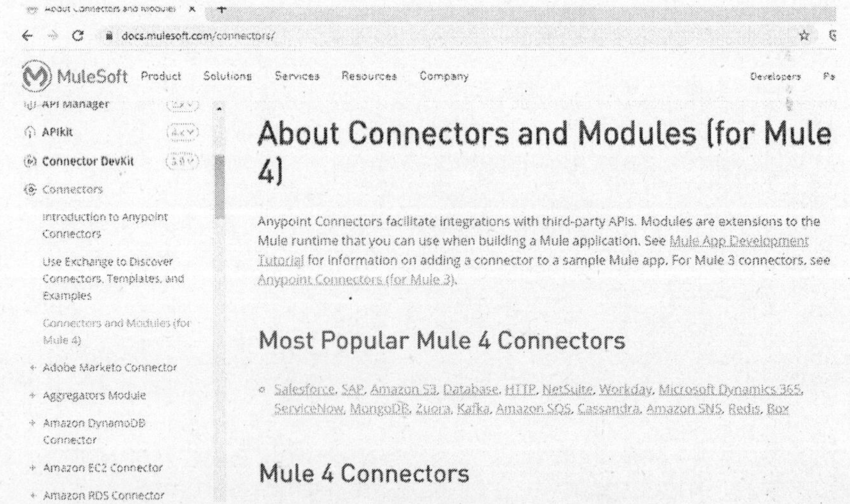


***Figure 5.11:** MuleSoft Connectors Documentation*

Templates will be used as a starting point of your project with basic settings. Examples are given to show you the scenarios expected out of the real-time SaaS applications:

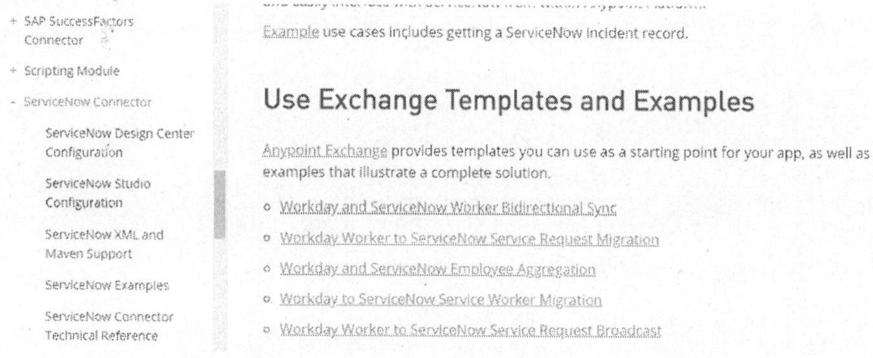


***Figure 5.12:** MuleSoft Connectors exploring samples*

The below table provides you a list of SaaS suites available in the market. You may have to Google individual SaaS suite websites to understand their business areas and API documentation:

| Adobe Marketo | CloudHub | IBM CTG | Oracle Siebel |
|---|---|---|---|
| Amazon Webn Services | Database | IBM MQ | Redis |
| AMQP | EDIFACT EDI | JMS | Roostify |
| Anypoint MQ Connector | TRADACOMS EDI | Kafka | RosettaNet |
| AS2 | X12 EDI | LDAP | SalesforceSAP Concur |
| Blend | Email | Microsoft .NET | SAP SuccessFactors |
| BMC Remedy | File | MongoDB | ServiceNow |
| Box | FTP | Neo4J | Slack |
| CAQH | FTPS | NetSuite | SFTP |
| Cassandra | HDFS (Hadoop) | Object Store | Sockets |
| Web Service Consumer | HL7 EDI | Oracle EBS 12.2 | Twilio |
| WebSockets | HTTP | Oracle PeopleSoft | Veeva Vault |
| Workday | Zuora | | VM |

***Figure 5.13:** MuleSoft Connectors*

The following list is having some specific SaaS suite names we have identified to explore further in our forthcoming chapters:

| | |
|---|---|
| Salesforce | ServiceNow |
| SAP | MongoDB |
| Amazon S3 | Zuora |
| Slack | Coupa |
| Database | Kafka |
| HTTP | Cassandra |
| NetSuite | Redis |
| Workday | Box |

***Figure 5.14:** MuleSoft Connectors to be explored*

# Why Cloud-based SaaS applications?

Cloud-based SaaS applications are having lots of advantages over traditional applications in terms of performance, maintenance, billing, quick customer onboarding, multi-tenant provisioning, etc. The following diagram gives us a clear picture of the current SaaS scenarios:

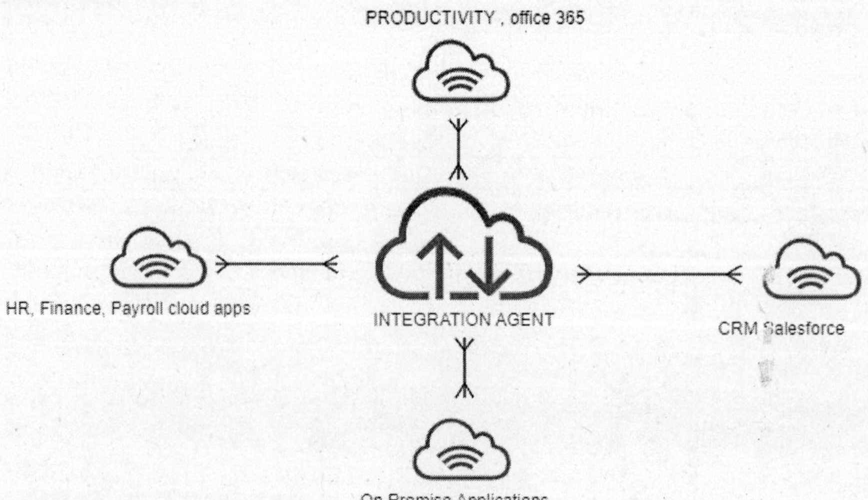


***Figure 5.15:** SaaS Demystified*

# How MuleSoft differ from other integration platforms?

MuleSoft flows are very lightweight compare to other integration platforms. MuleSoft comes with a cloud-based deployment platform so that developing, building, and deploying Mule applications will be automated and lightweight. Also, MuleSoft provides very good features for monitoring and controlling the Flows deployed into Mule Cloud.

# Getting familiarize with SaaS APIs

Play with the search in exchange features to identify more connectors, download those Modules, and check the API calls provided by them. The below screenshot shows you the NetSuite, ServiceNow, and Salesforce connector modules downloaded to the project:

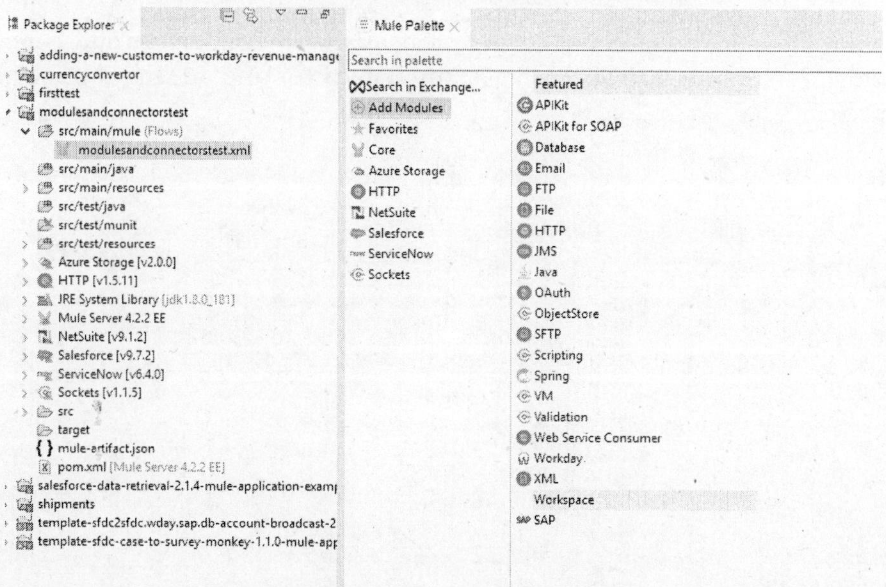


***Figure 5.16:*** *MuleSoft Featured Connectors and Modules*

Select the Salesforce connector and explore the API operations:

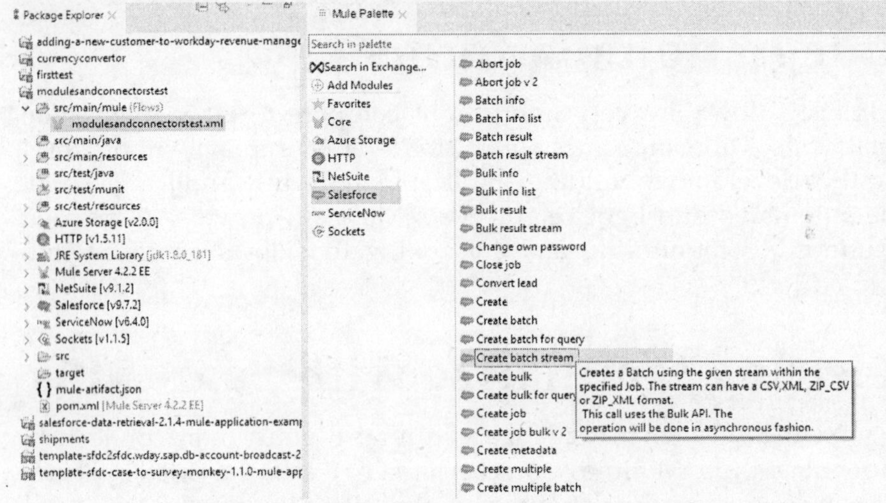


*Figure 5.17: MuleSoft Connectors API Explanation*

Follow the below screenshot to explore available connectors and here we are searching for Microsoft Azure connector and adding it to our project:

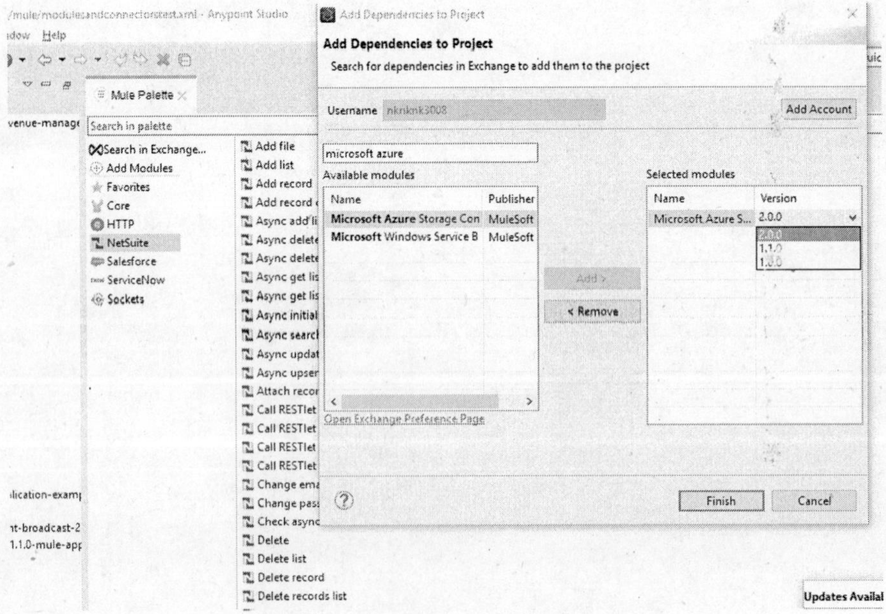


*Figure 5.18: Adding new Connector*

Once the Azure connector added you can browse the operational APIs given by Azure cloud:

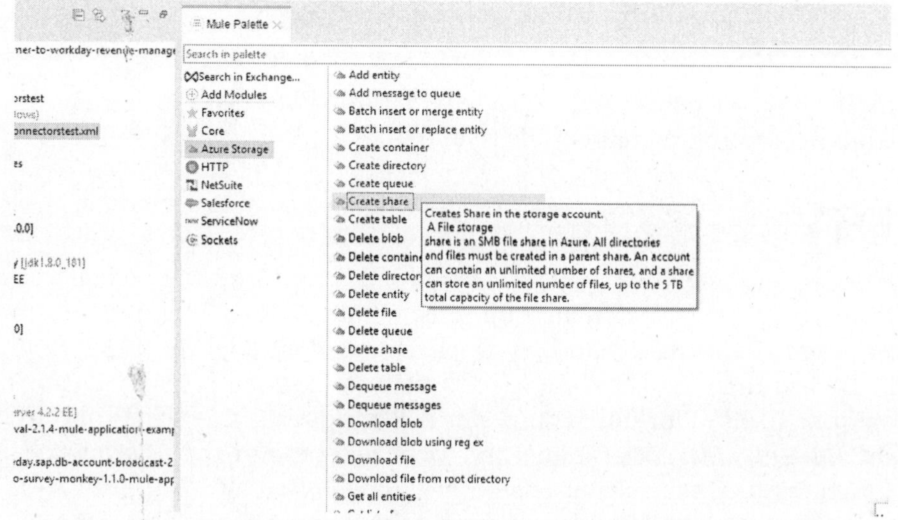


***Figure 5.19:** Exploring APIs of new Connector*

The below screenshot shows how to explore a new connector or existing connector from a SaaS Suite home site:

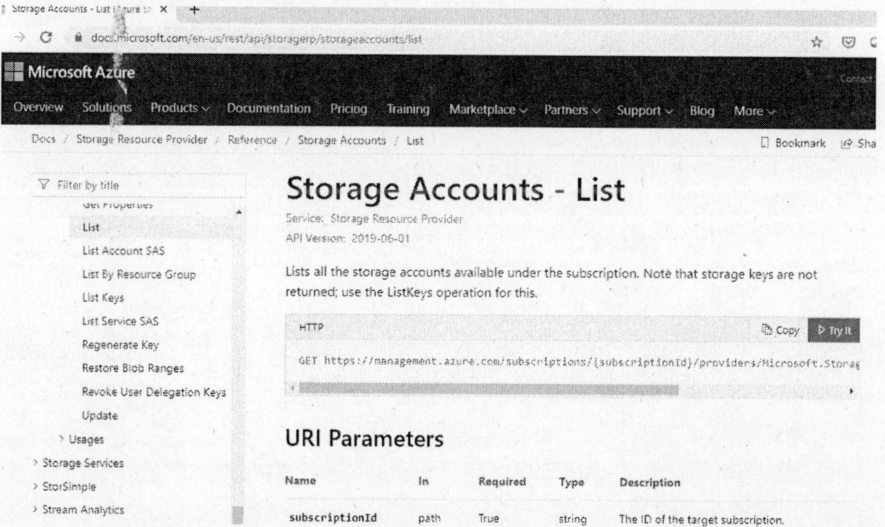


***Figure 5.20:** Exploring APIs of new Connector from Application Site*

We are trying to search Google for *azure storage api reference* and able to reach the following link:

**https//docs.microsoft.com/en-us/rest/api/storagerp/storageaccounts/list**

In this link, we can see the Storage Account API to List the number of storage accounts a customer is having.

# DIY

Refer the screenshot below, Download the Workday connector through Search in Exchange options, create a **`New Project`**, go to **`Message Flow`** panel, and try to check the **`Workday`** Module in the **`Mule Pallet`**. Then as shown in the below screenshot drag and drop any one of the Workday components like **`Upsert Customer`** and in the **`Upsert Customer`** panel try to select some of the operations/functions like submitting customers. Finally, try accessing the API documentation of Workday and crosscheck the API specifications:

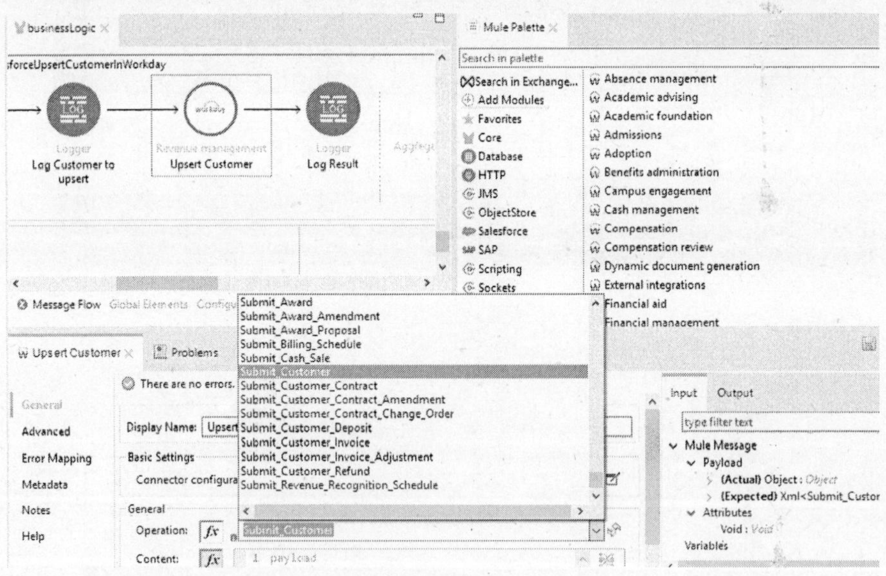


***Figure 5.21:** APIs Functions Retrieval*

# Conclusion

We explored the concepts like what is a SaaS cloud application, how the APIs are exposed for Enterprise Integrations. Also, the connectors provided by MuleSoft to access these SaaS APIs, how to configure, how to explore the assets provided by MuleSoft. We have downloaded some of the examples provided by MuleSoft and imported the examples inside the Anypoint Studio. We have gone through the structure of the example HTTP application provided by MuleSoft and understood the various available SaaS applications, connectors, and APIs. We have also discussed how MuleSoft differs from other Integrations Platforms and hope this chapter is useful to understand the MuleSoft Connector Ecosystem.

In our next chapter, we will be dealing with the topics like RAML basics and API designing specifications, Cheers.

# Points to remember

- This chapter does not require any technical prerequisites, anybody from any business domain can practice API designing using API designer, Anypoint Studio, and Console.
- This chapter tries to explain to you the available SaaS applications and how to understand and explore the APIs exposed by those SaaS applications.
- Readers are expected to study more about the usage of the majority of the industry-standard SaaS applications in their business acumen.
- Also, readers must be familiar now with MuleSoft Exchange, the assets provided by MuleSoft, how to reuse the same.
- From the API designer perspective, you are expecting to study these Cloud SaaS application fundamentals various APIs to gain confidence when you are designing project-specific APIs to interact with these SaaS APIs.

# Key terms to explore

- SaaS applications
- SaaS on Cloud
- Exchange Assets
- Templates, Examples, Connectors, etc.
- Downloading and exploring examples
- Why Cloud SaaS?
- MuleSoft advantage

# CHAPTER 6
# REST, SOAP, Postman, and Anypoint

In this chapter we will discuss the following topics:

- RESTful
- SOAP
- Invoking web services
- Postman client
- RESTful HTTP web service in Anypoint Studio

## Objectives

After studying this unit, you should be able to understand:

- What is web services
- RESTFul and SOAP web services
- Web services methods and types
- Postman client installation and invoking web services from Postman
- Developing an HTTP Listener in Anypoint Studio

- Implementing a RESTful web service and invoking the GET and POST method

# Pre-requisites

A few hands-on with Anypoint Studio is required for this chapter. Also, some basic understanding or exposure to the concepts of web services like submitting data to the server, invoking a server method from the browser or Postman client are expected. The chapter covers all these concepts and you can easily simulate these working flows in your system without many hurdles.

# Understanding sample RESTful web services

Visit the website **http://dummy.restapiexample.com/** where you can see an Employee RESTful web service developed and deployed for the testing purpose.

You can call these web services by clicking the full route links:

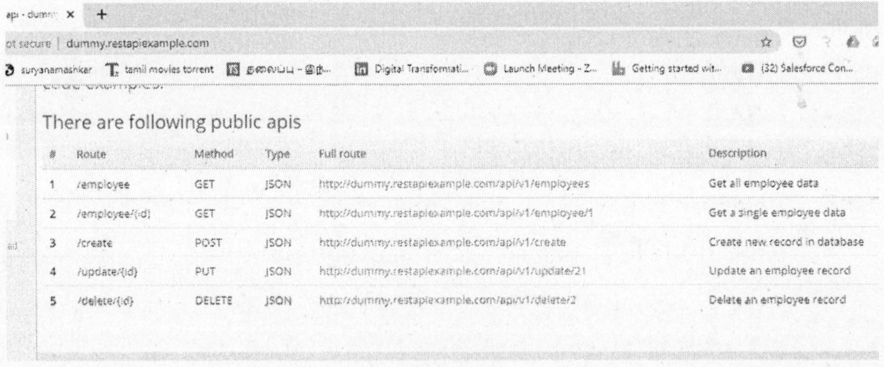


| # | Route | Method | Type | Full route | Description |
|---|---|---|---|---|---|
| 1 | /employee | GET | JSON | http://dummy.restapiexample.com/api/v1/employees | Get all employee data |
| 2 | /employee/{id} | GET | JSON | http://dummy.restapiexample.com/api/v1/employee/1 | Get a single employee data |
| 3 | /create | POST | JSON | http://dummy.restapiexample.com/api/v1/create | Create new record in database |
| 4 | /update/{id} | PUT | JSON | http://dummy.restapiexample.com/api/v1/update/21 | Update an employee record |
| 5 | /delete/{id} | DELETE | JSON | http://dummy.restapiexample.com/api/v1/delete/2 | Delete an employee record |

***Figure 6.1:*** *Dummy RESTful Service Online*

The below screenshot shows the result of calling an employees web service endpoint:

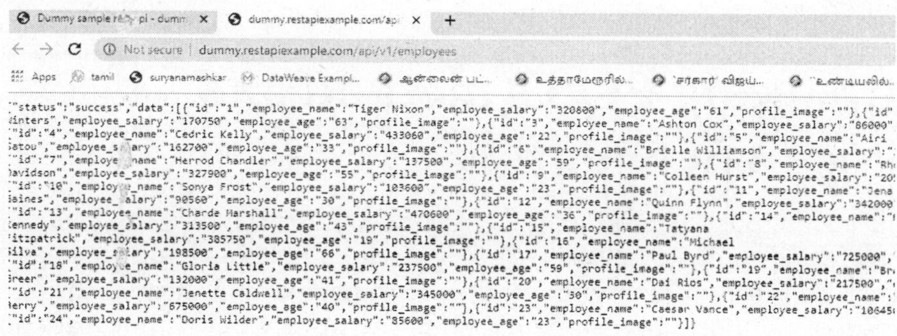


*Figure 6.2: Invoking Dummy RESTful Service*

This endpoint `/employees` lists all employees' records from a database:

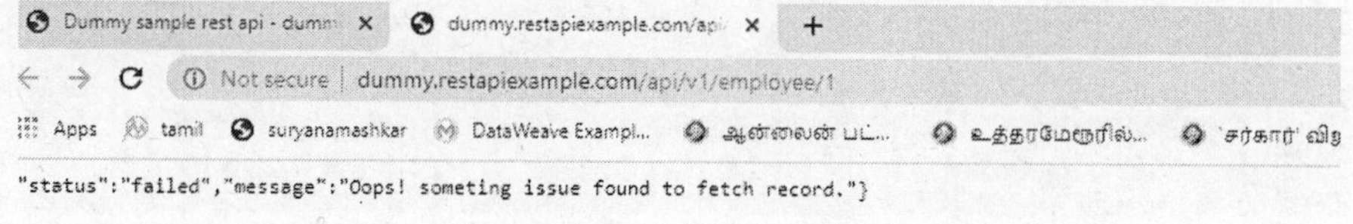


*Figure 6.3: Invoking RESTful Service using the query parameter*

The **http://dummy.restapiexample.com/api/v1/employee/1** link doesn't return any record since no employee records for employee ID 1. Revisit the all employees result and submit a valid available Employee ID as shown below:

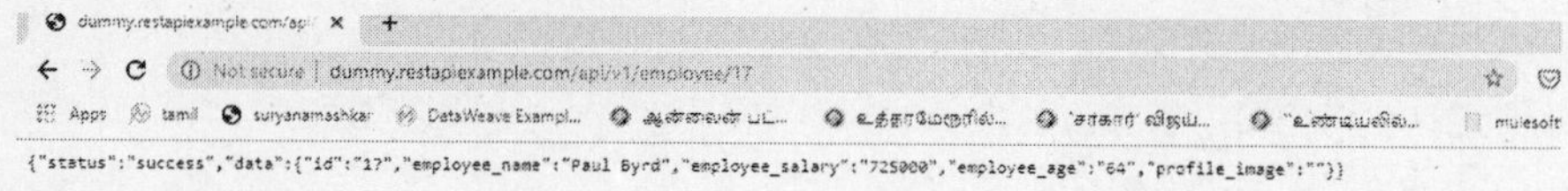


*Figure 6.3.a: Invoking RESTful Service using the query parameter*

The results for employee id 17 will be provided as shown above. Change the employee id of your preference and repeat the web service call.

# Invoking POST method and Postman client

To invoke post method to add a record into the database by calling create endpoint we need a Web service client like Postman. Postman is an API testing tool with multiple features like collections, storing results, etc. Postman can be integrated with continuous integration pipelines easily:

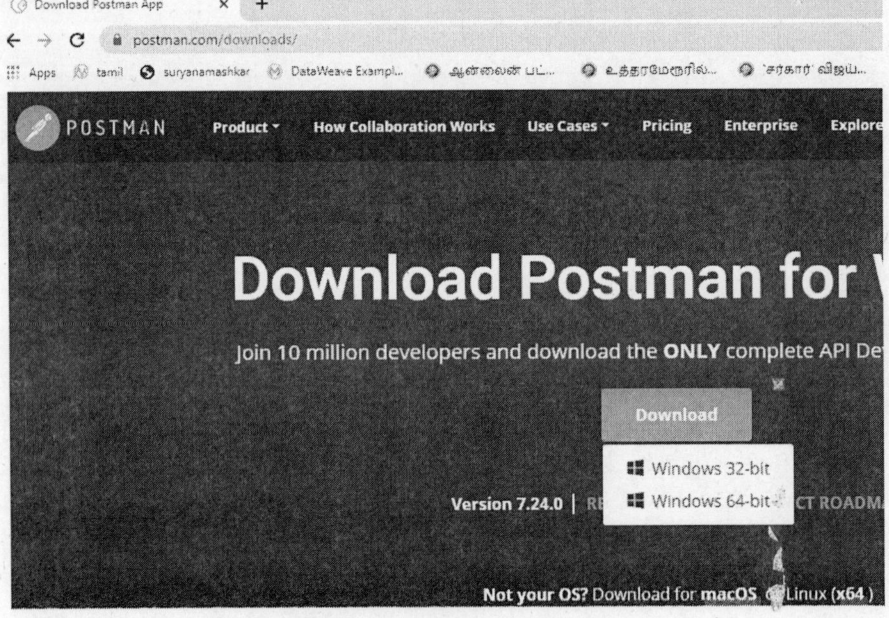


*Figure 6.4: downloading PostMan*

As shown above download the Postman and install:

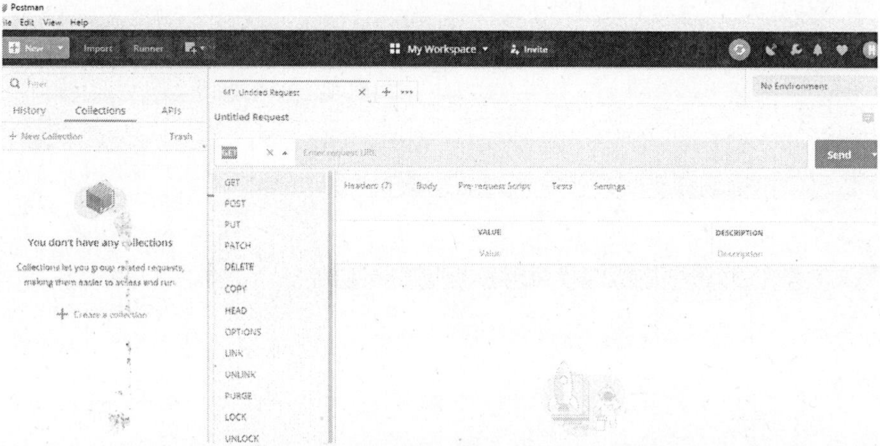

*Figure 6.5: Understanding PostMan*

The Postman comes with features like History, Collections, API spec storing, multiple web services methods like `GET`, `POST`, `PUT`, `DELETE`, etc. Also, Postman allows you to see the information shared by the server as **`Header`**, **`Body`**, etc. Multiple web service calls can be made using different tabs and can be revisited at any time:

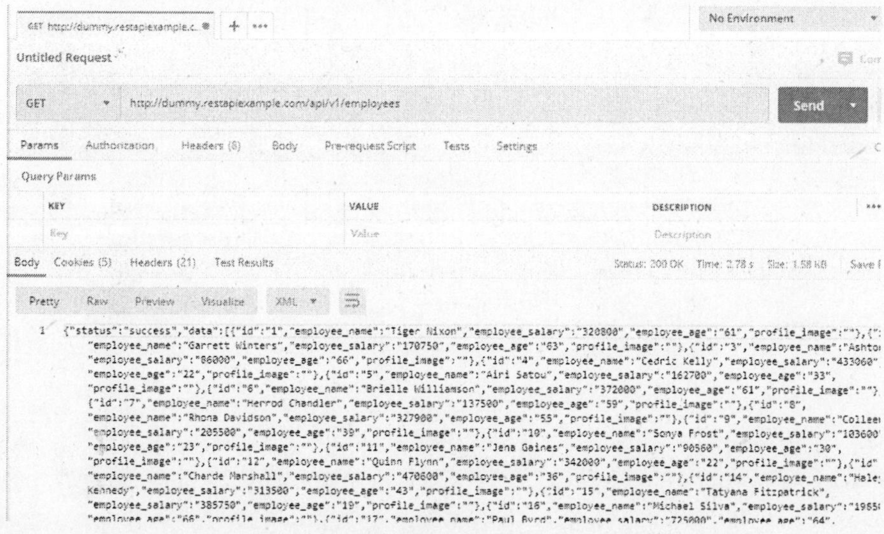


*Figure 6.6: Invoking Dummy Webservice using PostMan*

Try invoking the employees' details web service through Postman as shown above:

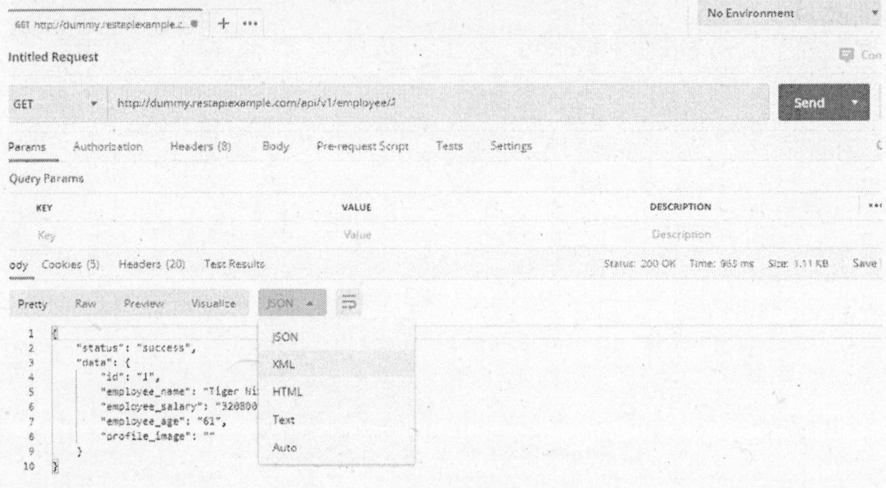

*Figure 6.7: Invoking Dummy web service using PostMan and checking the output*

Change and check the output type to XML or JSON in the body panel:

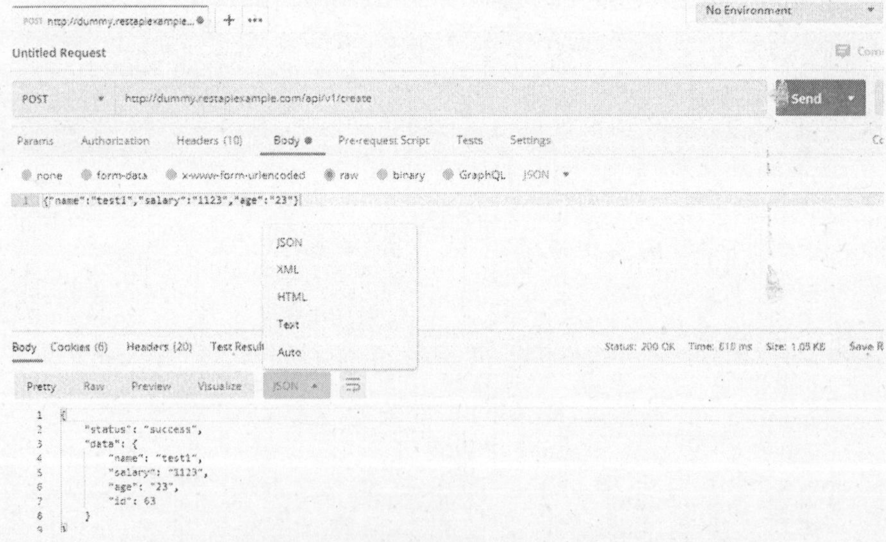

*Figure 6.8: Invoking POST web service*

Here are the steps to post a set of data to server-side web service to create an Employee record in the database. You have to change the method to `POST` and apply the **http://dummy.restapiexample.com/api/v1/create** URL as shown above. If you call the same URL from the browser you can see an error like method not allowed. Then in the **Body** tab choose datatype as raw and provide the JSON input for creating employee record:

*Figure 6.9: Invoking POST web service with different values*

In the bottom panel, you can see a success message and you can cross-check the entry by calling employee details web service:

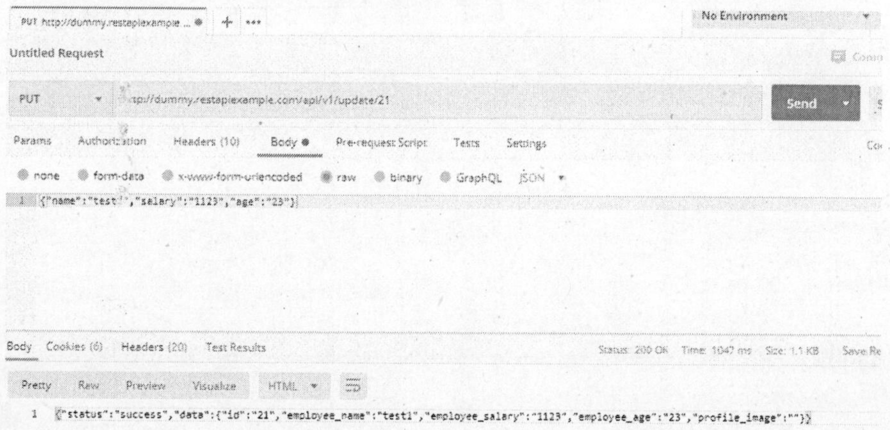


*Figure 6.10: Invoking PUT web service for updating values*

The PUT method is used for updating a specific record by inputting the employee id and other values to be updated as shown above:

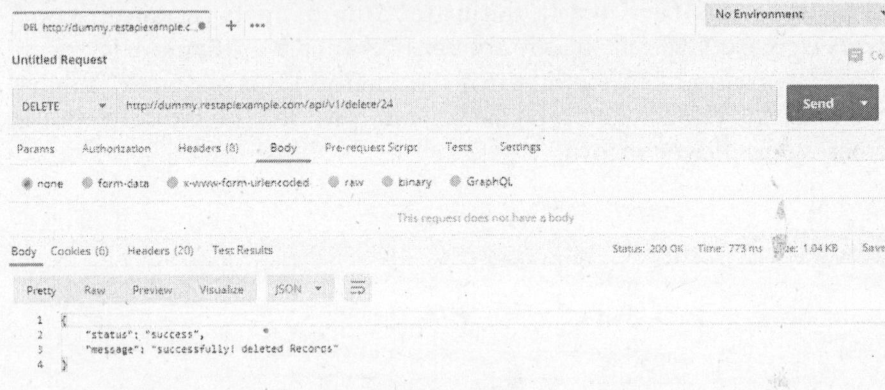


*Figure 6.11: Invoking DELETE web service for deleting*

Invoke the `delete` method by specifying employee record id and you can see a success message in the results panel:

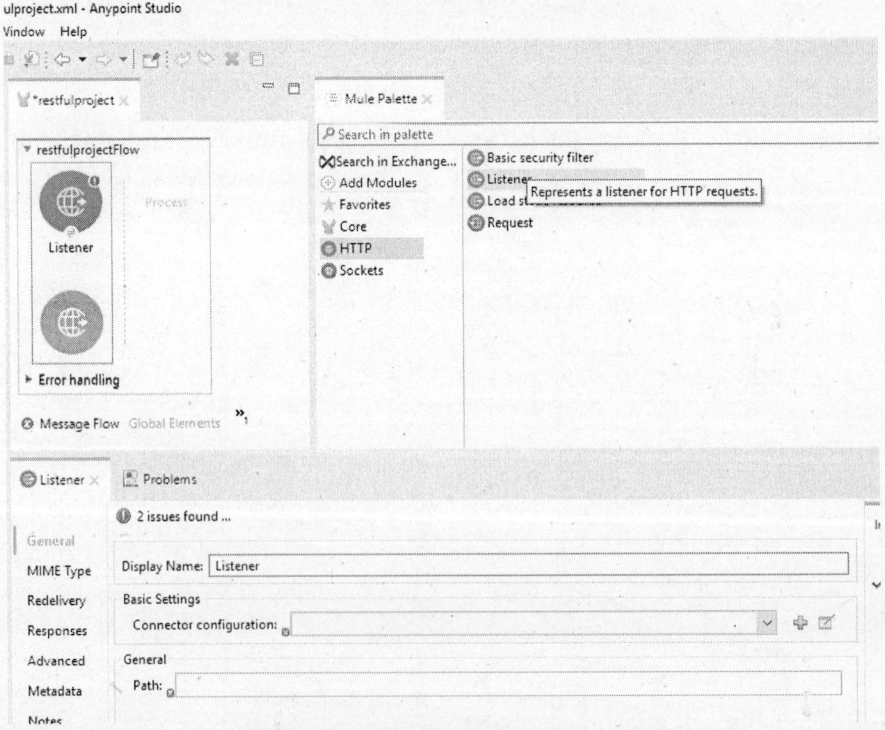


*Figure 6.12: Adding HTTP Listener*

Let us try to develop the RESTful HTTP web services using our Anypoint Studio. Create a basic flow with **`HTTP Listener config`** as shown above:

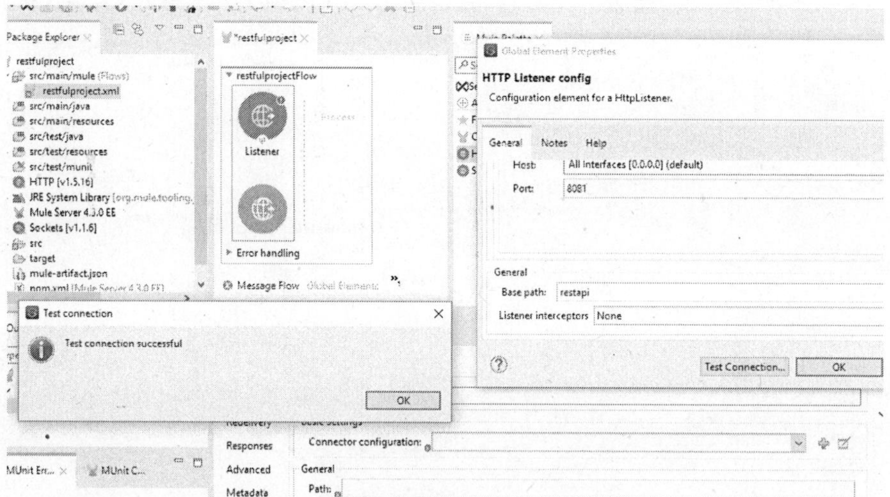


***Figure 6.13:** setting listener configurations*

The Listeners hostname will be localhost and if you need a base path you can set that in the base path field. The port number can be given as `8081` and you can test the connection and you will be getting a success message if the port number is not used by any other application servers:

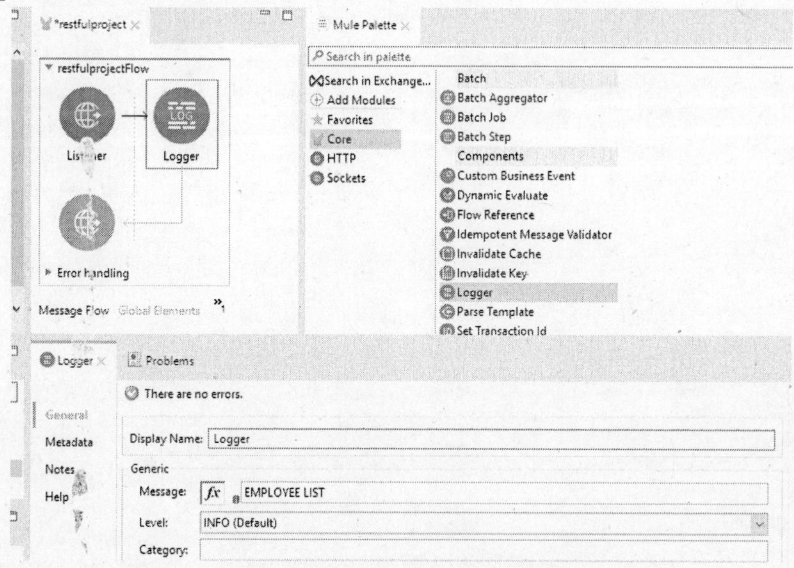


***Figure 6.14:** adding Logger element*

Add a **Logger** component and give some dummy information for testing purpose:

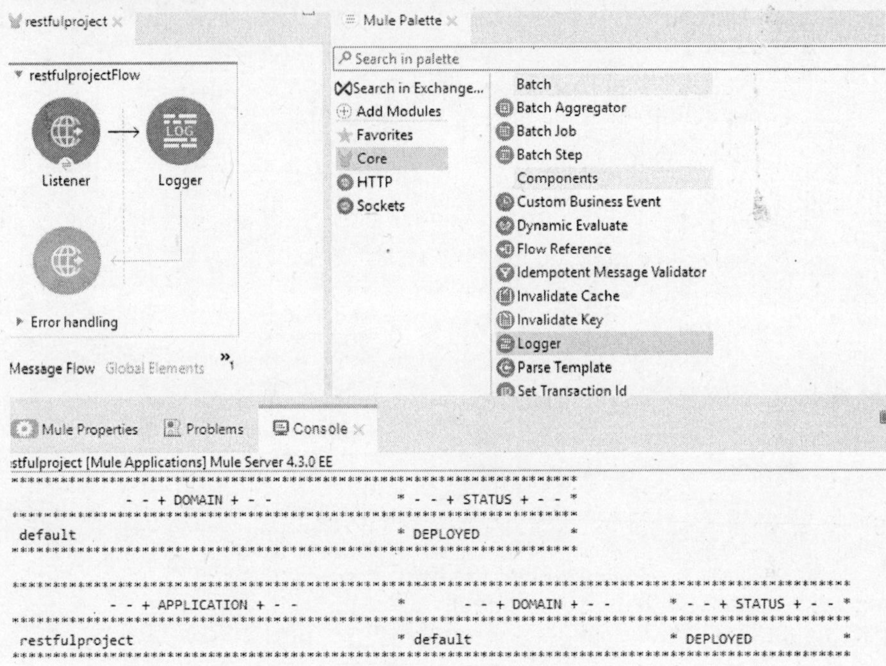


*Figure 6.15: Application Deployment*

Run and deploy the HTTP Listener flow:

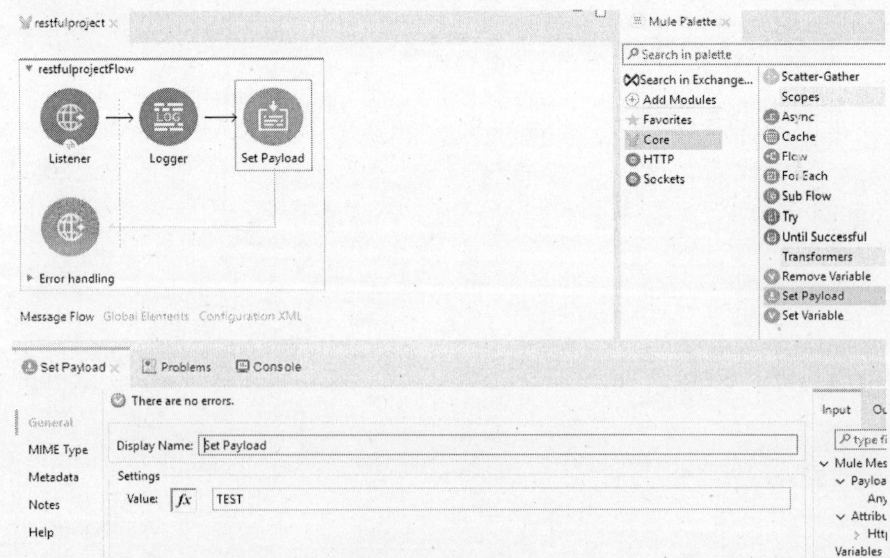


*Figure 6.16: Setting payload*

You can set a dummy payload value also:

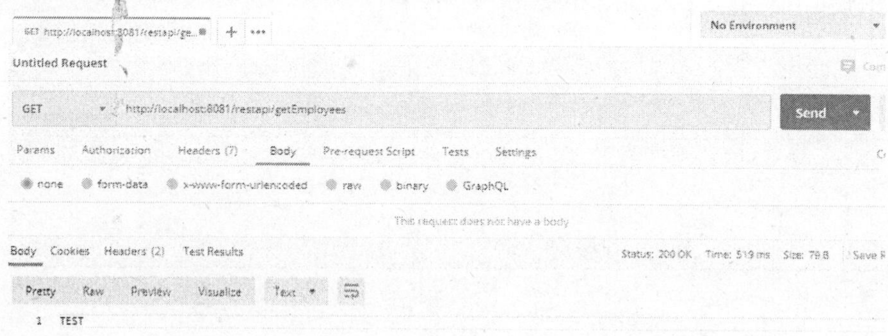


***Figure 6.17:*** *invoking employee service from the postman*

Invoke the `getEmployees` GET endpoint from Postman as above, you can get a success result:

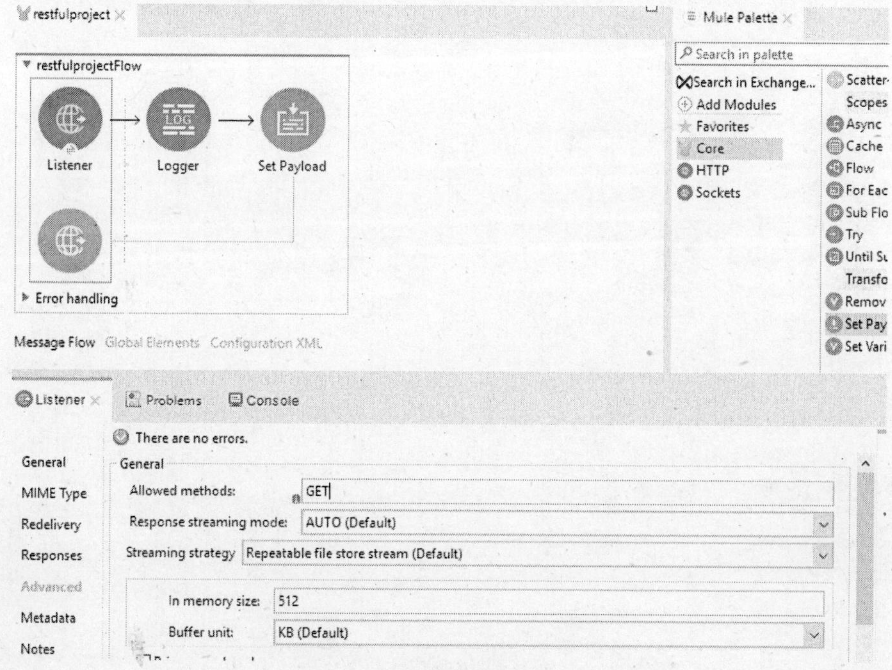


***Figure 6.17.a:*** *setting GET property*

You can notice that in the Listener dialogue we have explicitly mentioned the allowed method as `GET`:

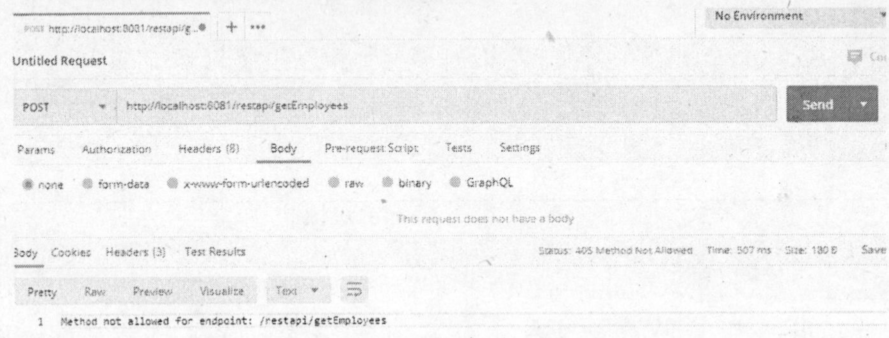


*Figure 6.18: checking the POST method*

Since we restricted the method type to `GET`, if we try to call the web service by choosing `POST` in postman, it would throw an error message saying method not allowed:

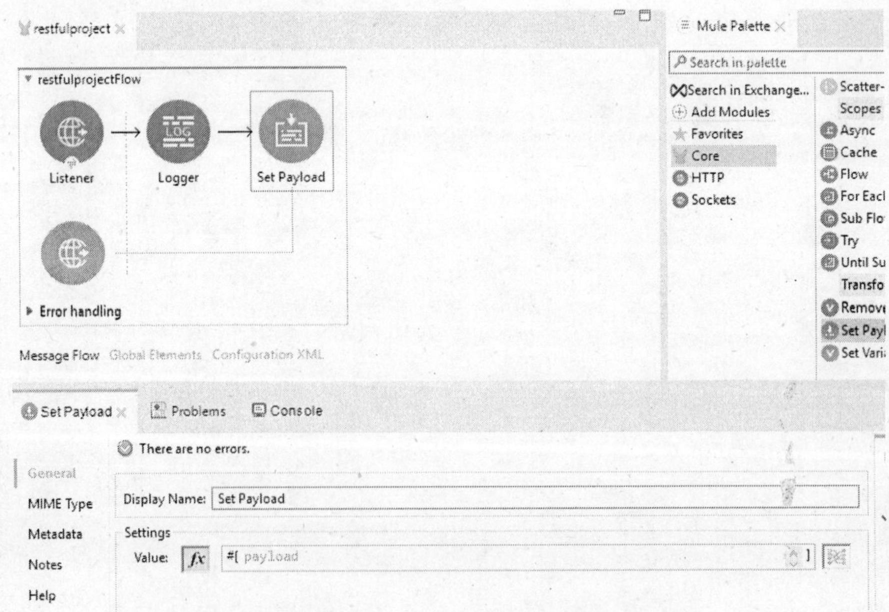


*Figure 6.19: POST method and Payload mapping*

So change the allowed method to **POST** and introduce a set payload component. In the payload component set the payload value to default payload value that means whatever payload submitted to server will be assigned as the server payload:

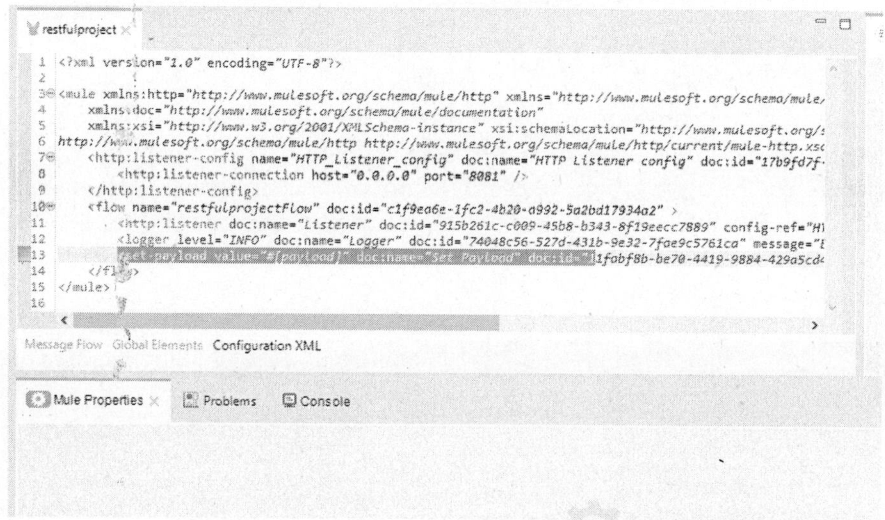

***Figure 6.20:** checking Payload related entries in the config file*

You can examine the config file settings for the **POST** endpoint:

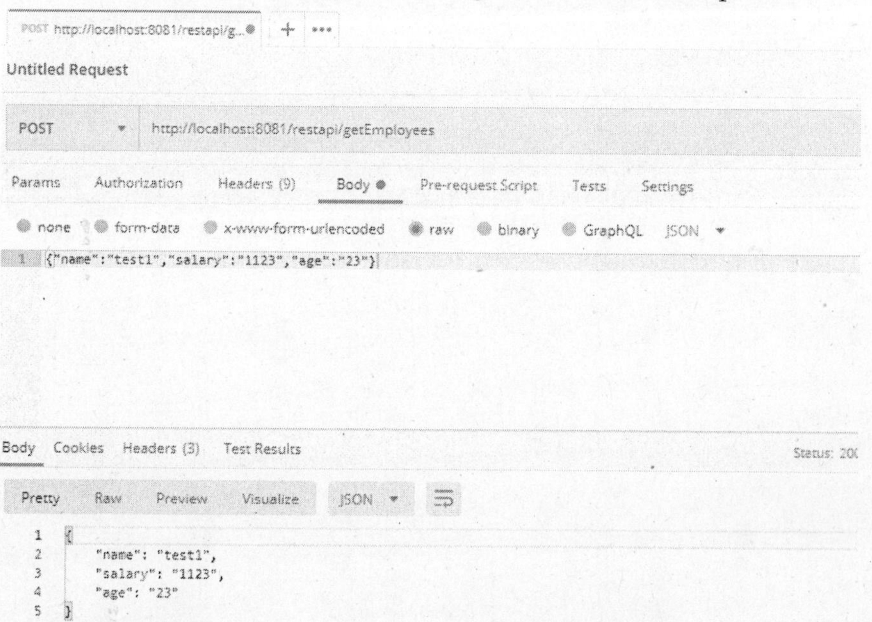

***Figure 6.21:** Retrieving the POSTed values through Payload mapping*

Invoke the `POST` web service from Postman and provide a dummy JSON data set as input that means a form submission kind of value set, now the value submitted will be set as a payload and will be posted back as a result.

# Invoking SOAP web services

To invoke post method to add a record into the database by calling creates endpoint we need a Web service client like Postman. SOAP stands for Simple Object Access Protocol and it is an XML based protocol. **WSDL** is the **Webservice Definition Language File** which will have information about all endpoints, inputs, and outputs.

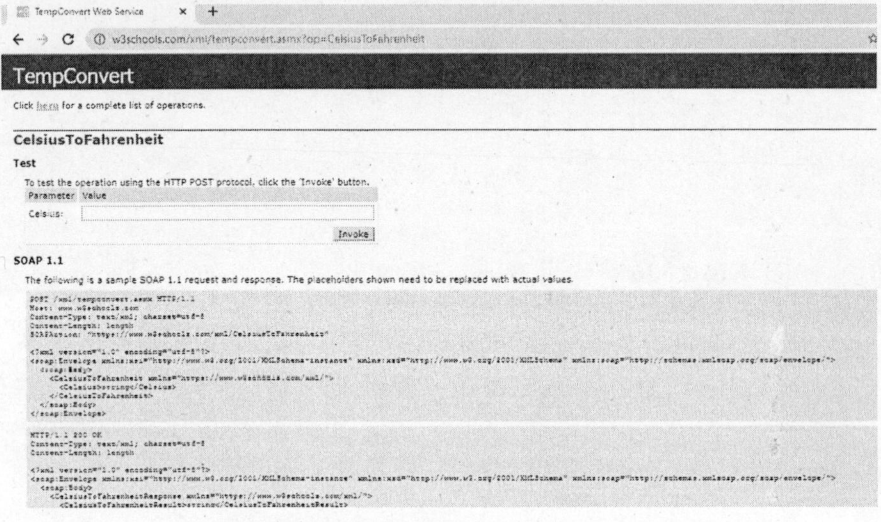


*Figure 6.22: Examining SOAP web service*

**https://www.w3schools.com/xml/tempconvert.asmx** access this link to have a look at the public WSDL provided by w3. Check out the `CelsiusToFahrenheit` and `FahrenheitToCelsius` web services details:

***Figure 6.23:*** *calling SOAP web service from HTTP Listener*

Let's us try to call SOAP web services inside our mule flow. Create an HTTP Listener as shown above and search for web service consumer and find the web service consumer component and add it to the MuleFlow:

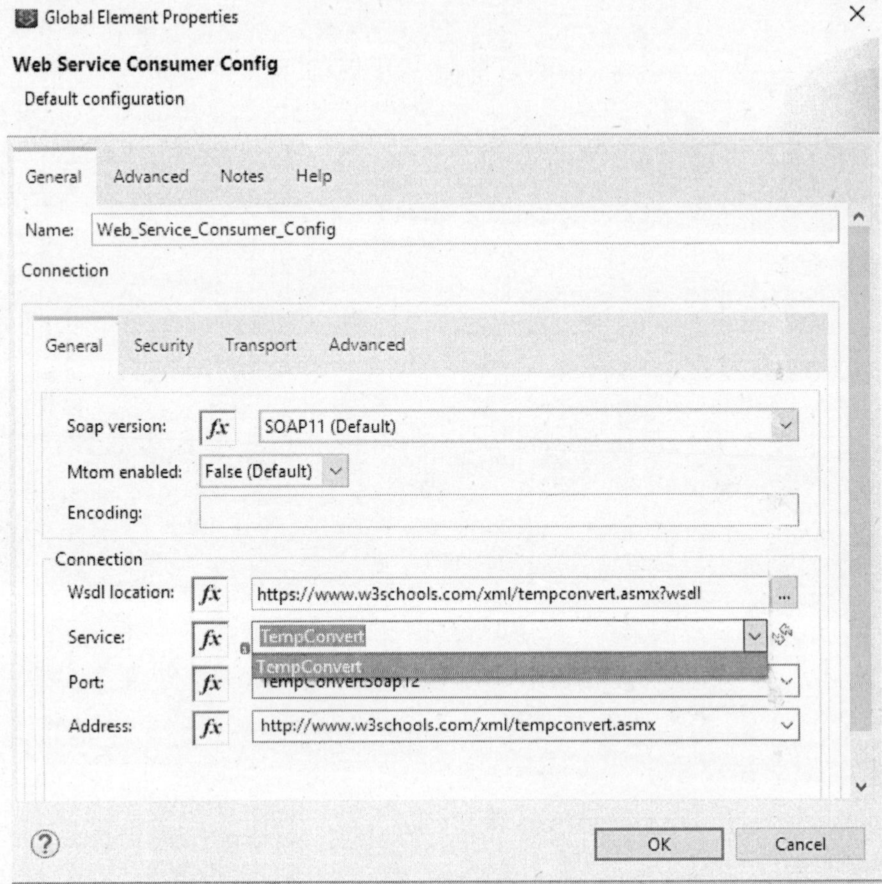


*Figure 6.23.a: calling SOAP web service from HTTP Listener*

Check out the connector configurations made above, provide the below link details in the WSDL Location field. **https://www.w3schools.com/xml/tempconvert.asmx?wsdl**

On successful configuration the fields Service, Port, and Address will be populated automatically:

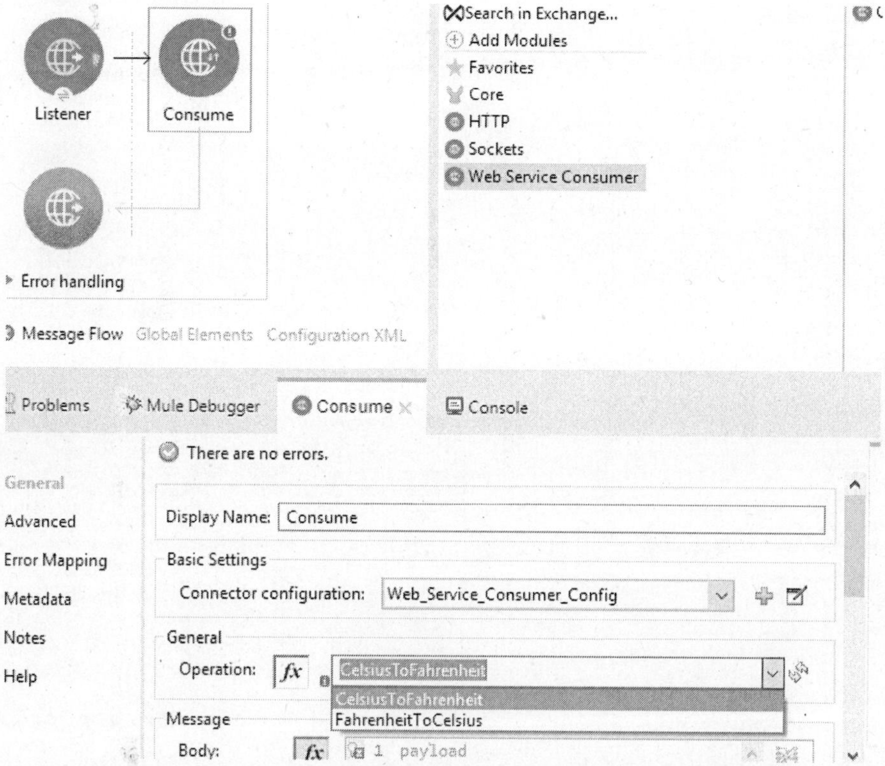

***Figure 6.23.b:** calling SOAP web service from HTTP Listener*

Once the configurations are done properly the SOAP web service operations will be visible in the `Consume` component panel. Choose the operation of your choice. Our idea is to invoke the SOAP web service rather getting the data from web service by providing some meaningful inputs, etc.:

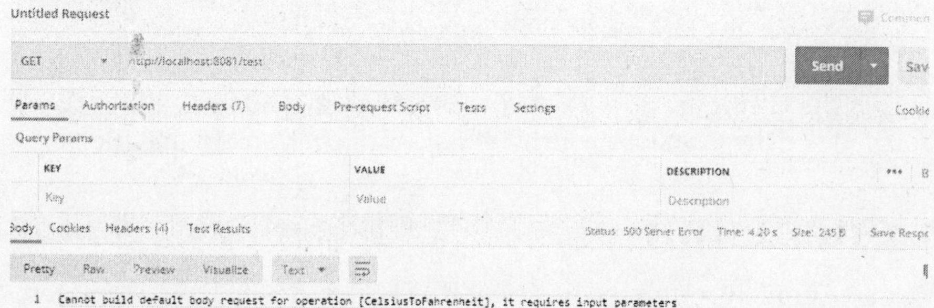


***Figure 6.24:** Calling SOAP web service through mule flow from the Postman*

So as shown in the above Postman screenshot, just try to run the flow and you can see an error message thrown from the public SOAP API:

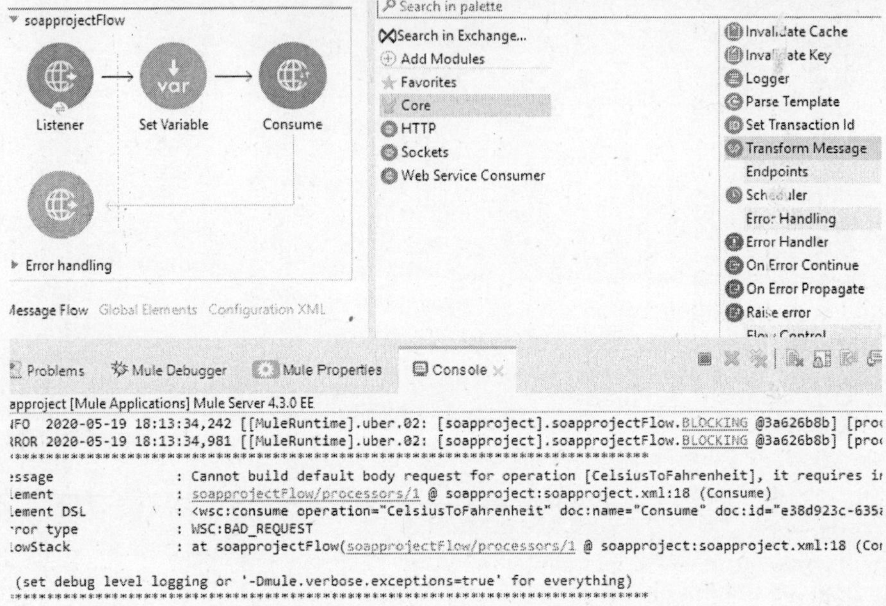


*Figure 6.25: Receiving error response from SOAP service*

Examine the console output to understand the `WSC:BAD_REQUEST` error and detail:

```
http://www.mulesoft.org/schema/mule/wsc http://www.mulesoft.org/schema/mule/wsc/current/mule-wsc.xsd
http://www.mulesoft.org/schema/mule/ee/core http://www.mulesoft.org/schema/mule/ee/core/current/mule-ee.xsd">
    <http:listener-config name="HTTP_Listener_config" doc:name="HTTP Listener config" doc:id="e171f370-82a5-4b7b-8ae0-a275534a383e" >
        <http:listener-connection host="0.0.0.0" port="8081" />
    </http:listener-config>
    <wsc:config name="Web_Service_Consumer_Config" doc:name="Web Service Consumer Config" doc:id="aa34bb81-7f91-48cc-a8d3-62211fa84995" >
        <wsc:connection wsdlLocation="https://www.w3schools.com/xml/tempconvert.asmx?wsdl" service="TempConvert" port="TempConvertSoap12"
        address="http://www.w3schools.com/xml/tempconvert.asmx" />
    </wsc:config>
    <flow name="soapprojectFlow" doc:id="120e2041-e88b-40df-aef4-b0b2c54e0613" >
        <http:listener doc:name="Listener" doc:id="1ce5a3d9-87c1-477b-85b7-2f427f9ba6f0" config-ref="HTTP_Listener_config" path="test"/>
        <set-variable value="#[message.attributes.queryParams.Temp]" doc:name="Set Variable" doc:id="bfbf2f1c-81fe-4ec7-b369-7db8cd3796ea" variableName="inputTemp"/>
        <wsc:consume operation="CelsiusToFahrenheit" doc:name="Consume" doc:id="e38d923c-635a-4958-88bd-0f218a69c4d9" config-ref="Web_Service_Consumer_Config"/>
    </flow>
</mule>
```

*Figure 6.26: SOAP service flow config file*

This is the configuration file of the SOAP web services calling flow. You can see the `Consume` components configurations in this file.

# Conclusion

We have gone through the basics of RESTful and SOAP web services. The postman client has been installed in our systems and we invoked

RESTful web service through Postman. In the RESTful web services we have invoked methods like `GET`, `POST`, `PUT`, and `DELETE` using a publicly available dummy web service like dummy employee web service.

We developed an HTTP Listener flow in Anypoint Studio and implemented endpoints for `GET` and `POST` methods. Through Postman we were able to invoke the web services which are locally deployed using Anypoint Studio.

In our next chapter, we will explore the RAML basics, designing a basic RESTful API with RAML specifications, and testing the same.

# Points to remember

- Try to implement more web services with methods like `GET`, `POST`, `PUT`, and `DELETE`.
- Understand the web service clients other than Postman and try to use them also to invoke web services.
- Go through the Postman features to understand the concepts like headers, body, application type, etc.

# Key terms to explore

- Postman
- Port number/URL
- RESTful
- SOAP
- GET, POST, PUT, and DELETE methods
- HTTP Listener
- API endpoints
- Posting data to the server
- JSON XML TEXT output types

# Chapter 7
# Start RAML

In this chapter we will discuss the following topics:

- RAML introduction
- Anypoint RAML Designer
- RAML specifications for GET, POST, PUT, and DELETE
- Testing RAML endpoints

## Objectives

After studying this unit, you should be able to understand:

- The basic structure of RAML specification
- Writing RAML specifications
- Integrating RAML specifications with Anypoint Studio
- Developing GET, POST, PUT, and DELETE endpoints
- Testing the RAML specifications
- Defining your RAML specs and integrating with Anypoint Studio

# Pre-requisites

Understanding of RESTful web services, Endpoint concepts like GET and POST methods, submitting data to server-side, Anypoint Studio, Anypoint Exchange are the few areas you must be familiar with by this time if you follow the previous chapters with some hands-on experience. It is also important to understand and practice publicly available REST and SOAP web services for testing purposes. Apart from Postman, you may try some other Web Services Clients like cURL, Fiddler, SoapUI, etc.

# RAML basics

RAML stands for RESTful API Modeling Language, which helps us to describe/specify all the information required to develop a clean pre-tested RESTful API. The API designers need not worry about how the internal technical aspects are handled by developers to execute the API and get the desired result out of various endpoints. But the API designers must have held about the whole API design, specifications like the name of the endpoint, input types, output types, input examples, output examples, response code handling, testing the API specification before releasing for development, testing, and user acceptance teams.

RAML is the best language for designing an API from scratch by providing all the required details. Also, RAML is having capabilities to handle repetitive specifications say, for example, the response example may be repetitive throughout the design and using RAML we can keep the example output in a separate file and we can provide the reference of the file where ever required.

In this chapter we will be designing the following endpoints in Anypoint Designer; we can test the specifications in the Designer itself before sharing it to developers or testers. Then we can integrate the specifications inside a MuleSoft Studio project for implementation. This is nothing but developing a CRUD operation API, means Create Retrieve Update and Delete for one entity like Employee:

- `GET: http://localhost:8081/api/getAllEmployeeDetails`
- `POST: http://localhost:8081/ api /postEmployees`
- `GET: http://localhost:8081/ api /getEmployeeDetail/{empid}`

- PUT: http://localhost:8081/ api /updateEmployees/ {empid}
- DELETE: http://localhost:8081/api/deleteEmployees/ {empid}

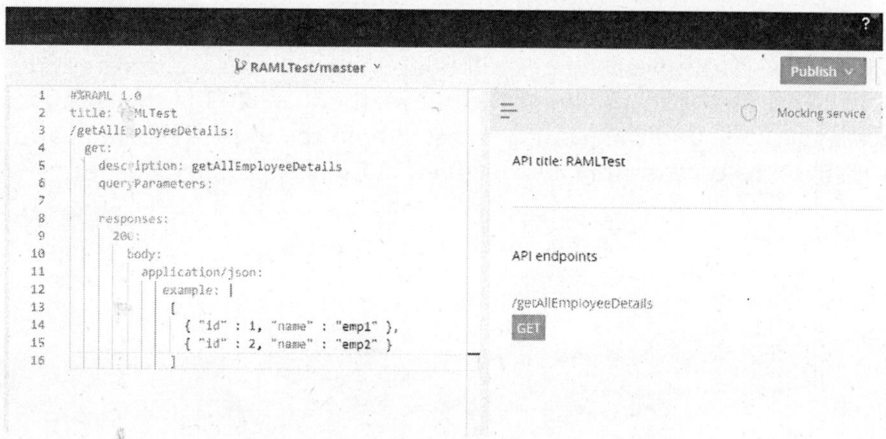


*Figure 7.1: Writing RAML code for getEmployees*

Login to the exchange and start designing an API as shown above. Here is the code of the RAML specification:

```
#%RAML 1.0
baseUri: https://anypoint.mulesoft.com/mocking/api/v1/
links/75f39179-12c4-4a72-a73c-cf8064b39894/ #
title: RAMLTest

/getEmployeeDetails:
  get:
    description: getEmployeeDetails;
    responses:
      200:
        body:
          application/json:
            example: |
              [
                { "id" : 1, "name" : "emp7" },
                { "id" : 2, "name" : "emp7" }
              ]
```

You can use the above code as it is in your designer. RAML version is 1.0 and the name is `RAMLTest`. In the next line we are mentioning the endpoint name `/getEmployeeDetails:`. If you are first-timer, you can directly type the endpoint name and press *Enter*. This will take you to the next line with proper indentation. The next line is to define the method type, it can be `GET, POST, PUT, DELETE`, etc. You can have a description of the get method. Next mandatory information what will be the response of the get method. So `200` is the positive response code and the result body will hold the in JSON format, and the JSON result example also is given in the RAML specification:

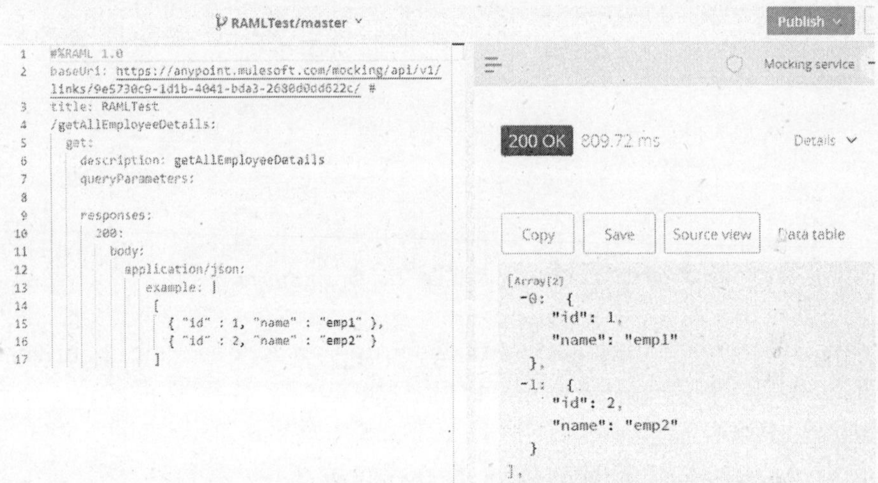


***Figure 7.2:** Executing RAML code for getEmployees*

You may not be having the `baseUri` while designing the API, once you are okay to test the `Spec` you can toggle the **`Mocking Service`** button on the right upper corner and a `Mock` service will be deployed for you to test the correctness of the spec. Click on the endpoint link shown after successful deployment click the **`GET`** button and **`TRY`**

**`IT`** button then **`SEND`** button, then you can see the `get` method got invoked and the expected result is populated:

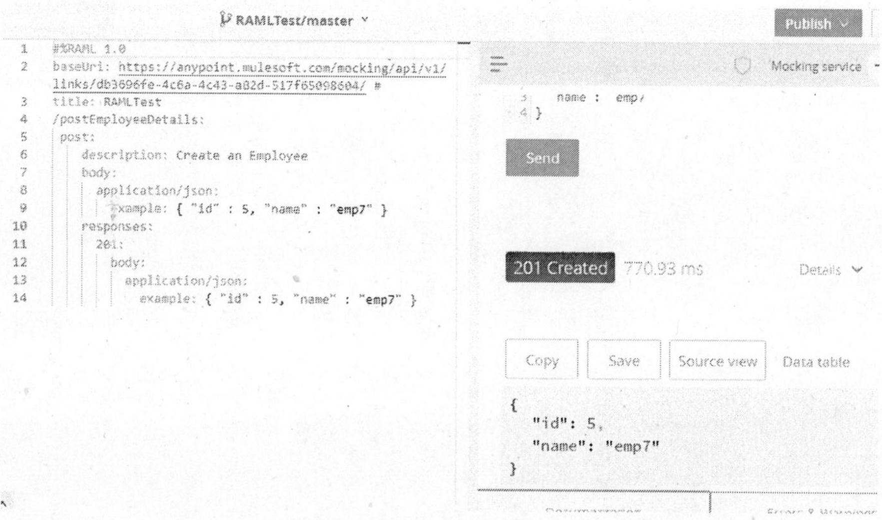


*Figure 7.3: Writing and executing RAML code for postEmployees*

Here is the code for `postEmployeeDetails` endpoint:

```
/postEmployeeDetails:
  post:
    description: Create an Employee
    body:
      application/json:
        example: { "id" : 5, "name" : "emp7" }
    responses:
      201:
        body:
          application/json:
            example: { "id" : 5, "name" : "emp7" }
```

Use the specifications as it is and you can see a difference that the body application type also comes with an example JSON data set:

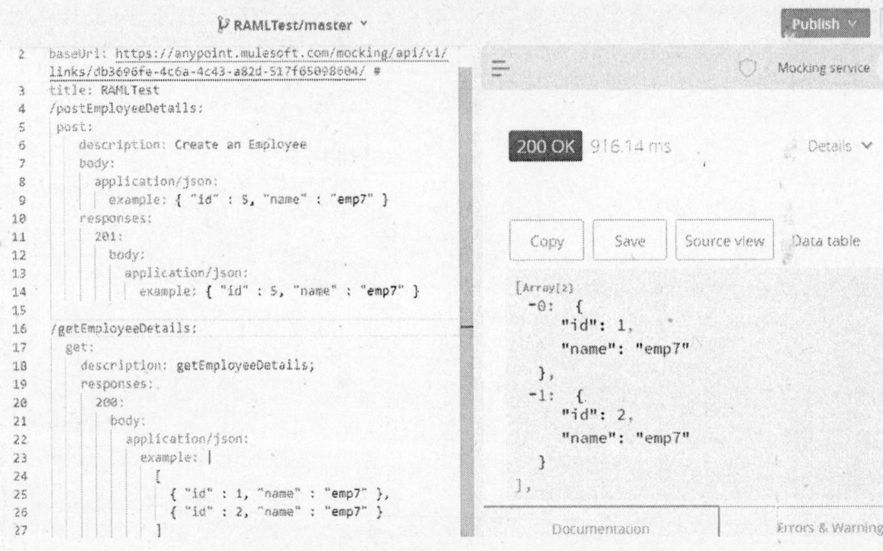

*Figure 7.4: merging get and post employees*

Add this code to the existing specification and follow the same steps. Click the Mock Service, click the endpoint link, click the **POST** button, **TRY IT** button and SEND button to invoke the POST method and get a response:

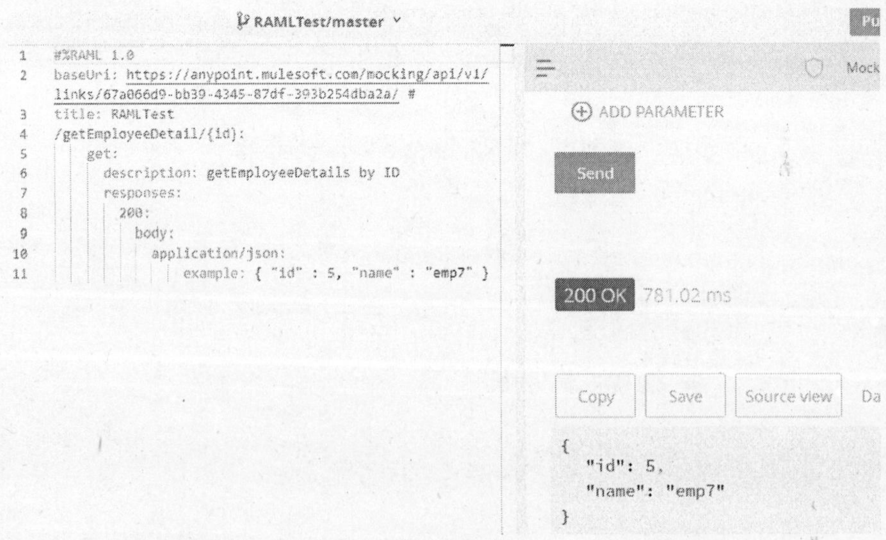

*Figure 7.5: Writing RAML code for getEmployees by ID*

Append the below code to existing RAML specification to create a `getemployee` get end point by passing a employee ID parameter:

```
/getEmployeeDetail/{id}:
 get:
    description: get EmployeeDetails;
    responses:
      200:
        body:
          application/json:
            example: |
              [
                { "id" : 2, "name" : "emp7" }
              ]
```

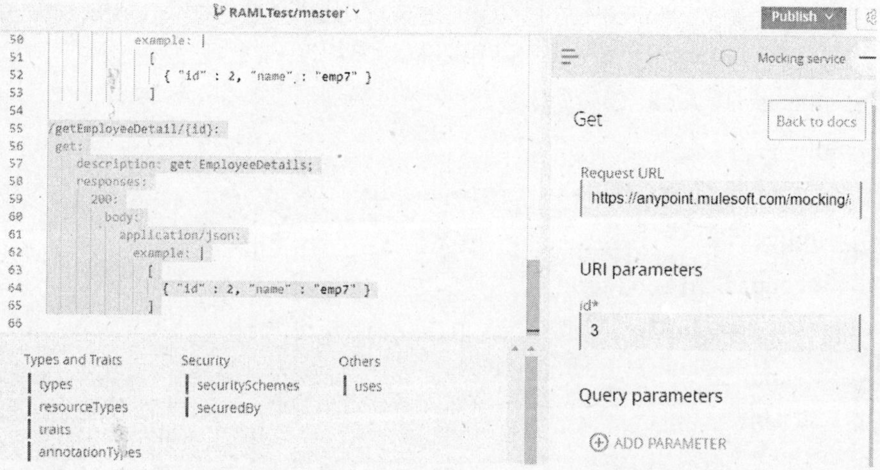

*Figure 7.5.a: executing RAML code for getEmployees by ID*

The **Mocking Service** panel automatically provides you a field for entering the employee ID go ahead and execute the API:

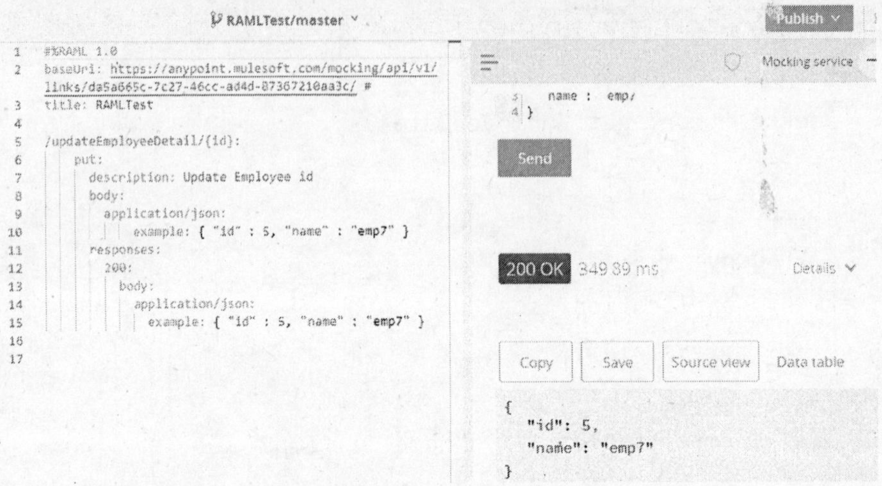

*Figure 7.6: Writing RAML code for update Employee by ID*

Here is the code for updating employee API:

```
/updateEmployeeDetail/{id}:
  put:
    description: Update Employee id
    body:
      application/json:
          example: { "id" : 5, "name" : "emp7" }
    responses:
      200:
        body:
          application/json:
            example: { "id" : 5, "name" : "emp7" }
```

Move this code to the designer editor and execute as shown above:

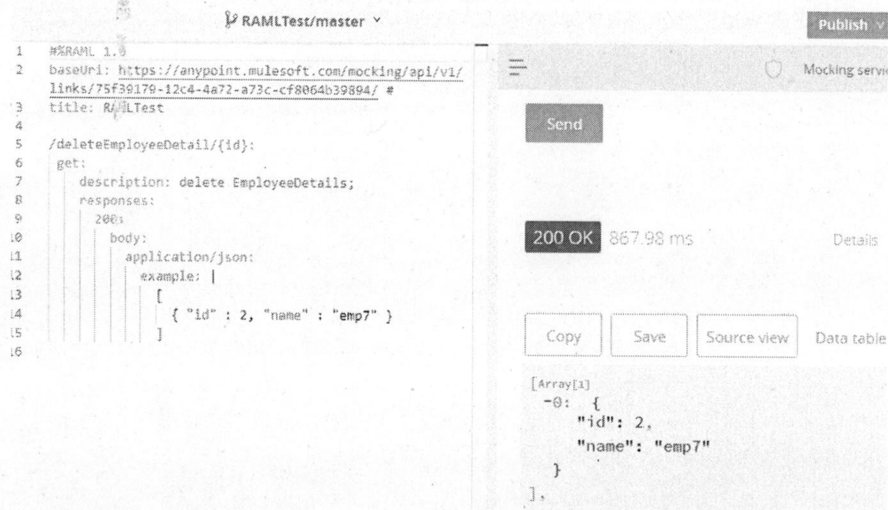


***Figure 7.7:*** *Writing RAML code for  delete Employee*

The code for delete endpoint. Update the specs and execute:

```
/deleteEmployeeDetail/{id}:
  get:
    description: delete EmployeeDetails;
    responses:
      200:
        body:
          application/json:
            example: |
              [
                { "id" : 2, "name" : "emp7" }
              ]
```

Now let us merge all the resources into a single file:

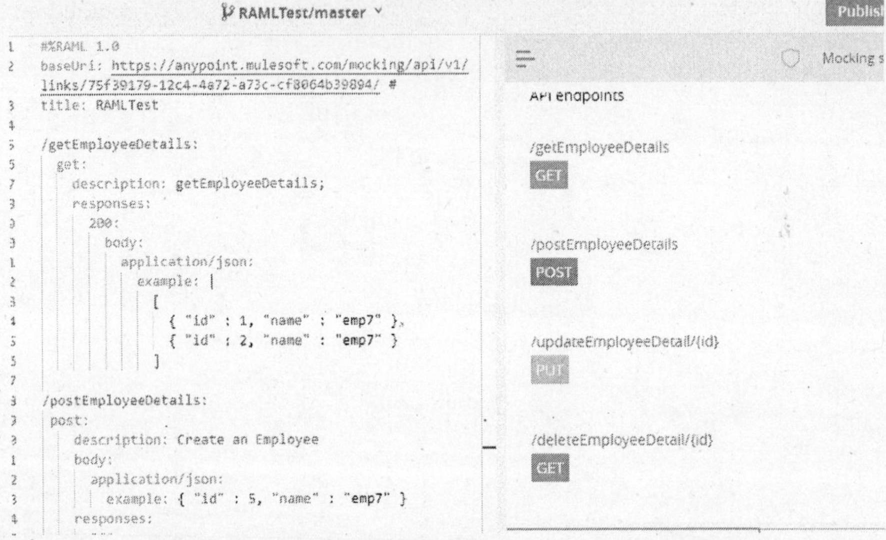


***Figure 7.8:*** *Merging get post put and delete employee methods*

The above screenshot shows the complete CRUD operations of the `EmployeeAPI` with all endpoints. Now it is time for integrating the developed specifications into Anypoint Studio, means the API designer done with his work and specifications are being shared with developers in real-time scenario, for our practice purpose we are integrating our specs with Anypoint Studio:

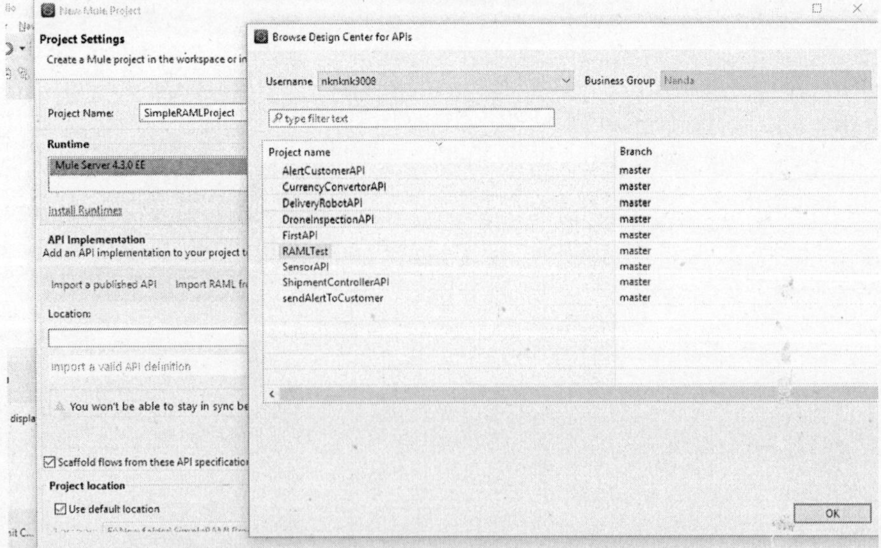


***Figure 7.9:*** *Import RAML specification to AnypointStudio*

But there is a possibility that the API Designer can work with Anypoint Studio as well in the future so that around 50 percent of API development can be completed by API designer, only the complex business logic will be implemented by MuleSoft developers by implementing advanced concepts like transformers, security, policies, encryption, etc.

By this time you must be familiar with importing API Specifications into an Anypoint Studio Project, go ahead and do it as shown in the screenshot above:

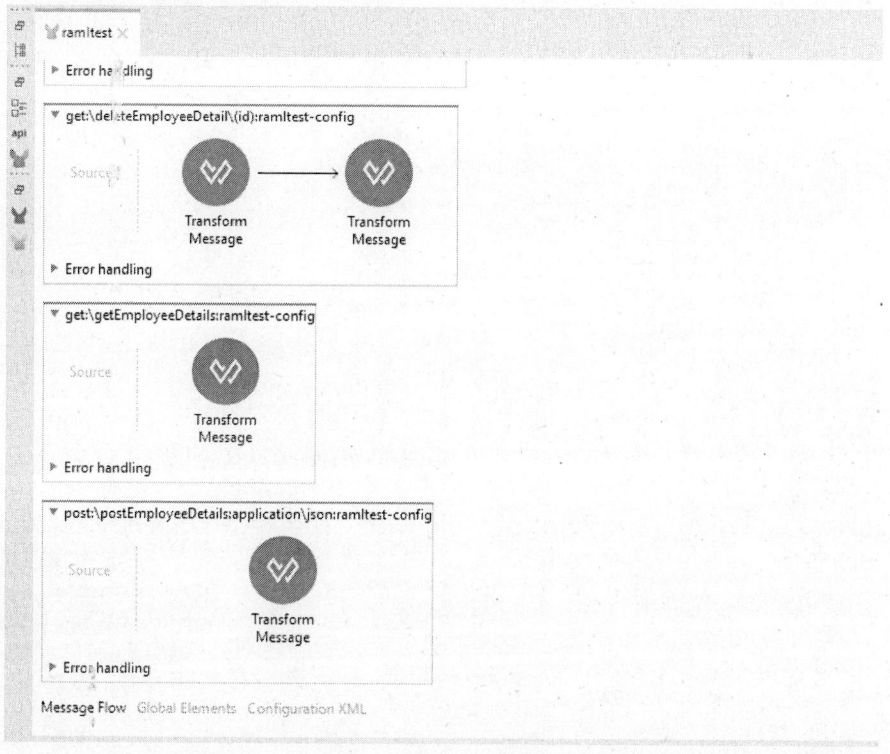


***Figure 7.10:*** *Result after completing the import.png*

The result of importing RAML API Spec from Exchange to Anypoint Project:

ramltest

```
    </flow>
    <flow name="get:\getEmployeeDetails:ramltest-config">
        <ee:transform xmlns:ee="http://www.mulesoft.org/schema/mule/ee/core" xsi:schemaLoca
            <ee:message>
                <ee:set-payload><![CDATA[%dw 2.0
output application/json
---
[
  {
    id: 1,
    name: "emp7"
  },
  {
    id: 2,
    name: "emp7"
  }
]]]></ee:set-payload>
            </ee:message>
        </ee:transform>
    </flow>
    <flow name="post:\postEmployeeDetails:application\json:ramltest-config">
        <ee:transform xmlns:ee="http://www.mulesoft.org/schema/mule/ee/core" xsi:schemaLoca
            <ee:message>
                <ee:set-payload><![CDATA[%dw 2.0
output application/json
---
{
  id: 5,
  name: "emp7"
}]]></ee:set-payload>
            </ee:message>
        </ee:transform>
    </flow>
</mule>
```

*Figure 7.10.a: The result after completing the import - checking config file entries*

Have a look at the configuration file where the RAML Specifications converted as MuleSoft code:

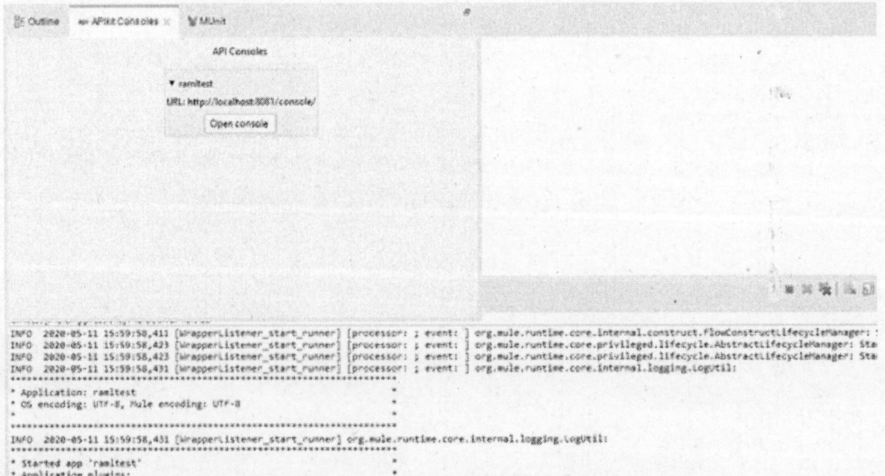


*Figure 7.11: Project deployed*

Go ahead and run the project:

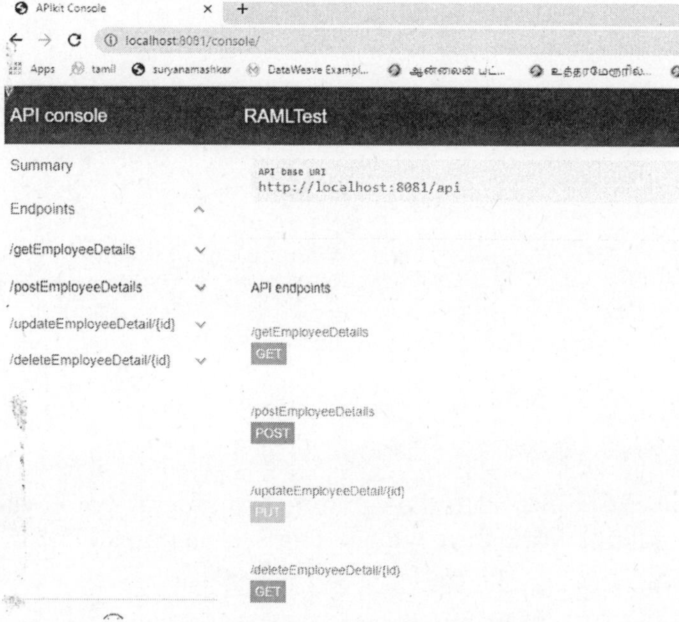


***Figure 7.12:*** *APIs running in console*

On successful deployment console will come out automatically and access the browser to explore all endpoints:

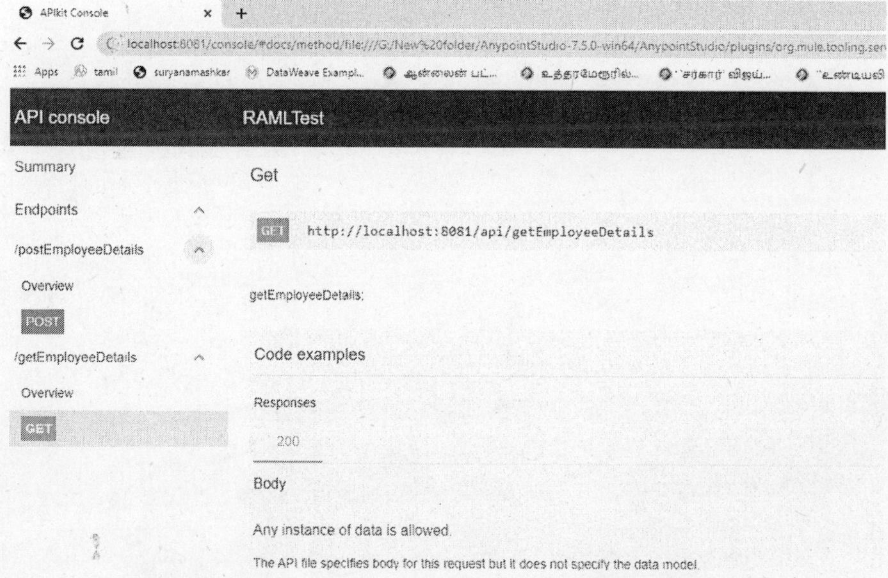


***Figure 7.12.a:*** *APIs running in the console - checking URLs*

Check the endpoints directly from the console:

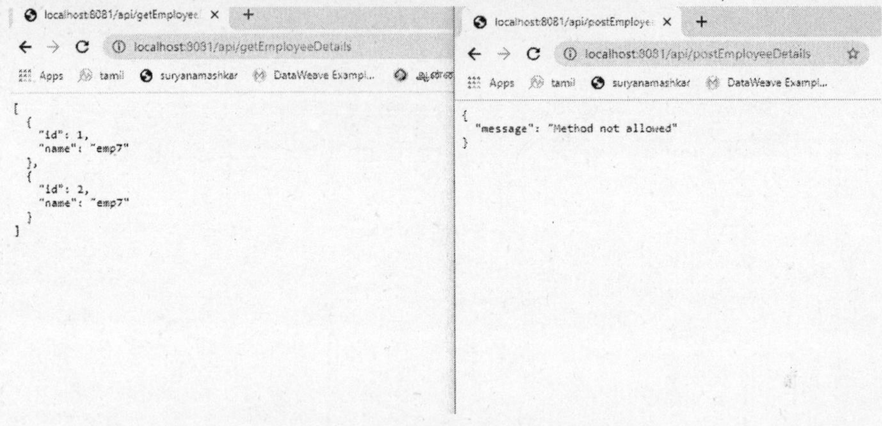


***Figure 7.12.b:*** *calling APIs from browser*

Check the endpoints from the separate browser, as you aware `POST` method will not work since we need a client to post data:

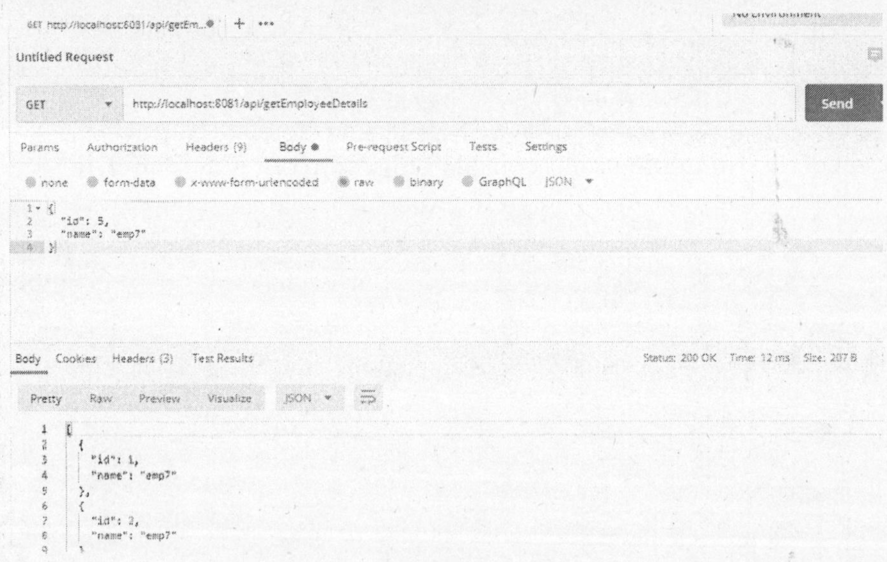


***Figure 7.13:*** *calling getEmployees*

Using Postman to invoke `GET` endpoint:

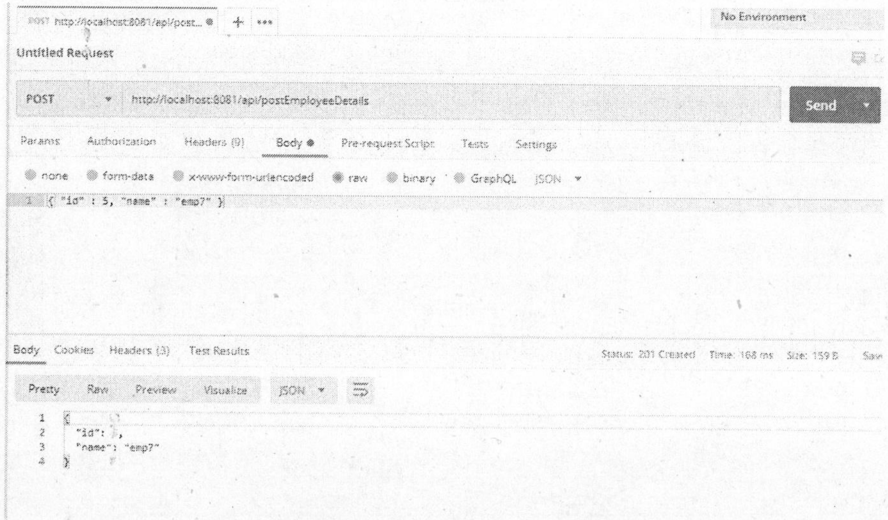


***Figure 7.14:** calling post employees*

Using Postman to invoke `POST` endpoint:

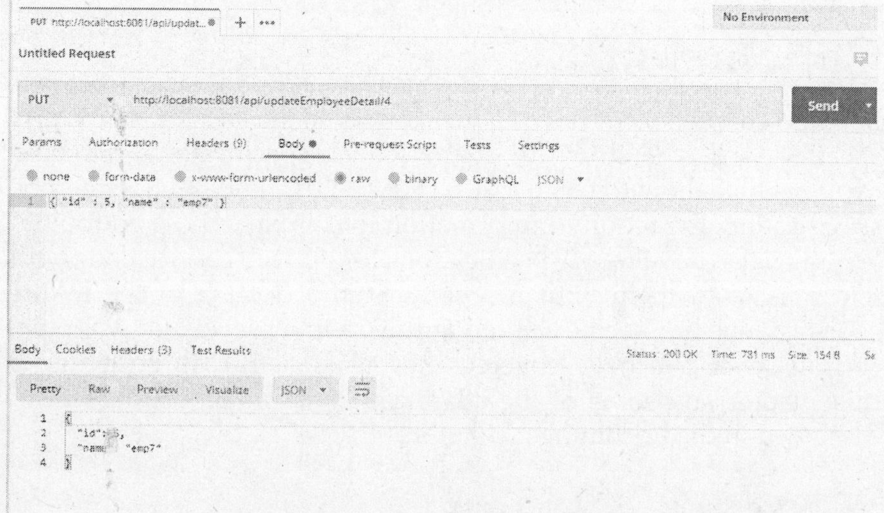


***Figure 7.15:** calling update Employees*

Using Postman to invoke `PUT` endpoint:

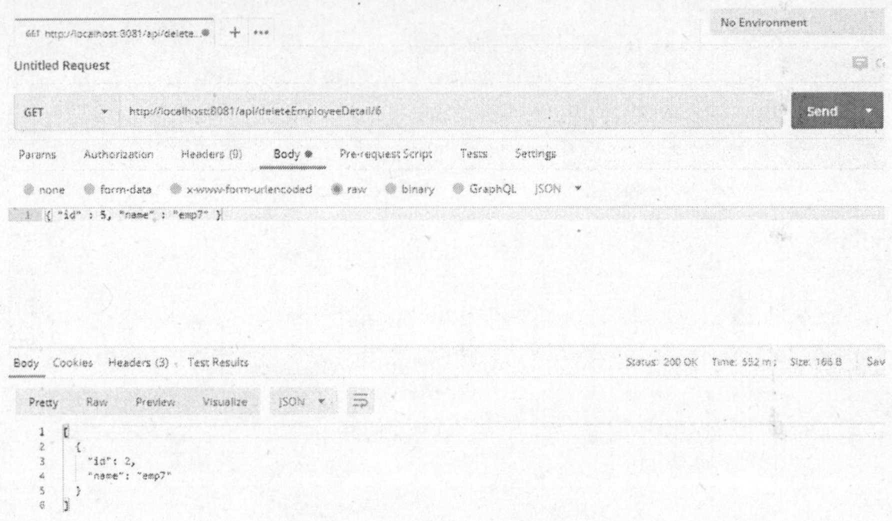

*Figure 7.16: calling delete Employees*

Using Postman to invoke delete endpoints.

# Conclusion

In this chapter, we have gone through the basics of RAML specifications. The structure of the RAML specifications has been explained like how to write a `GET`, `POST`, `PUT`, and `DELETE` method specification, the required information to complete these endpoints. We have also developed specifications for all web service endpoints and integrated them with Anypoint Studio. Testing of the RAML specifications has been executed at the designer level and Anypoint console level. We have covered the basics of RAML structure in this chapter and some of the advanced concepts of RAML will be discussed in the upcoming 2 chapters.

# Points to remember

- Now we can design the RAML specifications for different endpoints, integrate with Anypoint Studio, and can test using Postman.
- We can use any other web service client other than Postman.

- No need to limit yourself with the examples given in this project, try different endpoints for multiple domains and practice.
- The web services clients are having more features like automated testing, saving multiple requests for future use, etc. You can go ahead and try those options or understand the advanced features of such kind of clients.
- This chapter does not require any technical prerequisites, anybody from any business domain can practice API designing using API designer, Anypoint Studio, and console.
- This chapter demands you to focus more on Designing API Specifications rather than coding some implementations as an API designer.

# Key terms to explore

- RAML
- RAML structure
- GET, POST, PUT, and DELETE
- Postman
- Anypoint Studio, Exchange, Design center
- Mocking Service
- Response code

# CHAPTER 8
# RAML in Detail

In this chapter we will discuss the following topics:

- RAML examples importing
- Query parameter
- Media types
- Type definition and nested types
- RAML libraries
- Traits
- Extensions
- Resource types
- Schemas
- Type systems definition
- Autofill options in RAML editor
- The visual editor in the design center
- Exploring RAML specifications from Exchange
- HTTP response codes

# Objectives

After studying this unit, you should be able to understand:

- Develop RAML specifications using advanced techniques
- Understand the RAML specs in Exchange
- Handle data types in RAML
- Reusable error and example RAML files.
- Query parameters handling
- HTTP response codes
- Traits in RAML

# Pre-requisites

You must be familiar with basic RAML creation, importing to Anypoint Studio, and the structure of basic RAML. It is important to simulate the RAML specifications inside the Anypoint platform using the mock service. By the end of the chapter, you must be able to incorporate the topics covered in this chapter with the previous exercises.

# RAML

RAML is the popular markup language specifically designed for managing the complete API life cycle from designing, maintaining, and sharing. You have to visit the raml.org site to have complete insights about RAML. The site **https://github.com/raml-org/raml-spec** is having all information related to RAML like tutorials, examples, blogs, etc. The tutorial site **https://raml.org/developers/raml-100-tutorial** is explaining the following concepts in detail:

- Root Information – RAML version, title, and baseURI
- Resources – Endpoint names of a RESTful API specification like `/getCustomers`
- HTTP methods – `GET, POST`, etc.
- URI parameters – like `empid`

- queryparams of an endpoint
- HTTP responses like 200, 201, etc.

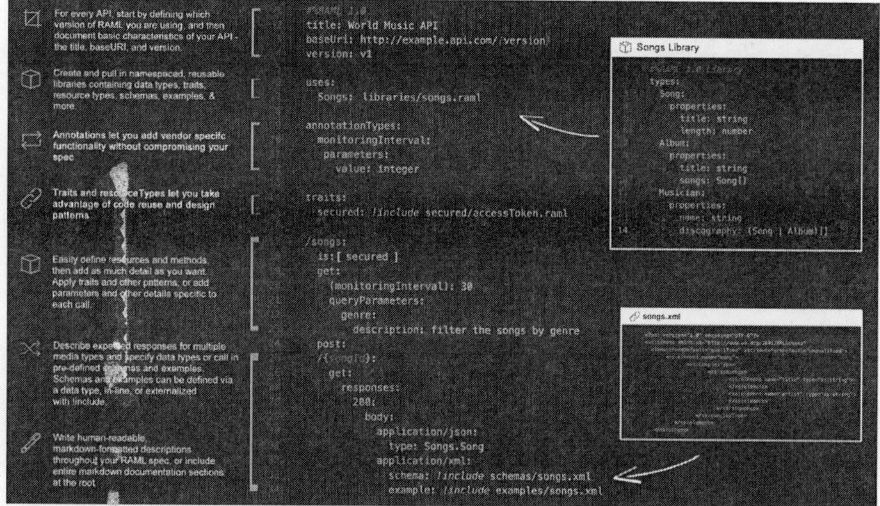


***Figure 8.1:*** *RAML quick guide from RAML org*

The above quick guide image explains the basics of RAML structure like:

- How to define the root elements
- How to reference the namespaces, reusable libraries
- How to call annotations
- How to link Traits
- Defining resources and methods
- Describing responses for each endpoint
- Writing descriptions

Let us quickly jump into the development of RAML by exploring the examples provided by **raml.org**:

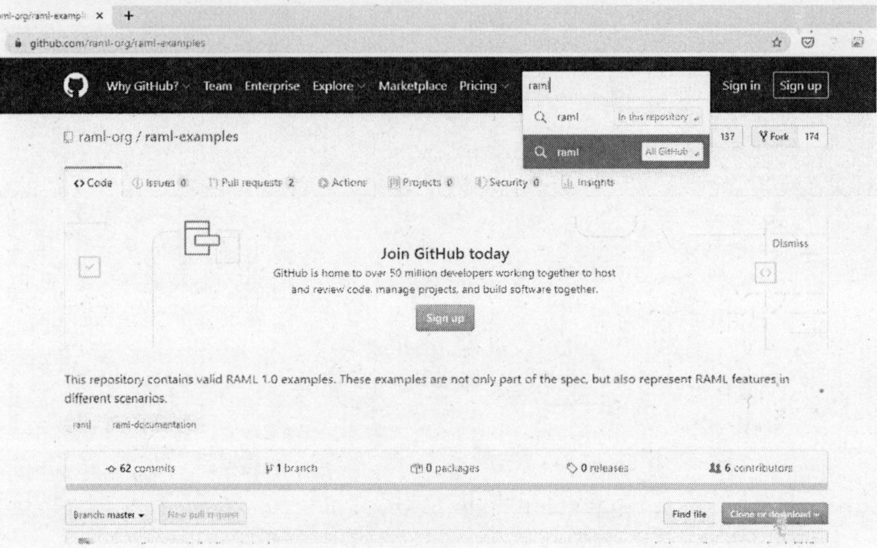


***Figure 8.2:*** *RAMl Examples in GitHub*

Visit GitHub site and search for RAML to reach out the official RAML example `project raml_examples`:

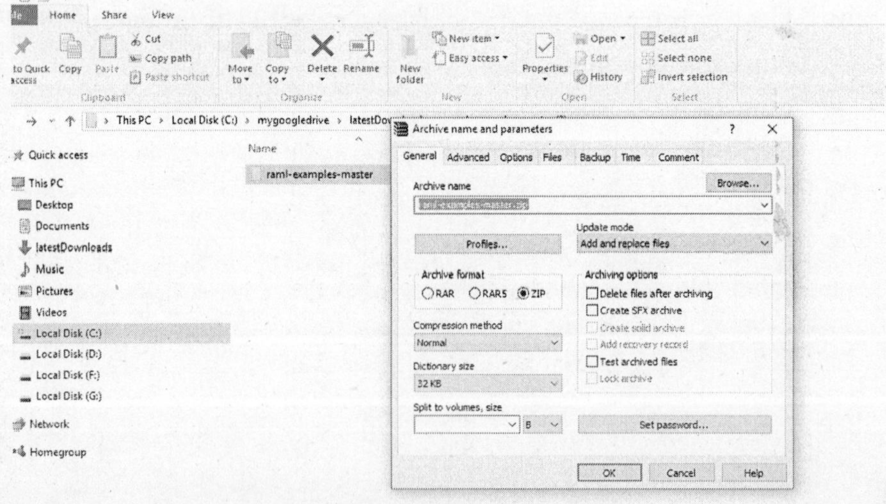


***Figure 8.3:*** *Zipping RAML examples*

Download the `raml_examples` and store them in the local folder. Unzip the archive and go to the `root` folder `raml-examples-master`. Bundle everything into `raml-example-master.ip` file as shown above:

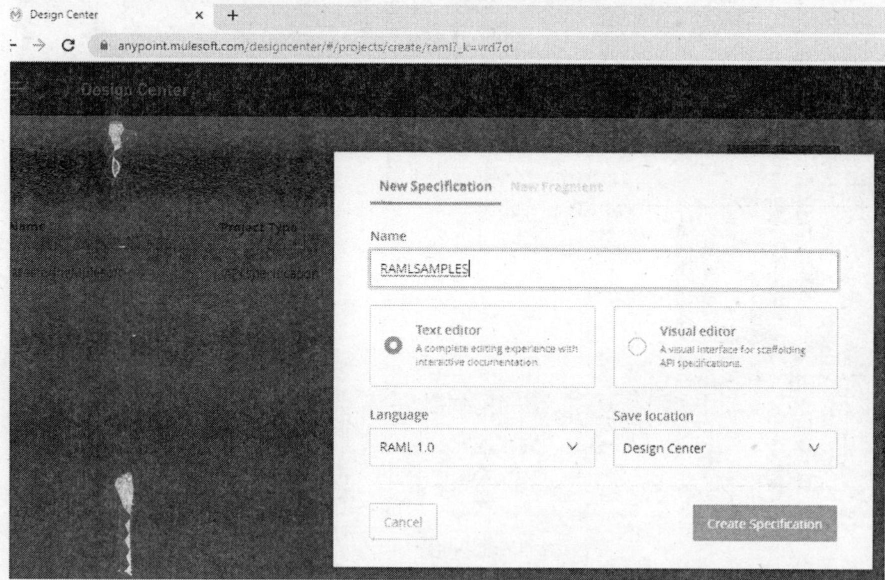


*Figure 8.4: Create new Specification in Designer*

Login to Anypoint portal and create a **`New Specification`** named `RAMLSAMPLES`:

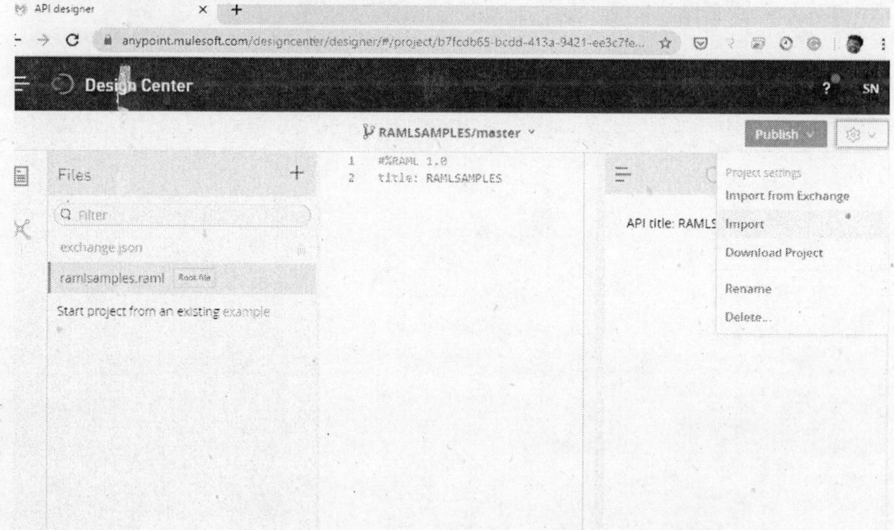


*Figure 8.5: Importing Zipped examples*

After the creation of new API specification tries to access the right corner **Import** menu item:

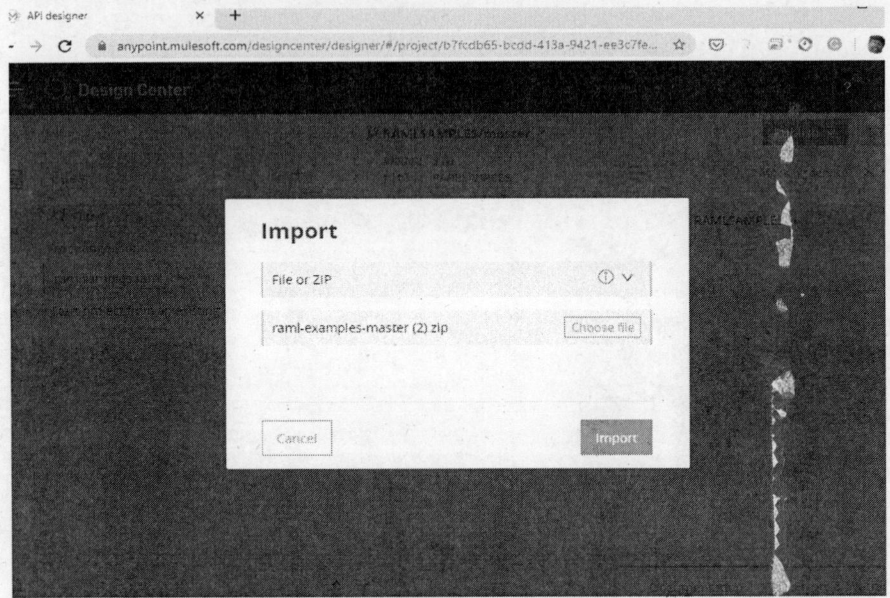


*Figure 8.6: Choose the ZIP file*

You must be able to select the ZIP file created out of RAML example masters and import into our API Specification project:

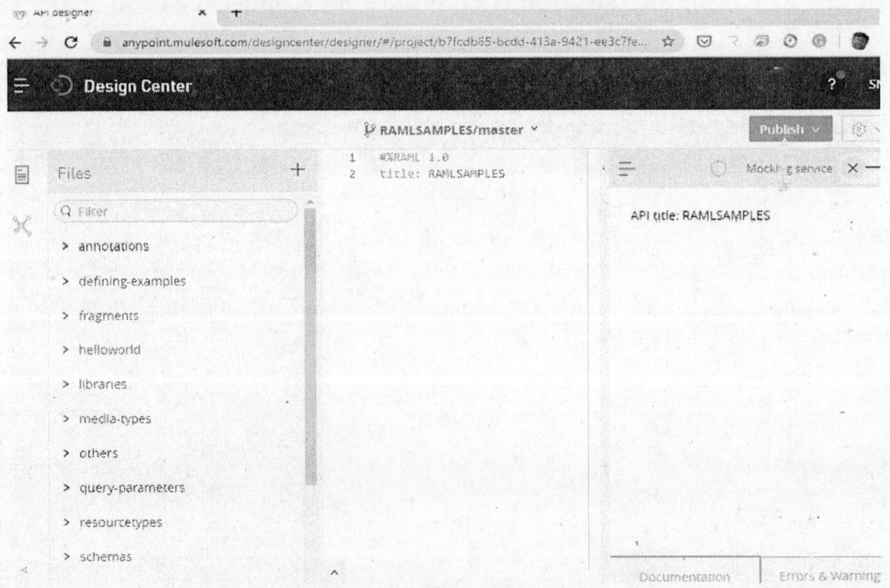


*Figure 8.7: After importing examples ZIP file*

This is the result of importing entire RAML examples into our design center:

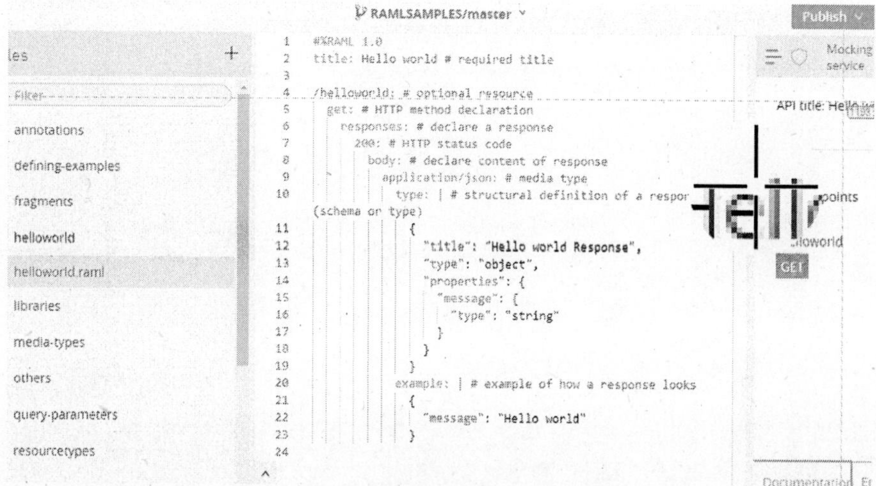


***Figure 8.8:*** *Hello World RAML*

Go ahead and open the `HelloWorld` RAML as shown above:

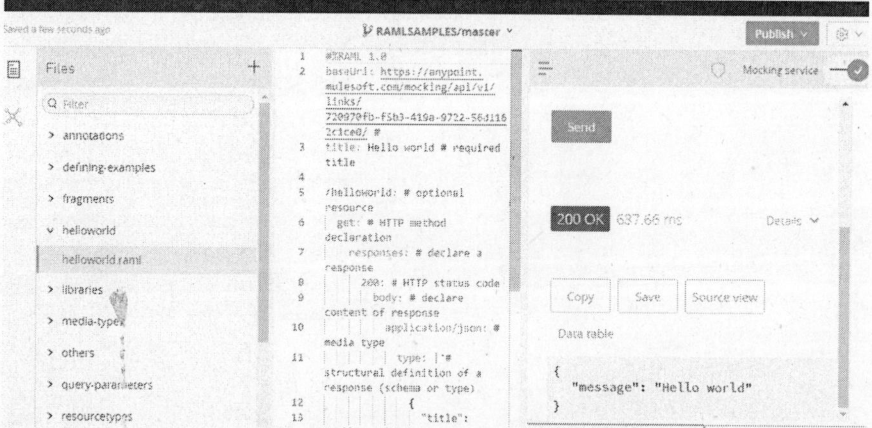


***Figure 8.9:*** *HelloWorld RAML Execution*

Toggle the **Mocking Service** and execute the `HelloWorld` RAML. Toggling the **Mocking Service**, examining the endpoints definitions, input, output parameters must be done for all examples:

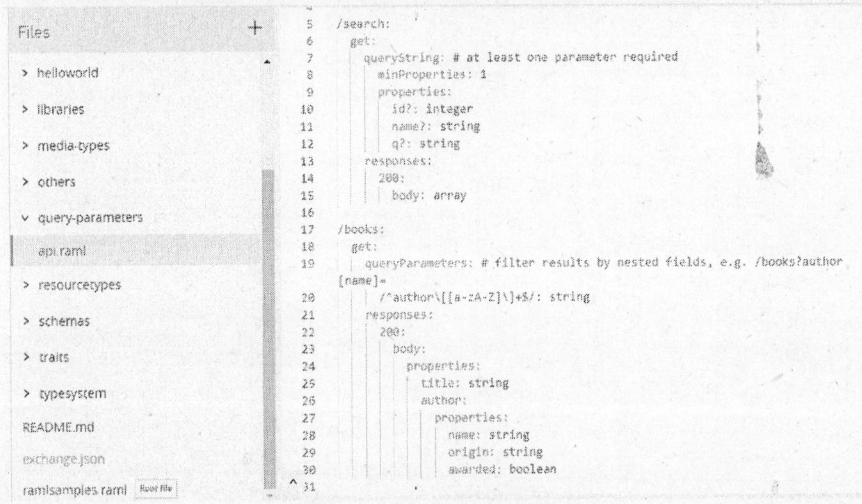

***Figure 8.10:*** *Query Parameter example*

Go to the `Query-parameters` folder and examine the RAML file. You can find 2 endpoints given with different query parameter settings:

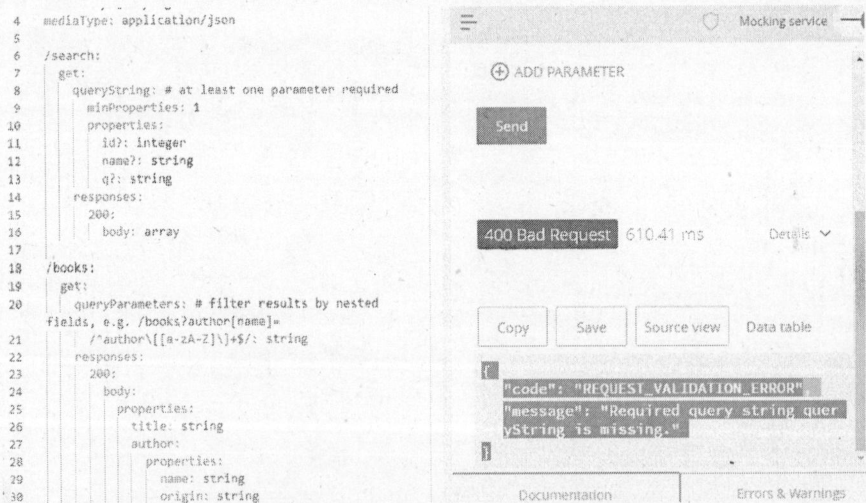

***Figure 8.11:*** *Required Query String Missing*

Run the search endpoint, you may see the error result as shown above which says required query string is missing:

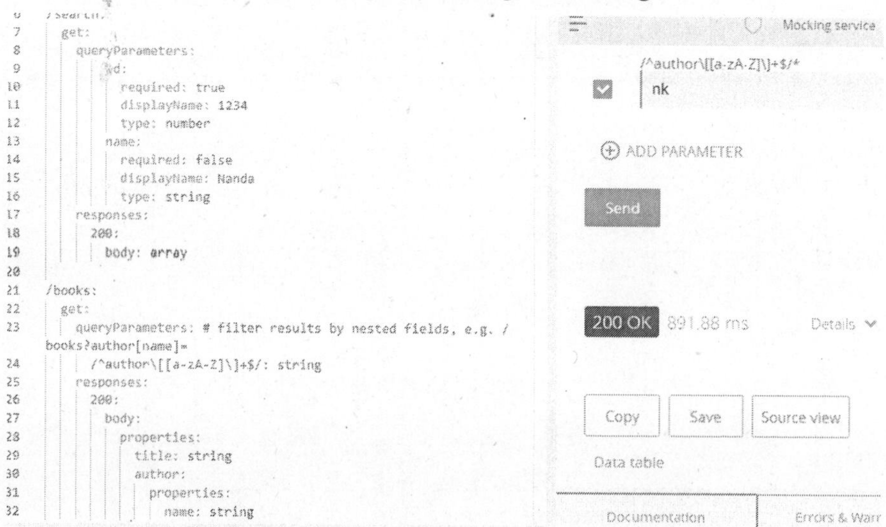


*Figure 8.12: Executing a Query Parameter example*

Run the books endpoint by giving some `queryParameter` value which matches the condition and executes the endpoint:

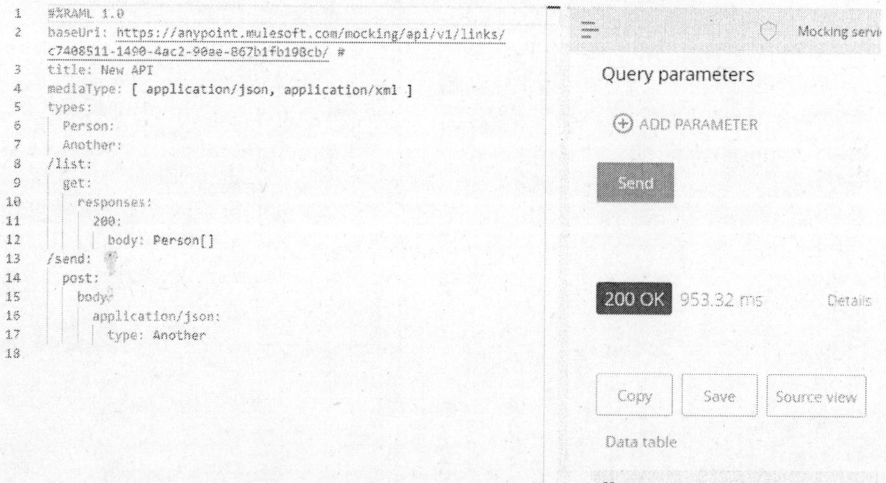


*Figure 8.13: Libraries implementation*

Open `mediatype | default | api.raml` to understand the basic declaration of `mediaType` and `Object` types as shown above:

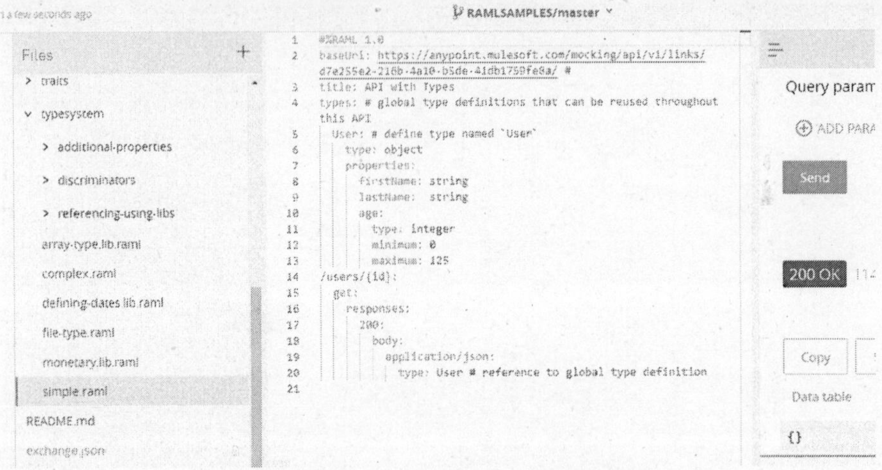


*Figure 8.14: Simple RAML with datatype*

Go to `Typesystem` folder and check out the `sample.raml` to understand how the type `User` is defined and from the `resources /users/{id}` how the type `User` has been referenced:

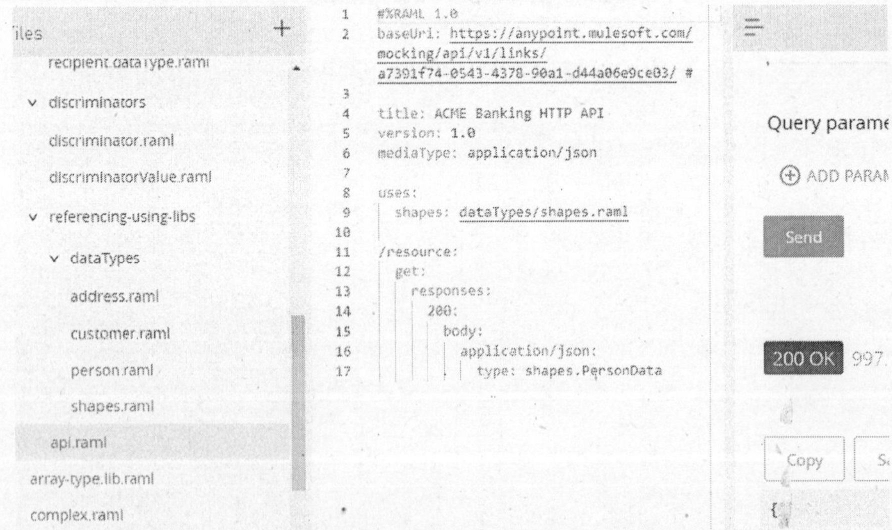


*Figure 8.15: RAML using Nested datatypes*

The above screenshot explains about the nested `Types` and how to access the `Types` in the RAML specification. The `/resources` endpoint referring the `shapes.PersonData` by including `shapes.raml` file:

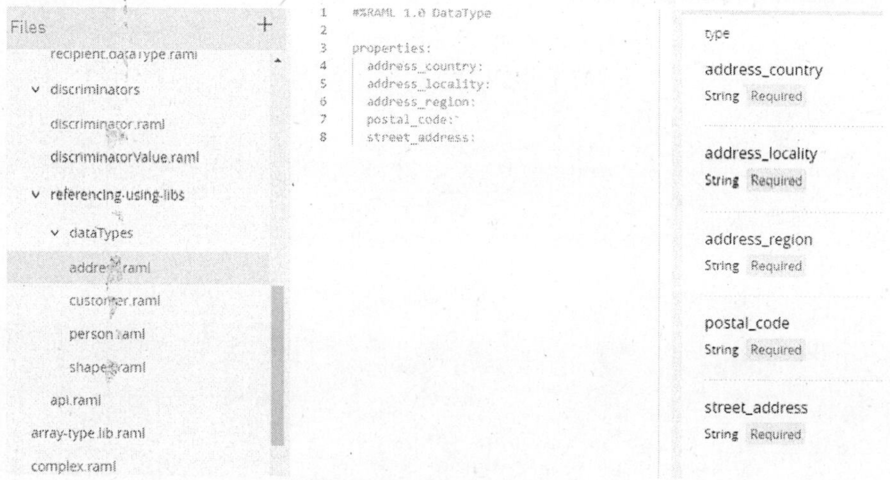


***Figure 8.16:*** *Address datatype*

To achieve this we have created four `raml` files in the `dataTypes` folder like `address.raml`, `customer.raml`, `person.raml`, and `shapes.raml`:

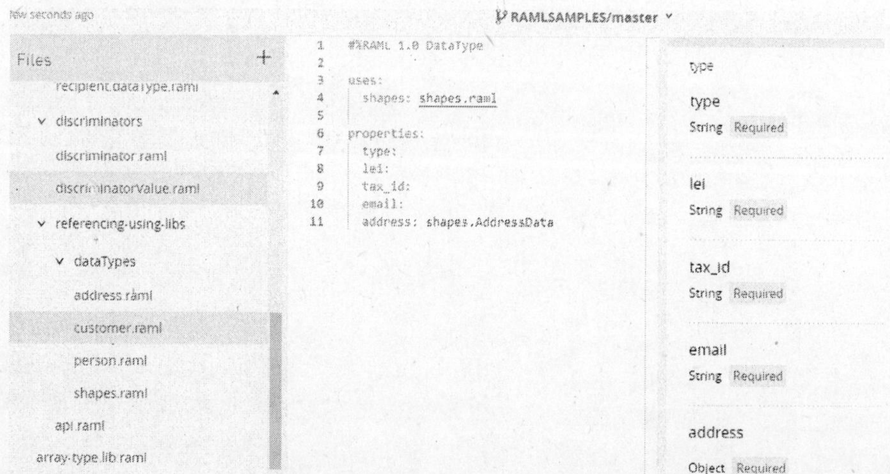


***Figure 8.17:*** *Customer datatype using Shape Data Reference*

The `customer.raml` file uses `addressData` property from `shapes.raml`:

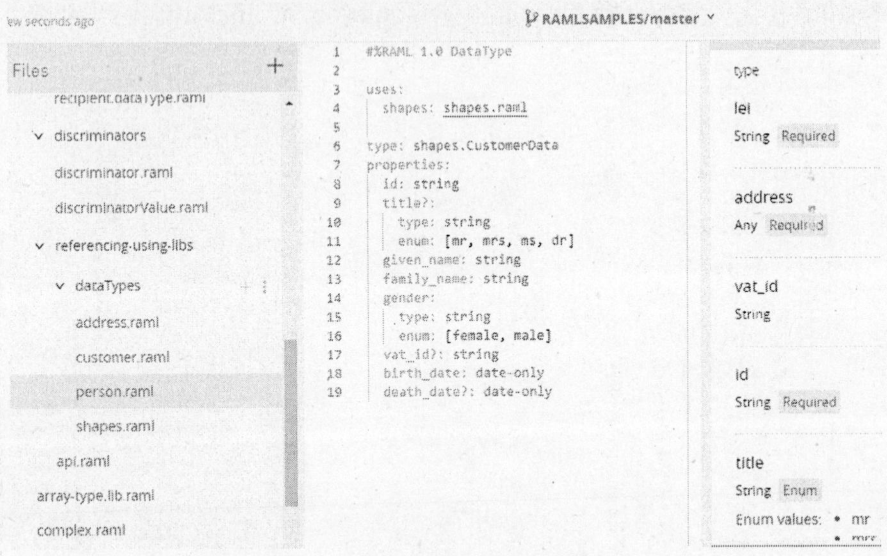


*Figure 8.18: Person datatype using Shape Data Reference*

The `person.raml` including a `customer.raml` datatype from `shapes.raml` file:

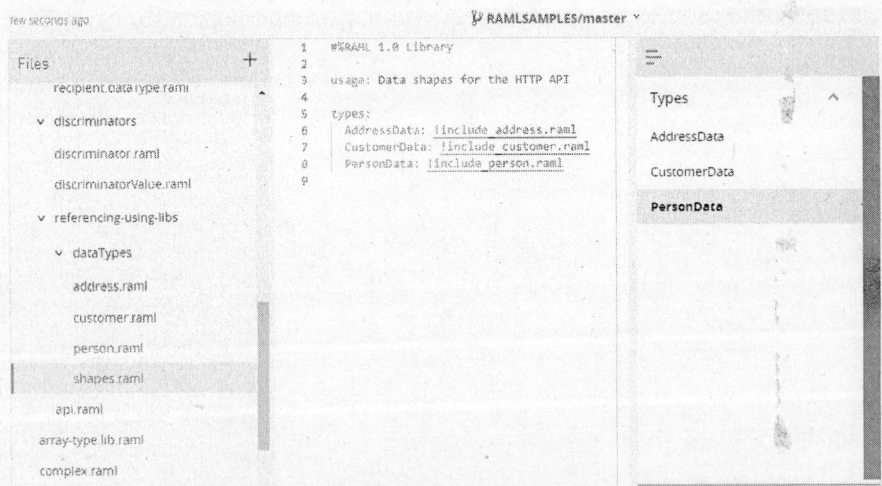


*Figure 8.19: Shapes Data RAML*

The `shapes.raml` datatype file includes all datatypes like `address.raml`, `customer.raml`, and `person.raml` files:

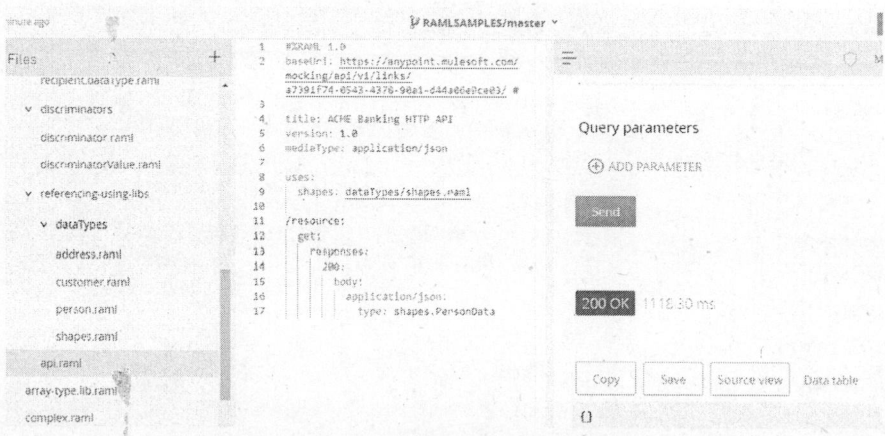

*Figure 8.20: Calling Person data from Shapes reference*

So when a RAML API root file includes `shapes.raml` data type then we can access all datatypes like `Persondata` by referencing the shapes datatype:

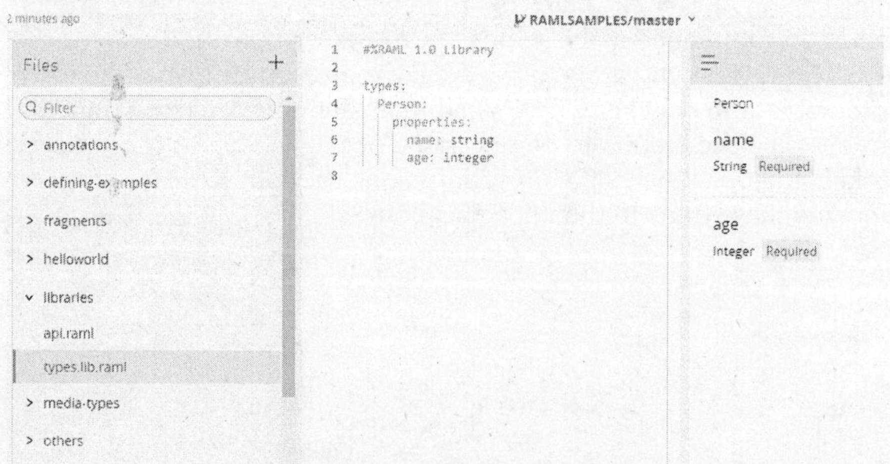

*Figure 8.21: Types of Library Creation*

The above example shows the usage of libraries in RAML. The `Libraries` folder is having a file called `types.lib.raml`, which is having definitions for type `Person`:

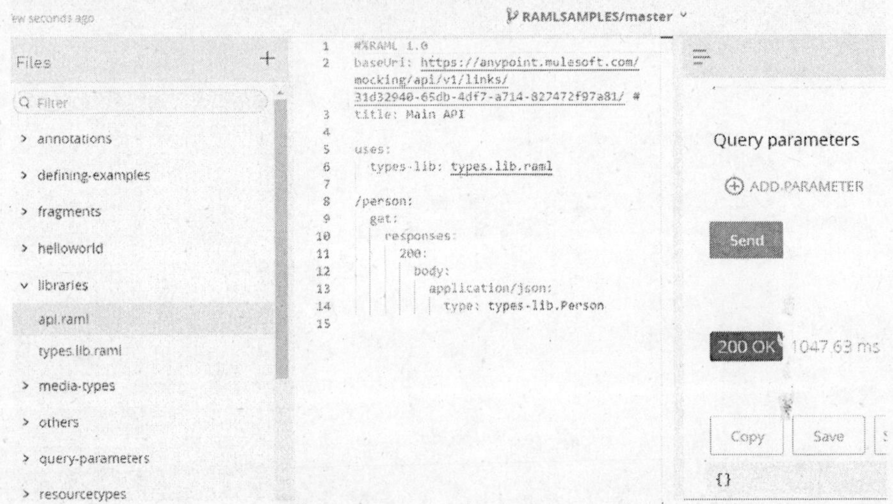


*Figure 8.22: Referencing Types Library in main RAML*

The Person library can be called from any root RAML files as shown above by referencing the `types-lib` keyword. To understand the Trait concept, in the traits folder we have three traits named security, orderable, and pageable. This is helpful in defining a query parameter to describe the results to be orderable or pageable and the security token must be a part of form submission. The root RAML can easily include these traits in their specifications:

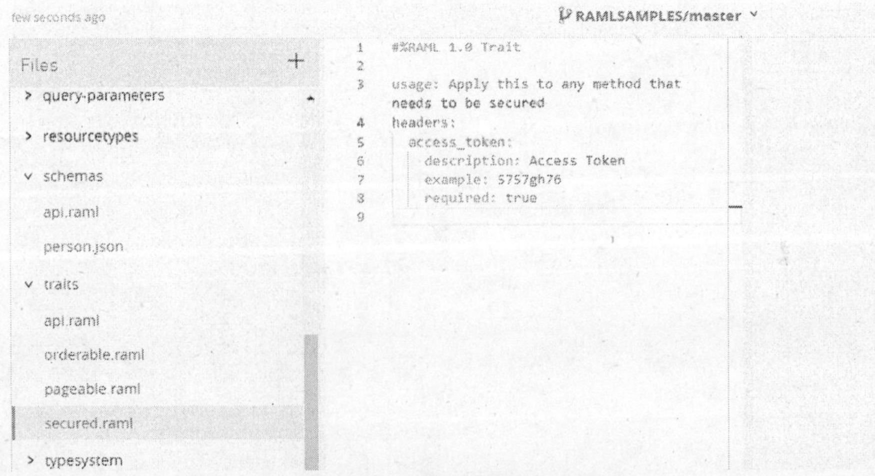


*Figure 8.23: Traits Security Fragment*

Create a `Security Trait` as shown above. The `access_token` will be passed through the header and it is mandatory to submit the data and the sample value also given:

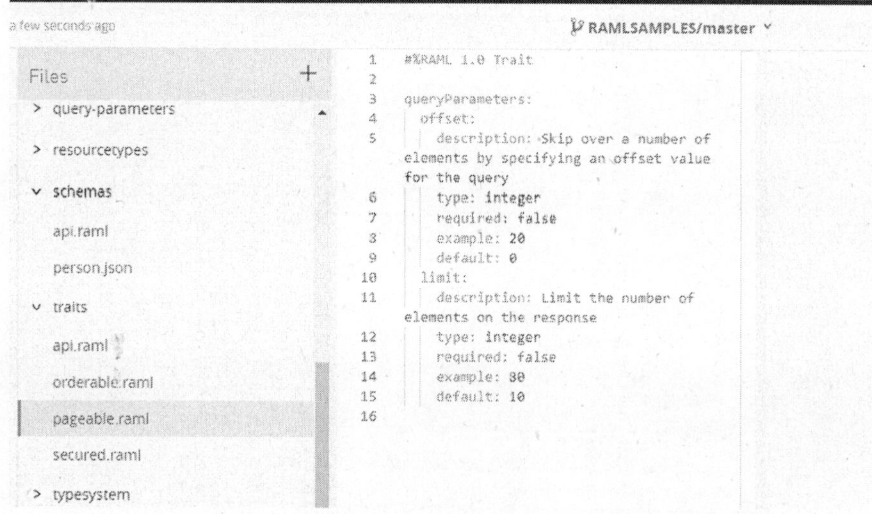


***Figure 8.24:*** *Traits Pageable Query Params Fragment*

The `pageable` trait, as shown above, is explaining the implementation of the pagination of the responses:

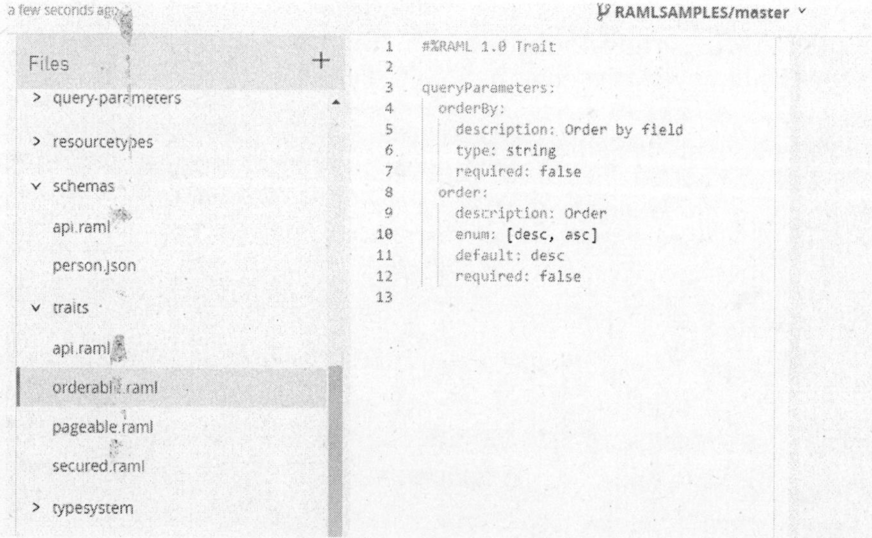


***Figure 8.25:*** *Traits Orderable Fragment*

The `orderable` trait is for sorting the responses:

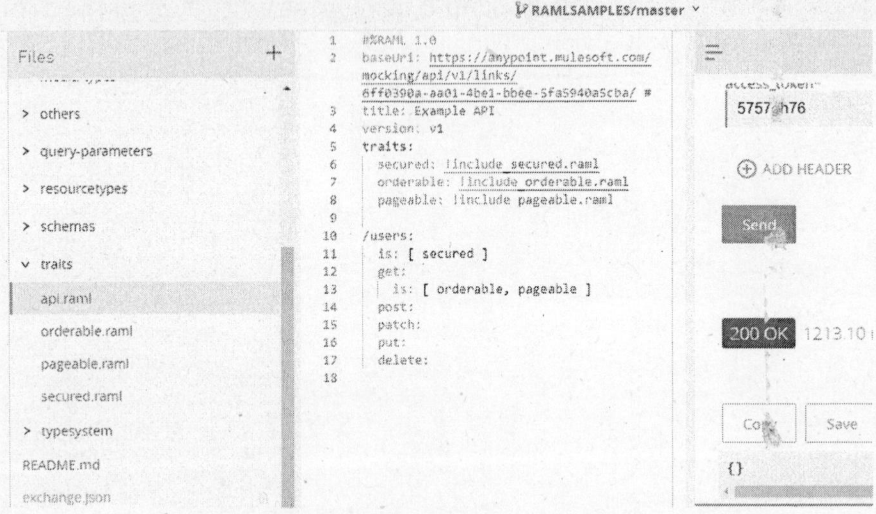


*Figure 8.26: Traits included in main RAML*

The root `api.raml` file includes all three traits and each trait will be called using their tag names like secured, orderable, and pageable. You can notice the secured trait is applied for both `GET` and `POST` methods and the orderable and `pageable` traits are applied only for the `GET` method.

In the RAML design, the fragments are classified into `datatype`, `extensions`, `overlays`, and `resourcetypes`. Let's see one-by-one:

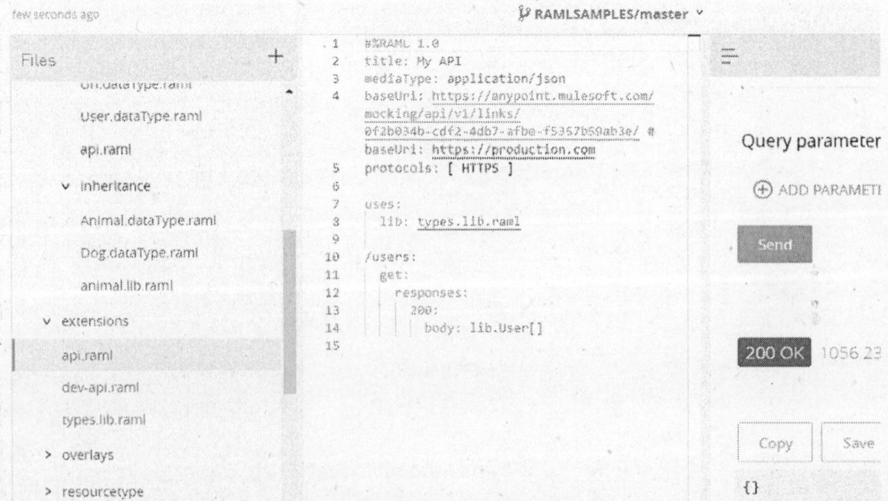


*Figure 8.27: Library Extensions*

Using library extensions we can define a datatype and call it in any RAML file. The above RAML calls an extension named `types.lib.raml`:

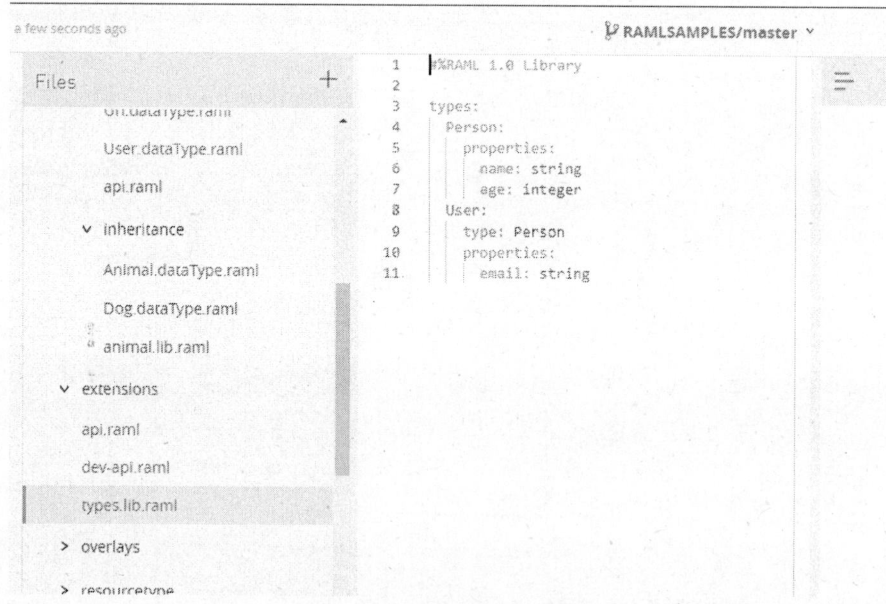


*Figure 8.28: Library definition*

The library is having definitions for a datatype called `Person` and `User` is a data type which is having `Person` as a property:

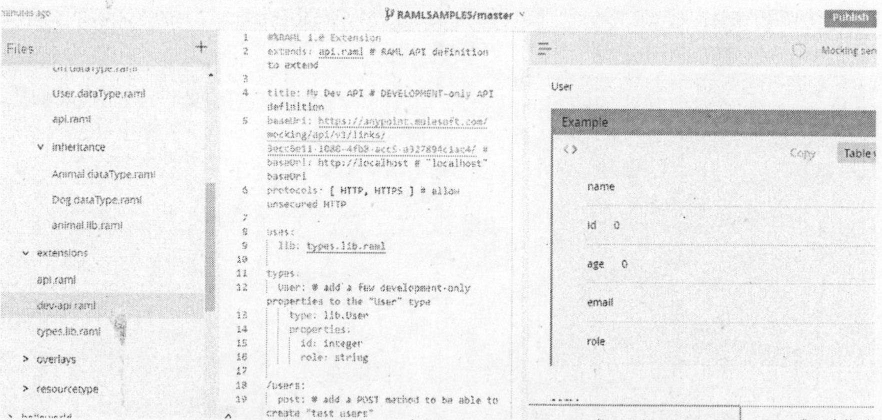


*Figure 8.29: Merging libraries and additional parameters*

The above API `api.raml` called the library as it is and the `dev-api.raml` is calling the `lib.raml` and also adding their parameters for the `User` datatype as shown above:

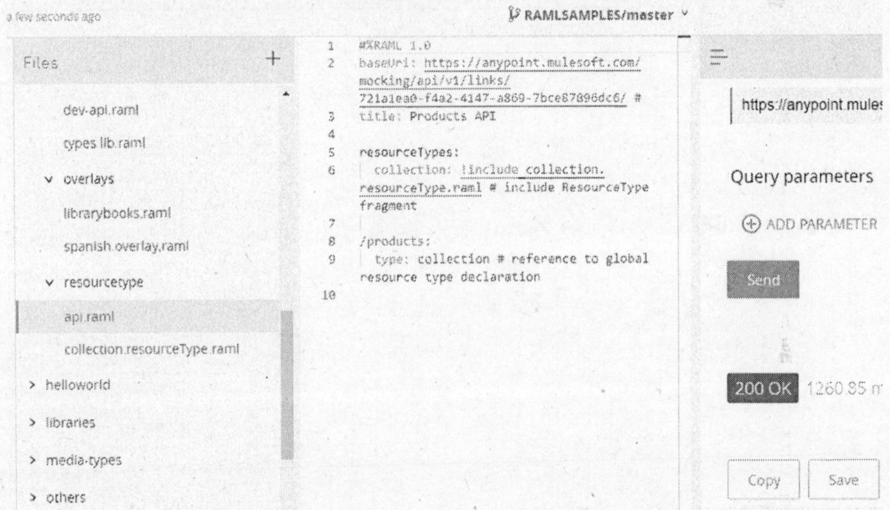


*Figure 8.30: collection resource types RAML*

The above `api.raml` is calling a collection resource type. You can see the resource type `/products` is including the definition of `get` and `post` methods by referring the `collection.resourcetype.raml`:

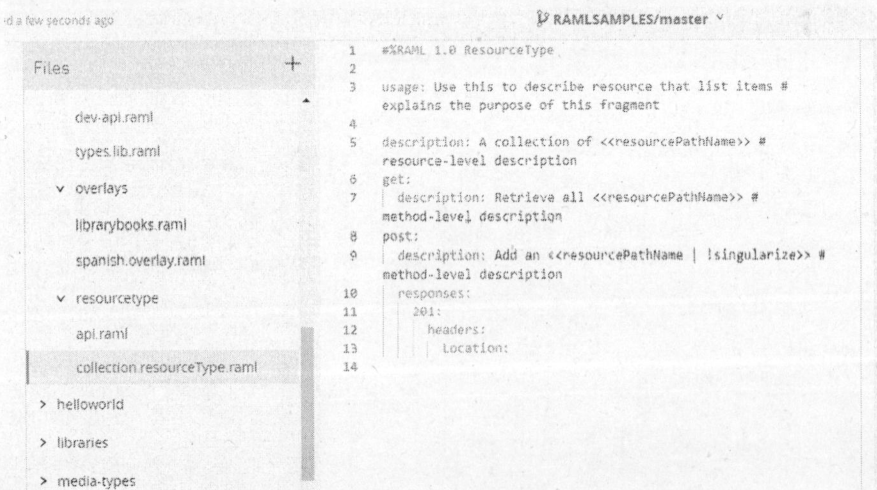


*Figure 8.31: Defining collections in a RAML file*

Here is the implementation of `resourcetypes` in a separate file called `collection.resourceType.raml`, this file is having specifications of `get` and `post` methods:

```
{
  "title": "Person Schema",
  "type": "object",
  "properties": {
    "firstName": {
      "type": "string"
    },
    "lastName": {
      "type": "string"
    },
    "age": {
      "description": "Age in years",
      "type": "integer",
      "minimum": 0
    }
  },
  "required": ["firstName", "lastName"]
}
```

***Figure 8.32:** Person Schema definition*

Schema and types are the same in RAML; the above `person.json` file is having details of `Person` datatype:

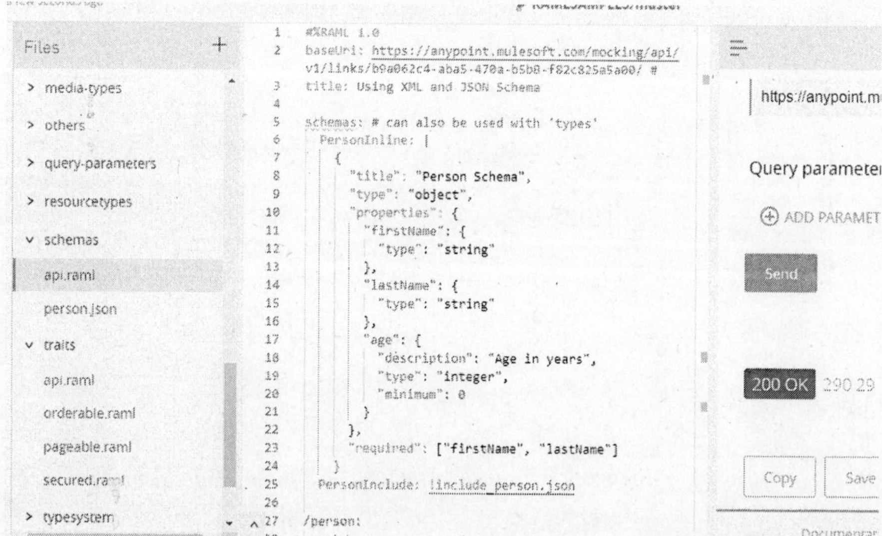


***Figure 8.33:** Including Person Schema in RAML*

The root `api.raml` is referencing `Person` JSON schema by including the `person.json` file:

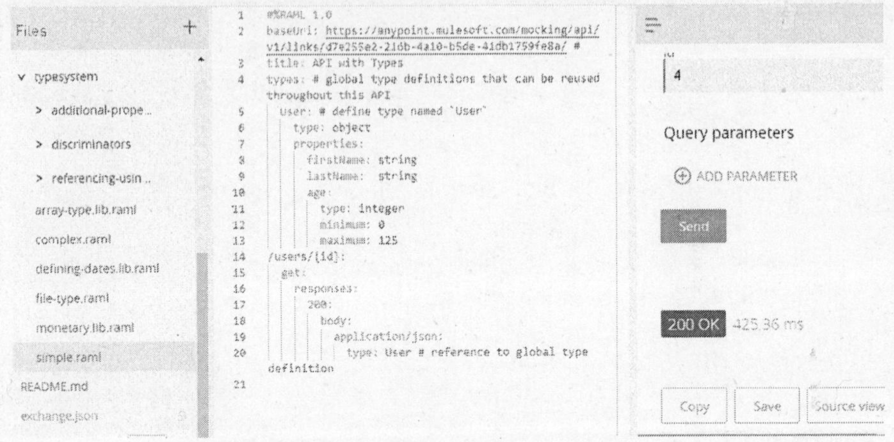

**Figure 8.34:** *Simple RAML with Types definition*

This `simple.raml` shows how to define the `User` type and using in the response body:

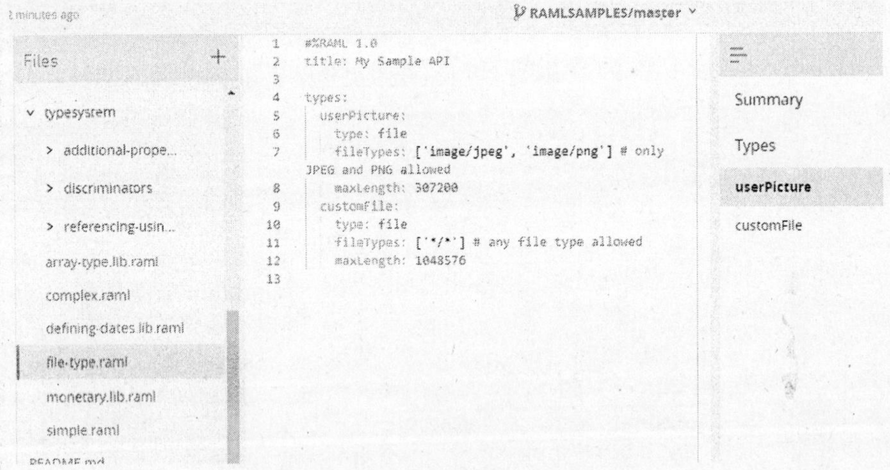

**Figure 8.35:** *Allowed File types definition*

This `file-type.raml` file shows how to define the allowed file types say a `userpicture` with proper file type extensions and `maxlength` kind of properties:

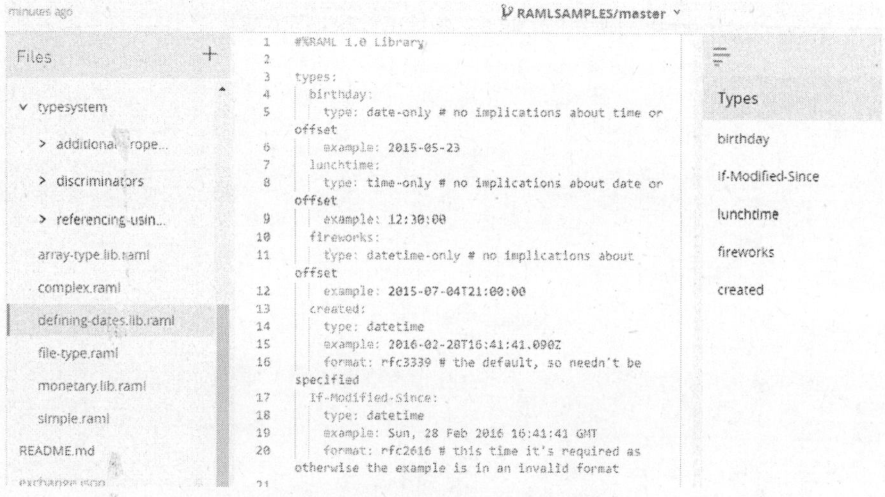


*Figure 8.36: Date Format definition*

This `defining-dates.lib.raml` file shows how to define the date formats to be used in a RAML specification. The example bundle comes with pre-defined projects which have implemented all the above concepts, please have a look at these projects so that we can create our project in the next chapter step-by-step using the reusable codes of these projects:

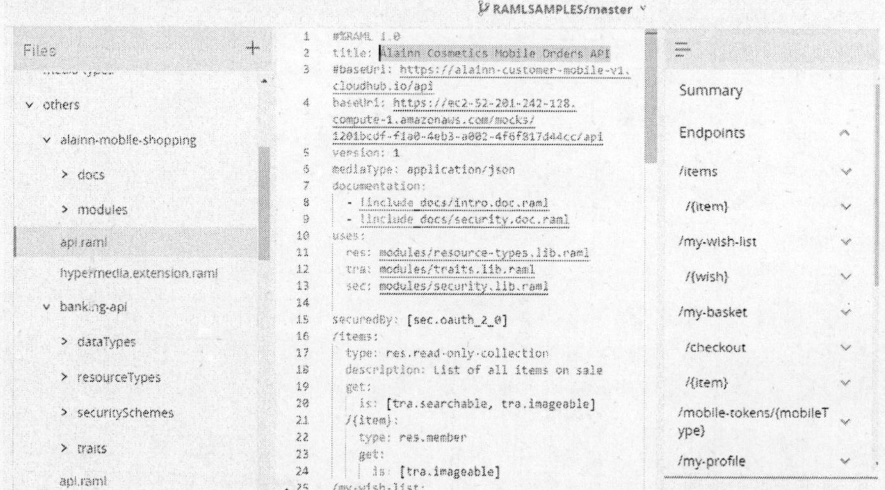


*Figure 8.37: Mobile Shopping RAML*

Mobile shopping RAML project, try to run the project, examine various endpoints, toggle mock service, and enter input parameters for better practice:

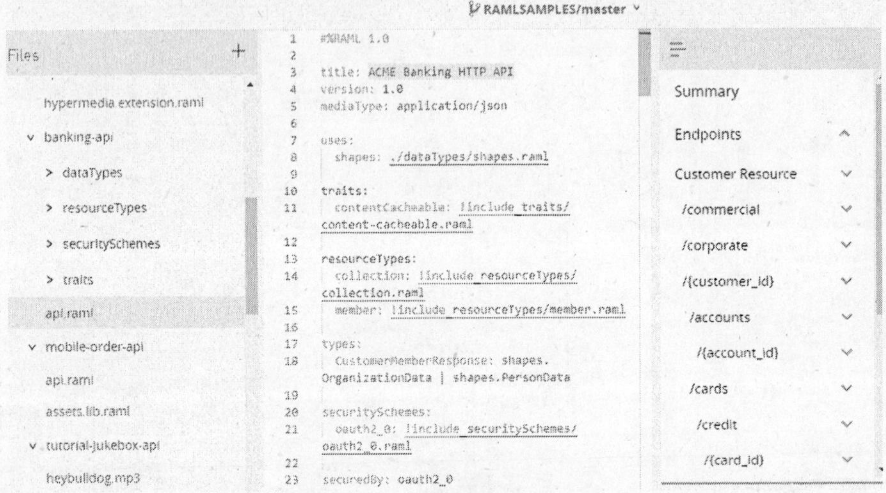


*Figure 8.38:* *Banking API RAML*

Banking RAML, try to run the project, examine various endpoints, toggle mock service, and enter input parameters for better practice:

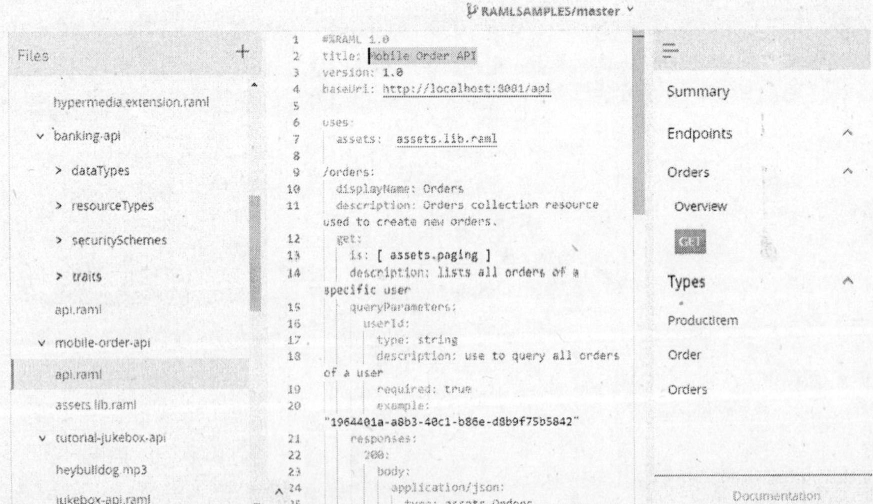


*Figure 8.39:* *Mobile RAML*

Mobile orders RAML project, try to run the project, examine various endpoints, toggle mock service, and enter input parameters for better practice:

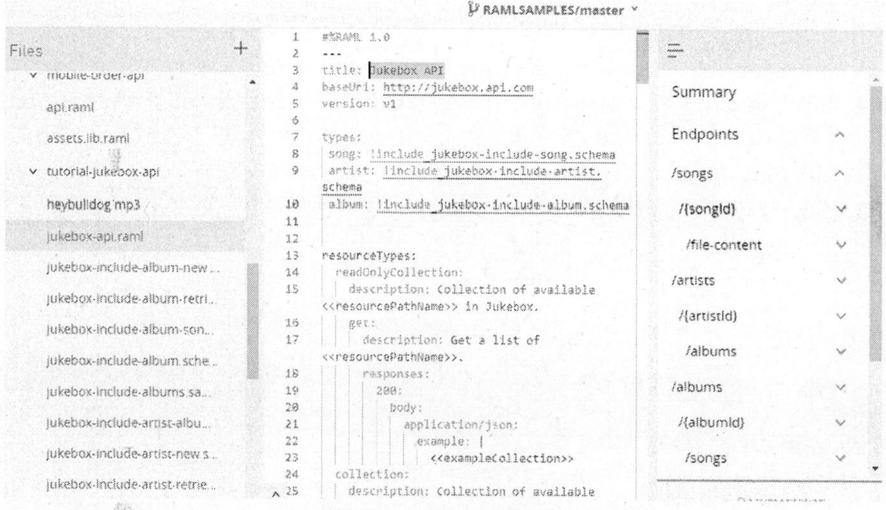


*Figure 8.40: JukeBox RAML*

JukeBox RAML, try to run the project, examine various endpoints, toggle mock service, and enter input parameters for better practice:

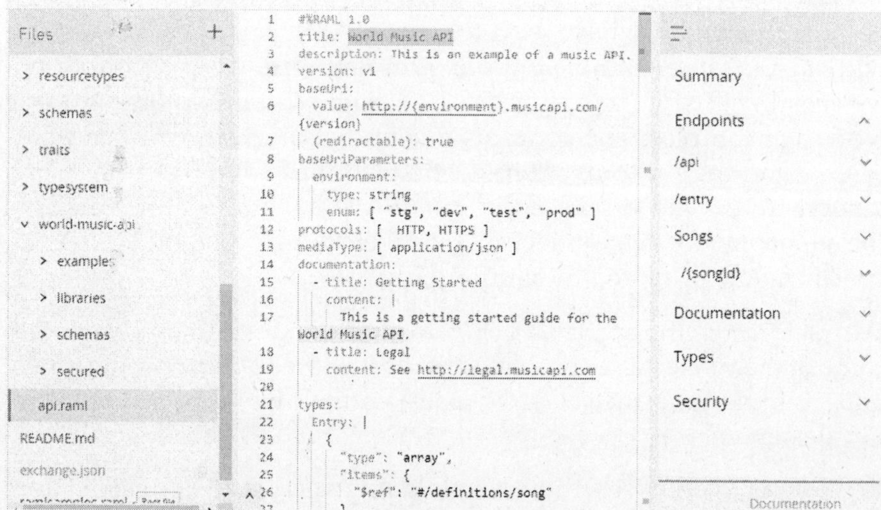


*Figure 8.41: World Music RAML*

WorldMusic RAML, try to run the project, examine various endpoints, toggle mock service, and enter input parameters for better practice.

# DIY

Don't limit yourself with the examples given here; try various samples available on the internet by downloading and importing them into the designer. Follow the HTTP response codes given below in some of your examples:

| **1xx Informational** | **3xx Redirection** | 408 Request Timeout | 429 Too Many Requests |
|---|---|---|---|
| 100 Continue | 300 Multiple Choices | 409 Conflict | 431 Request Header Fields Too Large |
| 101 Switching Protocols | 301 Moved Permanently | 410 Gone | 444 Connection Closed Without Response |
| 102 Processing | 302 Found | 411 Length Required | 451 Unavailable For Legal Reasons |
| **2xx Success** | 303 See Other | 412 Precondition Failed | 499 Client Closed Request |
| 200 OK | 304 Not Modified | 413 Payload Too Large | **5xx Server Error** |
| 201 Created | 305 Use Proxy | 414 Request-URI Too Long | 500 Internal Server Error |
| 202 Accepted | 307 Temporary Redirect | 415 Unsupported Media Type | 501 Not Implemented |
| 203 Non-authoritative Information | 308 Permanent Redirect | 416 Requested Range Not Satisfiable | 502 Bad Gateway |
| 204 No Content | **4xx Client Error** | 417 Expectation Failed | 503 Service Unavailable |
| 205 Reset Content | 400 Bad Request | 418 I'm a teapot | 504 Gateway Timeout |
| 206 Partial Content | 401 Unauthorized | 421 Misdirected Request | 505 HTTP Version Not Supported |
| 207 Multi-Status | 402 Payment Required | 422 Unprocessable Entity | 506 Variant Also Negotiates |
| 208 Already Reported | 403 Forbidden | 423 Locked | 507 Insufficient Storage |
| 226 IM Used | 404 Not Found | 424 Failed Dependency | 508 Loop Detected |
| | 405 Method Not Allowed | 426 Upgrade Required | 510 Not Extended |
| | 406 Not Acceptable | 428 Precondition Required | 511 Network Authentication Required |
| | 407 Proxy Authentication Required | | 599 Network Connect Timeout Error |

***Figure 8.42:*** *Response codes*

# Conclusion

In this chapter, we have covered the RAML specification details with an available example bundle from **raml.org**. We have imported the existing RAML bundle into our designer and explored all the working examples. The concepts like queryparameter, for example, error handling, resource types, traits, types, and schema were demonstrated and discussed in detail. We have also gone through the available working projects like a jukebox, banking, music RAML specifications provided by **raml.org**.

We got to know the available HTTP response codes and implemented some of them. We have completed exploring the RAML specifications and examples and the set-up is ready with all working examples in our designer.

In the next chapter, we will start developing a new RAML specification for a particular domain say ticketing system for any Airlines and test it.

# Points to remember

- In our next chapter, we will be developing a RAML specification for a specific business case by implementing all concepts discussed in this chapter.
- Make sure you have enough hands-on and understanding of the topics covered so far.

# Key terms to explore

- RAML query parameter
- Examples
- Error
- Response code
- Schema
- Types
- Traits
- Extensions
- Security
- Resource types

# CHAPTER 9
# RAML Project

In this chapter we will discuss the following topics:

- Exploring public APIs
- Recreating RESTful specifications from existing examples
- Understanding the raml.org sample projects
- Modifying existing projects
- Developing a new project
- Moving the new project to Anypoint Studio
- Deploying and testing projects through Anypoint Studio

## Objectives

After studying this unit, you should be able to understand:

- Understand the existing project structure
- Exploring various RAML concepts implemented
- Reusing RAML project specification
- Developing a new RAML specification
- Testing the RAML specification at Exchange level

- Moving the RAML APIs to Anypoint Studio
- Deploying and testing the APIs through Anypoint Studio Console

# Pre-requisites

Try to understand the various business domains which are looking for a major change in digital transformation space, so that you can easily connect with the business use cases coming in the future. Go back and make sure you have understood the concepts like the Center for Excellence, API LED connectivity so that you can visualize the importance of API designer in the Enterprise Integrations Paradigm. You need to understand the difference between API design and API Implementation so that you can focus more on API design using RAML kind of language rather than bothering about how this will be technically implemented by a developer. Overall clarity of SaaS applications on the cloud, the way they expose data through APIs will be a great help for you to design APIs to handle data from SaaS endpoints.

# Exploring public APIs

For a practice purpose, it is nice to explore some of the publicly available RESTful services to understand more about their design and implementation. The aim of exploring the free APIs must be to check the input-output values; you can reuse these data in your practice specifications. Also, you can get some fair idea about how the APIs are designed for various domains and how to execute the same.

Try to visit **reqres.in** website to explore the APIs provided for testing purpose:

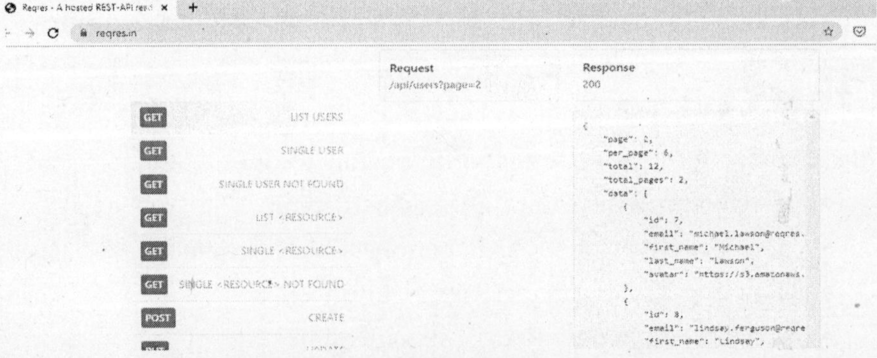


*Figure 9.1: Exploring Public APIs for List Users*

Execute the **`LIST USERS`** endpoint and check out the endpoint URL, input, and output:

*Figure 9.2: Calling Public APIs from Postman*

Execute the **`LIST USERS`** endpoint through Postman and check out the endpoint URL, input, and output:

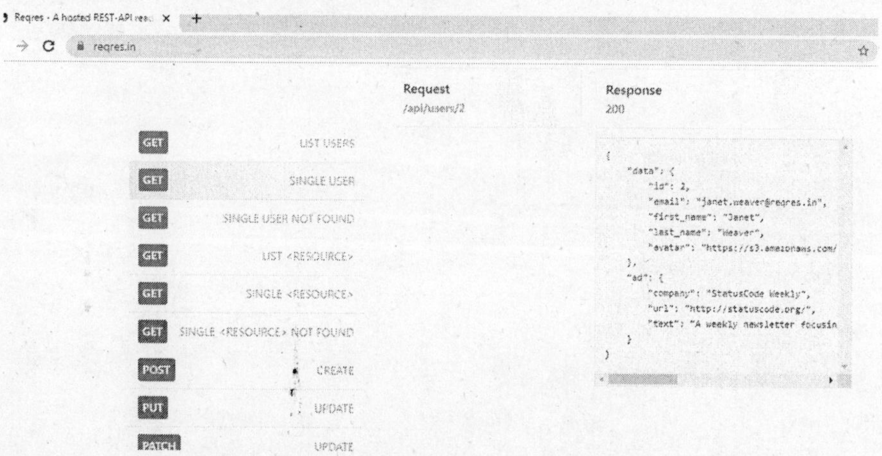

*Figure 9.3: Exploring Public APIs for Single User*

Execute the **`SINGLE USERS`** endpoint and check out the endpoint URL, input, and output:

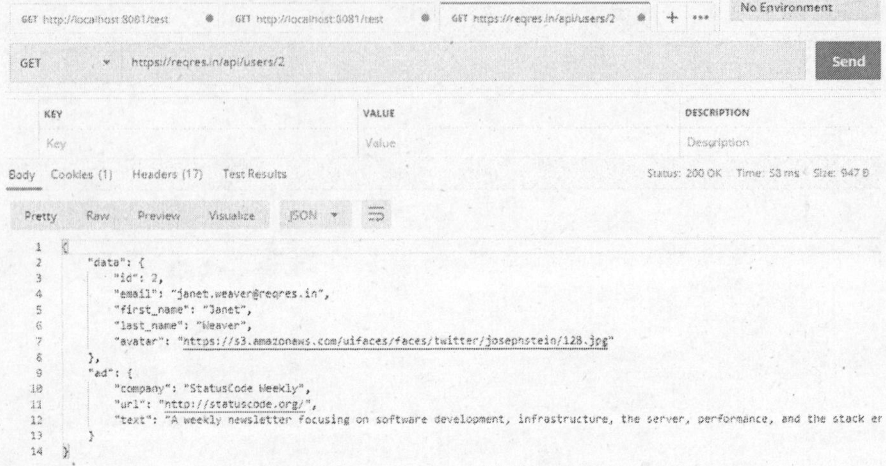

*Figure 9.4: Calling Public APIs from Postman*

Execute the **`SINGLE USERS`** endpoint through Postman and check out the endpoint URL, input, and output:

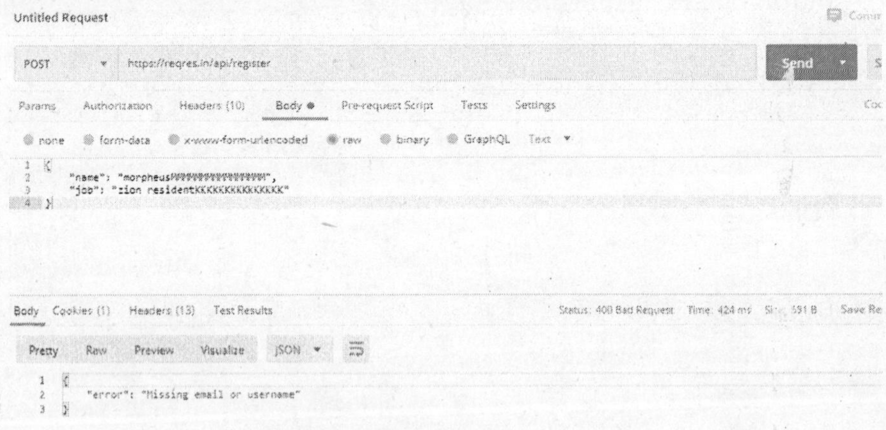

*Figure 9.5: Public API Post method*

Execute the **`REGISTER USERS`** endpoint and check out the endpoint URL, input, and output. The site is having the following endpoints:

- `LIST USERS`
- `SINGLE USER`
- `SINGLE USER NOT FOUND`

- `LIST <RESOURCE>`
- `SINGLE <RESOURCE>`
- `SINGLE <RESOURCE> NOT FOUND`
- `CREATE`
- `UPDATE`
- `UPDATE`
- `DELETE`
- `REGISTER - SUCCESSFUL`
- `REGISTER - UNSUCCESSFUL`
- `LOGIN - SUCCESSFUL`
- `LOGIN - UNSUCCESSFUL`
- `DELAYED RESPONSE`

Try the following URLs to invoke various endpoints:

- **https://reqres.in/api/users/2**
- **https://reqres.in/api/users**
- **https://reqres.in/api/users/2**
- **https://reqres.in/api/users/2**
- **https://reqres.in/api/register**
- **https://reqres.in/api/register**
- **https://reqres.in/api/login**
- **https://reqres.in/api/login**

# Exploring commercial APIs

There are numerous commercials API websites are available, Most of them will allow you to access 2-3 basic APIs to get a feel of their Web Services, when it comes to commercial usage then the customers must go for purchasing a license and get responses by providing security key.

The website `openweathermap.org` provides API services for weather related data. If a portal needs to be developed for Weather related business then they can use these web services by subscribing:

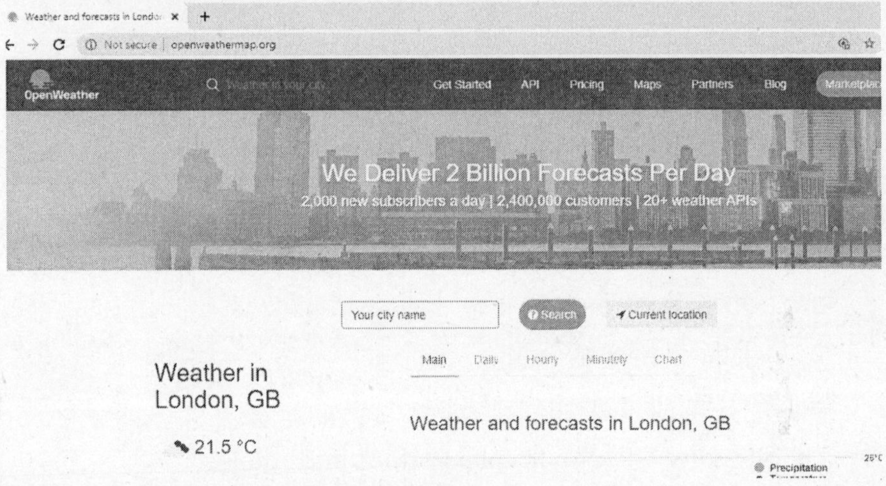


***Figure 9.6:*** *openweathermap*

Visit **openweathermap.org** and understand their API model:

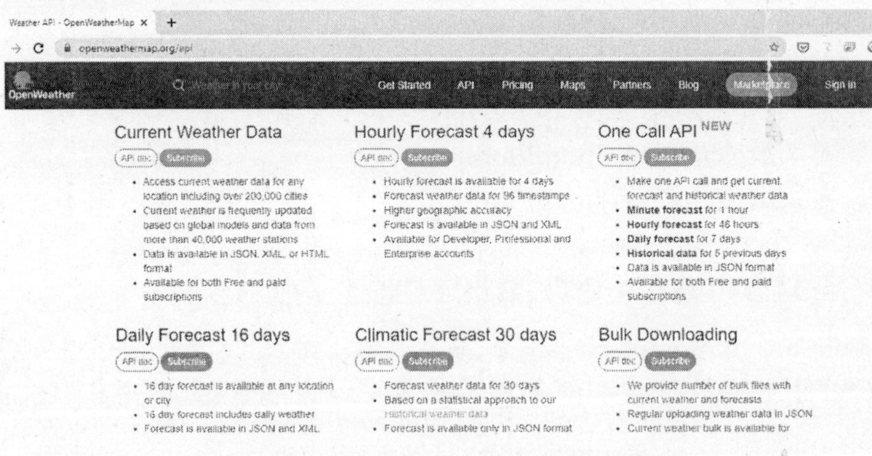


***Figure 9.7:*** *openweathermap Available APIs*

**openweathermap.org** API page provides you the details of available APIs:

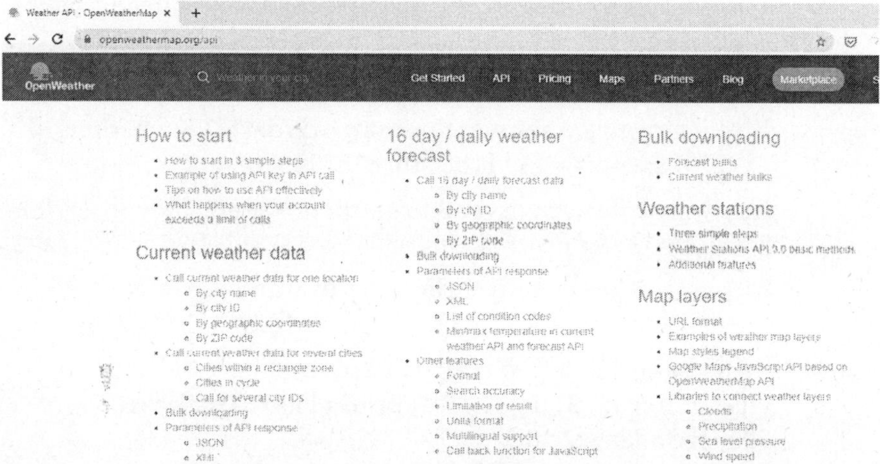

***Figure 9.8:** openweathermap API details*

**openweathermap.org** API details page provides details about data provided by various web services:

***Figure 9.9:** openweathermap calling APIs from browser*

Try to call these links to get responses as given in above screenshots:

- **http://samples.openweathermap.org/data/2.5/weather?q=London,uk&appid=439d4b804bc8187953eb36d2a8c26a02**
- **http://samples.openweathermap.org/data/2.5/weather?q=London,uk&appid=439d4b804bc8187953eb36d2a8c26a02**
- **http://samples.openweathermap.org/data/2.5/weather?id=2172797&appid=439d4b804bc8187953eb36d2a8c26a02**
- **http://samples.openweathermap.org/data/2.5/weather?lat=35&lon=139&appid=439d4b804bc8187953eb36d2a8c26a02**
- **http://samples.openweathermap.org/data/2.5/weather?zip=94040,us&appid=439d4b804bc8187953eb36d2a8c26a02**
- **http://samples.openweathermap.org/data/2.5/ box/city?bbox=12, 32,15,37,10&appid=439d4b804bc8187953eb36d2a8c26a02**

The following screenshot explains about current weather API details:

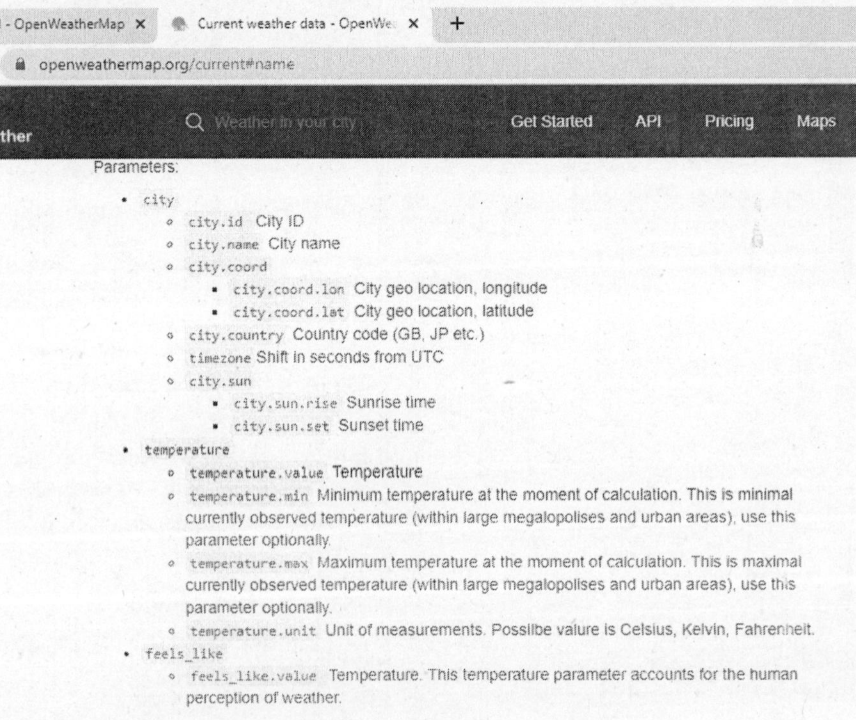


*Figure 9.10: openweathermap API Details*

**Figure 9.11:** *GoRest fake rest API*

Another `fakeAPI` website, **gorest.co.in**:

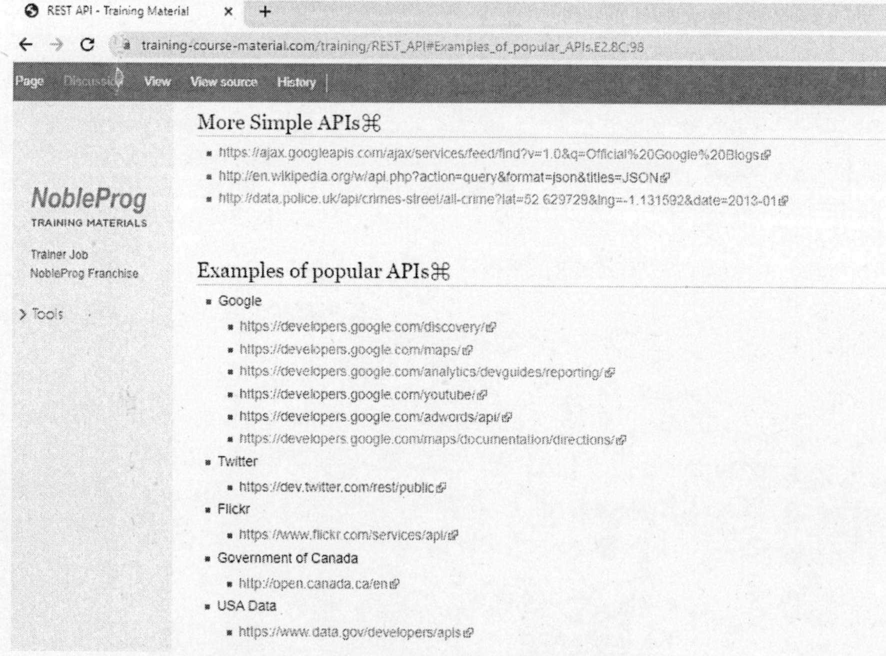


**Figure 9.12:** *Some more examples of public APIs*

This training site talks about popular commercial social media APIs:

*Figure 9.13: openweathermap calling API from Postman*

Try calling the weather API using Postman, as shown above; the results from the APIs can be reused for your practice APIs:

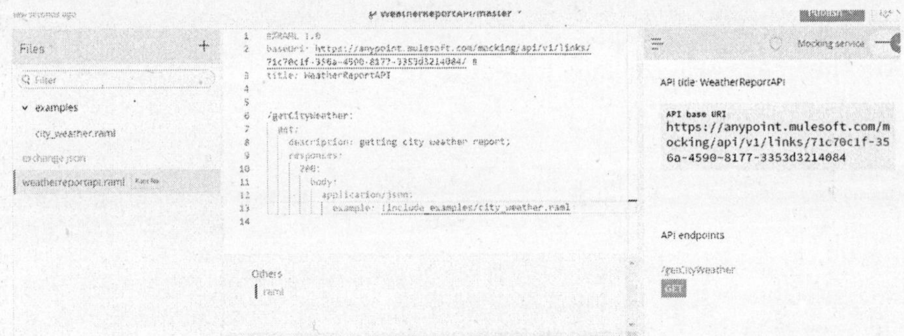


*Figure 9.14: Create Local REST RAML Specification based on public APIs*

Create an example folder and move the JSON results and store, then try creating an API specification as shown above:

```
#%RAML 1.0 NamedExample
example:
  {
  "coord": {
      "lon": -0.13,
      "lat": 51.51
  },
  "weather": [
      {
          "id": 300,
          "main": "Drizzle",
          "description": "light intensity drizzle",
          "icon": "09d"
      }
  ],
  "base": "stations",
  "main": {
      "temp": 280.32,
      "pressure": 1012,
      "humidity": 81,
      "temp_min": 279.15,
      "temp_max": 281.15
  },
  "visibility": 10000,
  "wind": {
      "speed": 4.1,
      "deg": 80
  },
```

**Figure 9.15:** *Using example output in our Local API*

The above screenshot shows the example file moved inside the `examples` folder file called `city_weather.raml`:

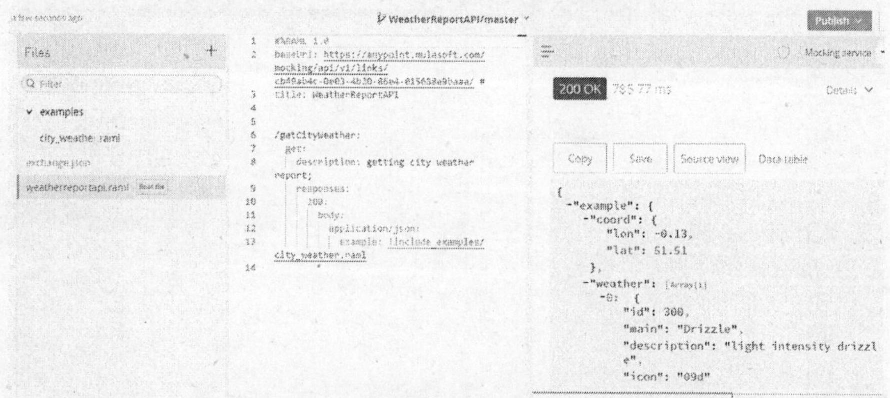


**Figure 9.16:** *Executing local API from Browser*

Execute the RAML API created from the designer:

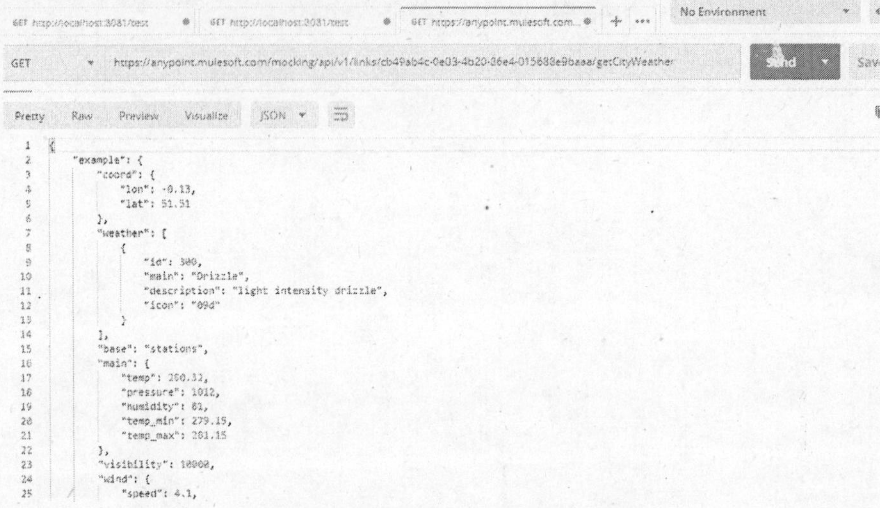


*Figure 9.17: Executing local API from Postman*

Call the mock API link from Postman as shown above:

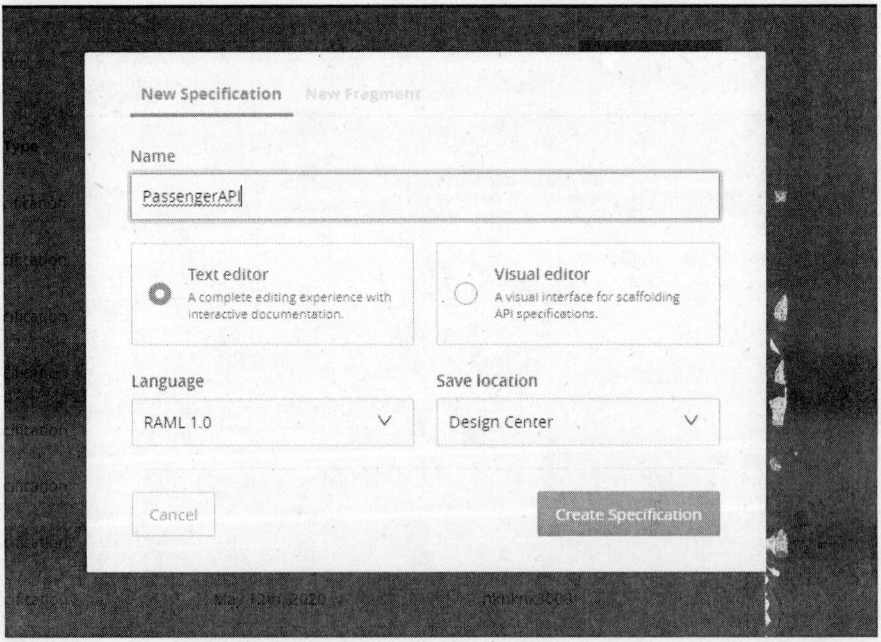

New Specification
New Fragment
Name
PassengerAPI
Text editor
A complete editing experience with interactive documentation.
Visual editor
A visual interface for scaffolding API specifications.
Language
RAML 1.0
Save location
Design Center
Cancel
Create Specification

*Figure 9.18: Making a meaningful REST API spec*

Make the samples more meaningful by giving domain-specific functional names:

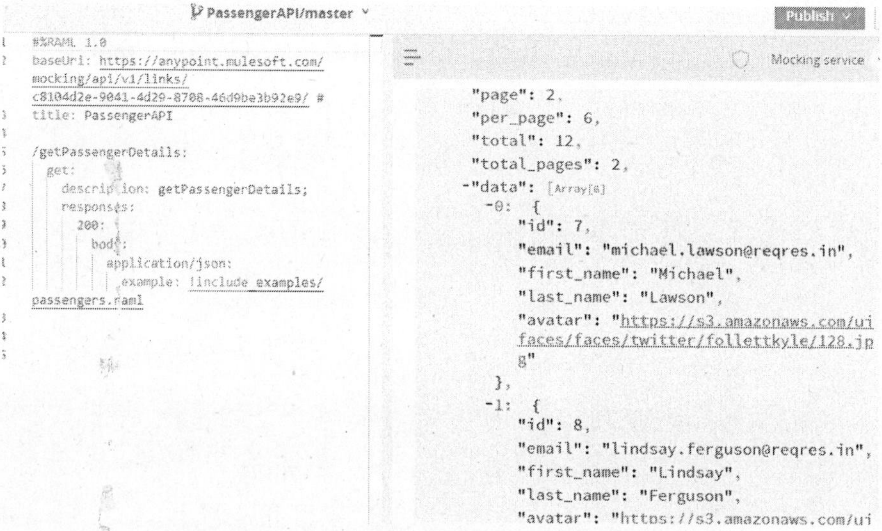

Figure 9.19: PassengerAPI and getPassengerDetails resource

Develop a passenger details API as shown above:

```
/getPassengerDetails:
  get:
    description: getPassengerDetails;
    queryParameters:
      conuntry:
        type: string
        displayName: Country
        description: Passenger Country
        example: India
        required:  false
      conuntryTravelling:
        type: string
        displayName: conuntry Travelling
        description: Passenger conuntry Travelling
        example: India
        required:  true
```

```
    responses:
      200:
        body:
          application/json:
            example: !include examples/passengers.raml
```

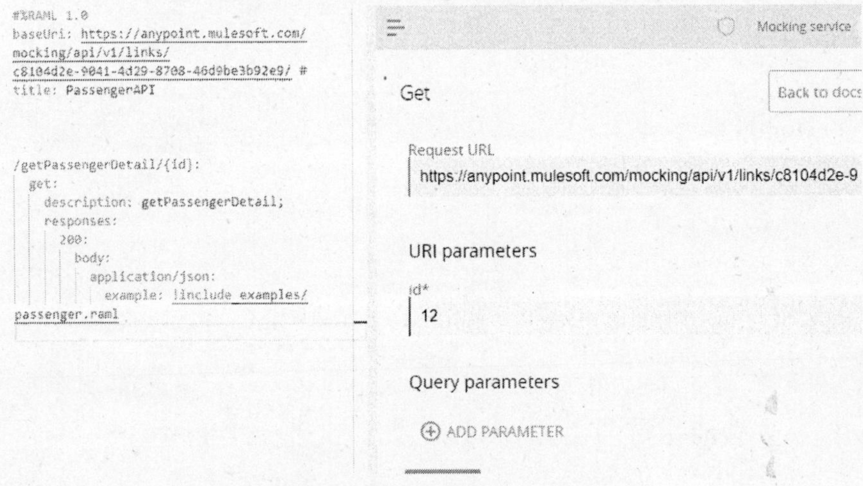


***Figure 9.20:** Executing getPassengerDetails*

Add the passenger details retrieving resource by passing an ID:

```
/getPassengerDetail/{id}:
  get:
    description: getPassengerDetail;
    responses:
      200:
        body:
          application/json:
            example: !include examples/passenger.raml
```

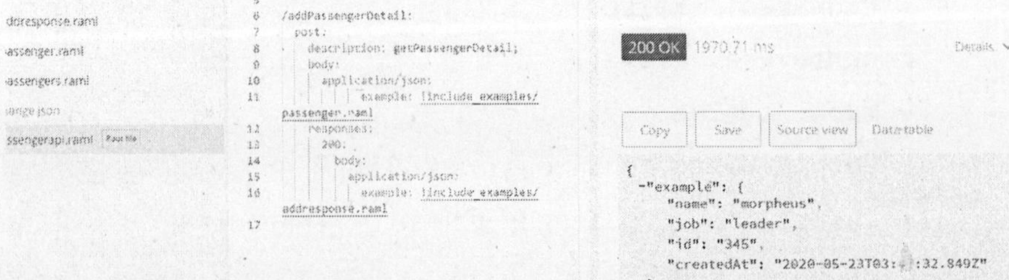


***Figure 9.21:** including examples and executing getPassengerDetails*

Add a passenger details creating resource using `POST` method:

```
/addPassengerDetail:
  post:
    description: getPassengerDetail;
    body:
      application/json:
            example: !include examples/passenger.raml
    responses:
      200:
        body:
          application/json:
            example: !include examples/addresponse.raml
```

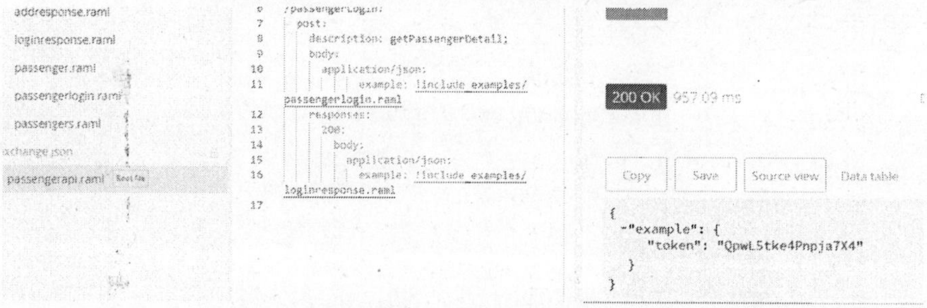

***Figure 9.22:*** *passengerLogin*

Add the passenger login resource as shown below:

```
/passengerLogin:
  post:
    description: getPassengerDetail;
    body:
      application/json:
            example: !include examples/passengerlogin.raml
    responses:
      200:
        body:
          application/json:
            example: !include examples/loginresponse.raml
```

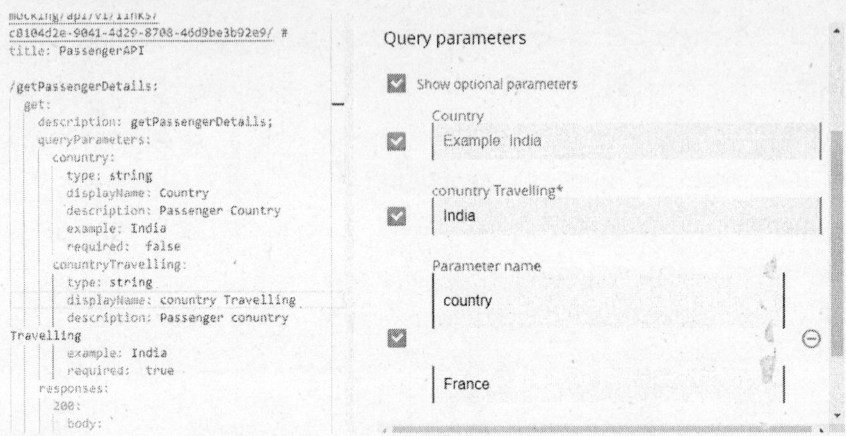


*Figure 9.23: passenger with the query parameter*

Add a get passenger detail resource to retrieve passenger details:

```
/getPassengerDetails:
  get:
    description: getPassengerDetails;
    queryParameters:
      conuntry:
        type: string
        displayName: Country
        description: Passenger Country
        example: India
        required:  false
      conuntryTravelling:
        type: string
        displayName: conuntry Travelling
        description: Passenger conuntry Travelling
        example: India
        required:  true
    responses:
      200:
        body:
          application/json:
            example: !include examples/passengers.raml
```

The above practice examples given and the public fake APIs and commercials APIs will be giving you some hands on experience for you to get comfort with the API usage scenarios.

# Understanding the raml.org sample projects

Now we will check the available sample projects given by **raml.org,** we can understand the real-time project structure; we can reuse the code snippets given by **raml.org** for our practice purpose:

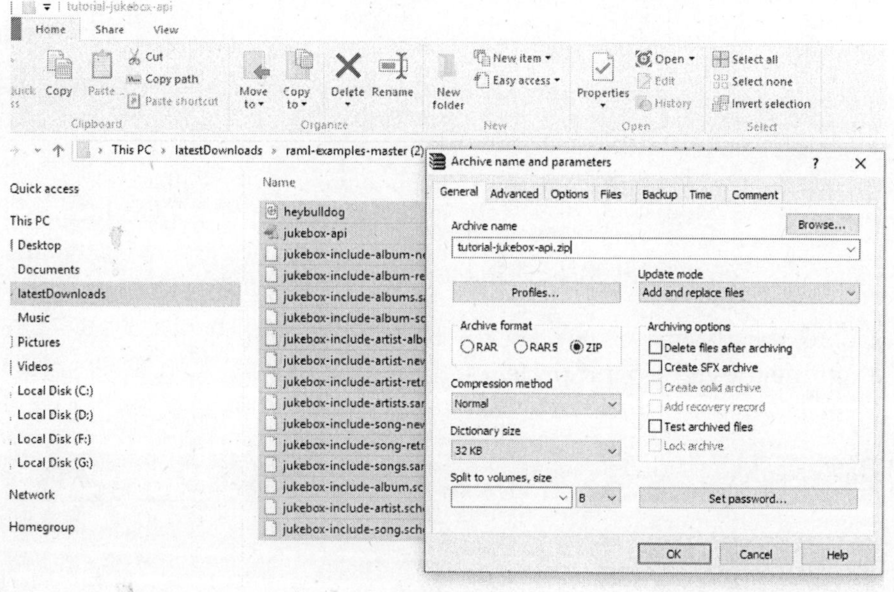


*Figure 9.24: Download RAML examples and ZIP jukebox example*

Practice Download the RAML examples master file from GitHub as we have seen in our earlier chapters, now, go to `\raml-examples-master\others\tutorial-jukebox-api` folder and ZIP it into a `.zip` file as shown above:

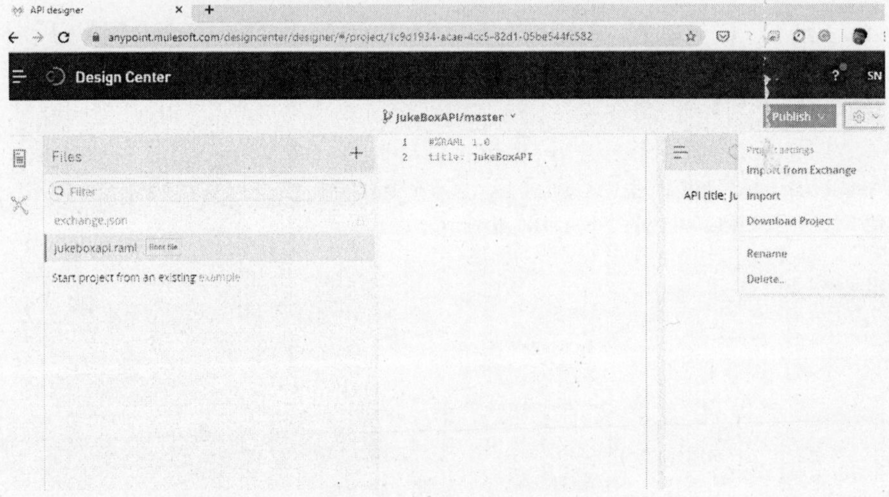


***Figure 9.25:*** *Import the ZIP file to Designer Project*

Go to the design center, create an API specification project, and examine the right-hand project setting tool:

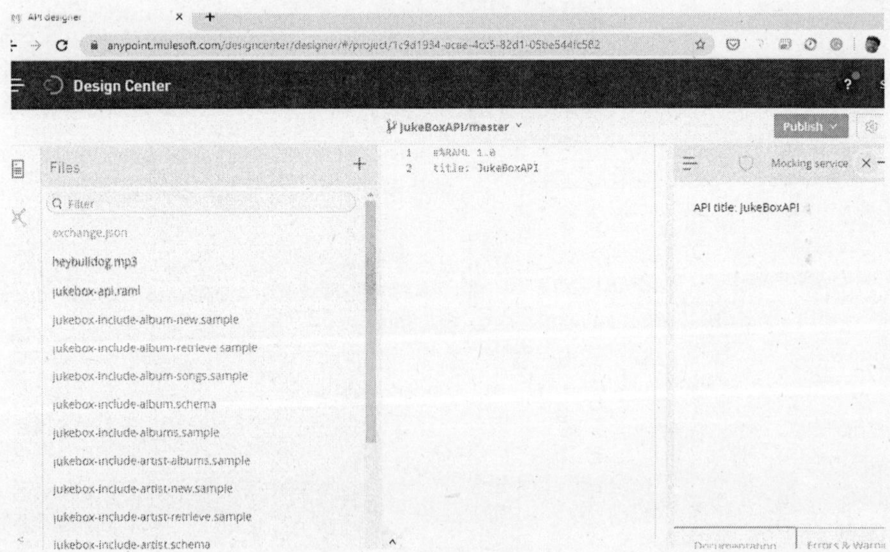


***Figure 9.26:*** *Import Result*

Choose the import menu item and import the ZIP file created in your local folder. The above screenshot shows you the result of importing the ZIP file:

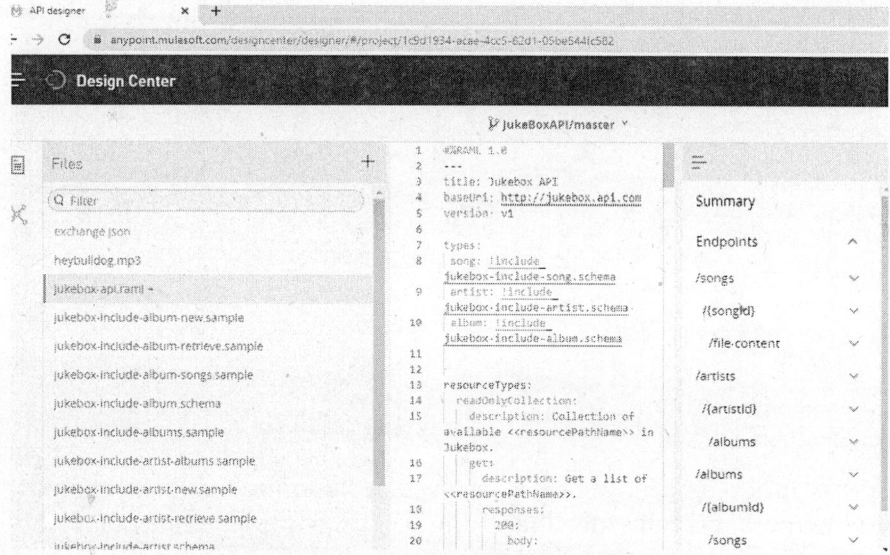

*Figure 9.27: Juke Box API RAML Inspection*

Examine the Jukebox API as shown above:

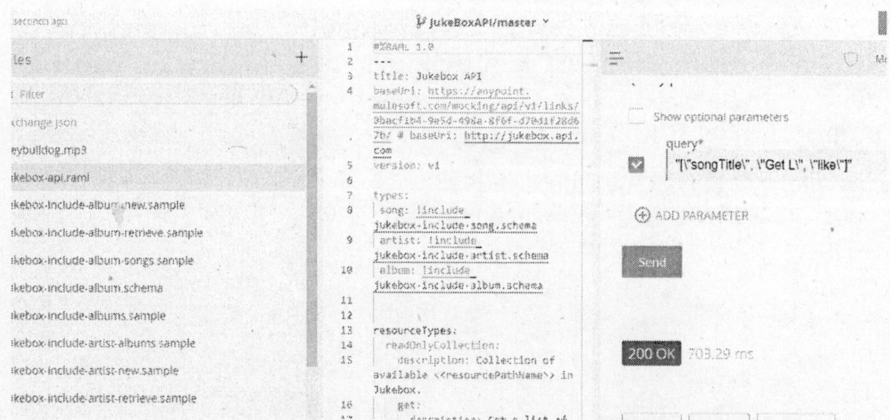

*Figure 9.28: Juke Box API RAML Execution*

Execute all endpoints as shown above:

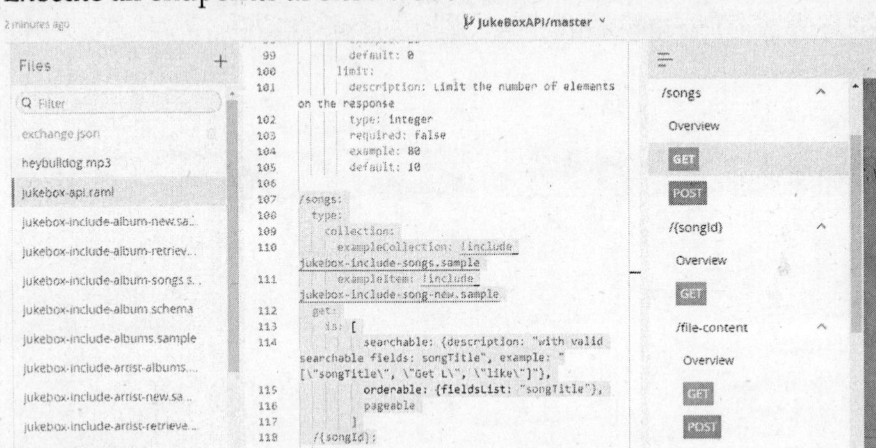

***Figure 9.29:*** *Exploring Songs resource*

Try to understand how the examples are handles, how the schemas are defined and referenced, and the resource implementation in the Jukebox API.

# Modifying existing projects

Now we will see how easily we can modify the existing project to meet our domain-based requirements, this is just a short cut to make your hands-on as quickly as possible and also to make you understand the simplicity of RAML language:

```
"albumId": "183100e3-0e2b-4404-a716-66104d440550",
"albumName": "Random Access Memories",
"year": "2013",
"imageURL": "http://upload.wikimedia.org/wikipedia/en/a/a7/Random_Access_Memories.jpg",
"genreCode": "ELE",
"artistId": "110e8300-e32b-41d4-a716-664400445500"
```

Replace
Find what: albumId
Replace with: BookID
Case sensitive
Whole word only
Regular expression
Support \U \L \E
Upward search
Wrap at the end of file
Continue to next file
Replace all range
Current file
Selection
All open files

***Figure 9.30:*** *Modifying Juke Box Source Files*

Use a text editor like *EditPlus* and open all the files from your jukebox folder as shown above. Now you can find and replace the keywords used in the projects to meet your domain needs. Find and replace all `albumIDs` to `BookID` if you want to develop a specification for *Book Selling Business:*

```
"BookID": "183103e3-0e2b-4404-a716-66104d440550",
"bookName": "Random Access Memories",
"year": "2013",
"genre": "Electric Funk",
"imageURL": "http://upload.wikimedia.org/wikipedia/en/a/a7/Random_Access_Memories.jpg",
"genre": {
  "countryCode": "ELE",
  "countryName": "Electronict"
},
"songs": [
  {
    "bookID": "550e8400-e29b-41d4-a716-446655440000",
    "bookName": "Get Lucky"
  },
  {
    "bookID": "550e8400-e29b-41d4-a716-446655440111",
    "bookName": "Loose yourself to dance"
  },
  {
    "bookID": "550e8400-e29b-41d4-a716-446655440222",
    "bookName": "Gio sorgio by Moroder"
  }
],
"artist": {
  "Author": "110e8300-e32b-41d4-a716-664400445500",
  "publisher": "Daft Punk",
  "imageURL": "http://travelhymns.com/wp-content/uploads/2013/06/random-access-memories1.jpg"
}
```

Replace
Find what: artistName
Replace with: publisher
Case sensitive
Whole word only
Regular expression
Support \U \L \E
Upward search
Wrap at the end
Continue to ne
Replace all range
Current file
Selection
All open f

***Figure 9.31:*** *Modifying Juke Box Source Files*

Try to check all the object data used in this project and modify it meaningfully:

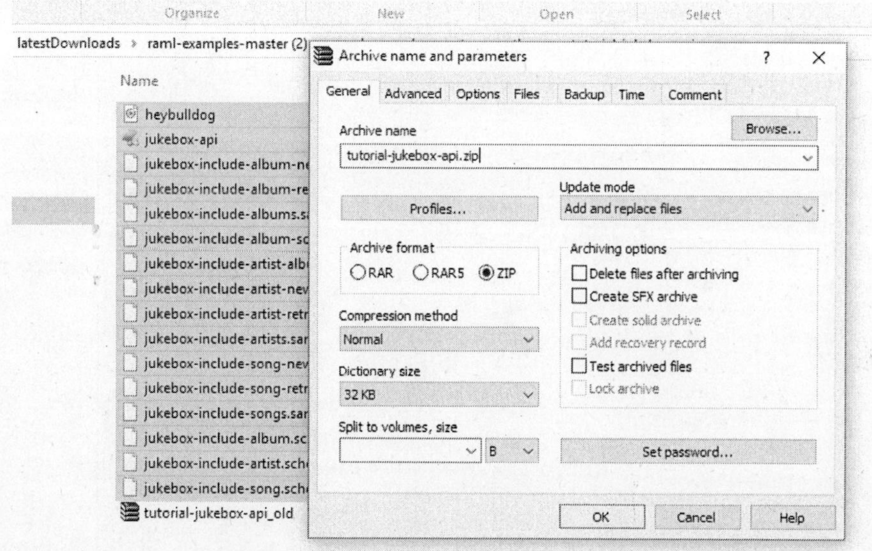


***Figure 9.32:*** *ZIP the modified source files*

Repeat the zipping steps as we did before:

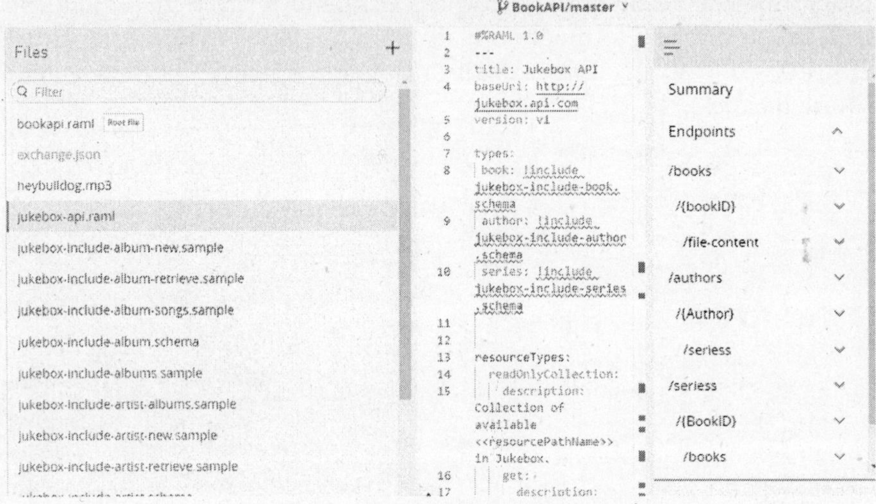

**Figure 9.33:** *import into BookAPI master*

Repeat importing the new ZIP file into a new project. You can notice some conflicts in file names reference:

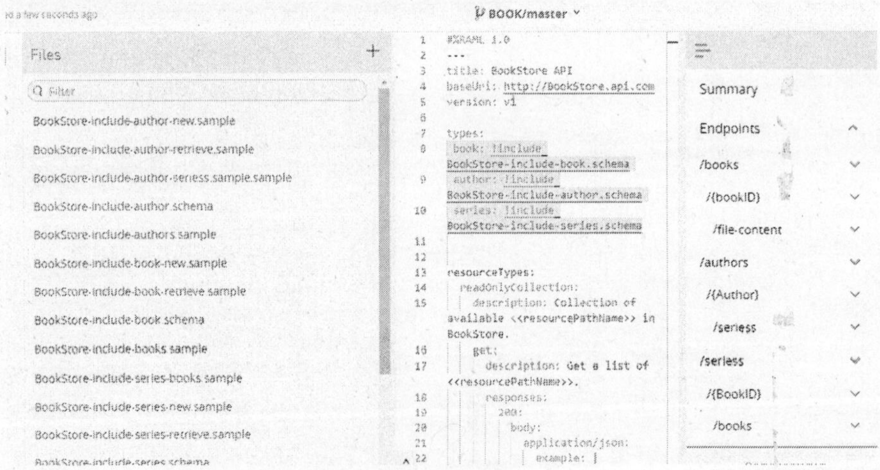

**Figure 9.34:** *Modify File names*

Resolve the file name conflicts as shown above:

```
Files
BookStore-include-book-retrieve.sample
BookStore-include-books.sample
BookStore-include-series-books.sample
BookStore-include-series-new.sample
BookStore-include-series-retrieve.sample
BookStore-include-seriess.sample
schema
BookStore-include-author.schema
BookStore-include-book.schema
BookStore-include-series.schema
book.raml  Root file
exchange.json
heybulldog.mp3

#%RAML 1.0
---
title: BookStore API
baseUri: http://BookStore.api.com
version: v1

types:
  book: !include schema/BookStore-include-book.schema
  author: !include schema/BookStore-include-author.schema
  series: !include schema/BookStore-include-series.schema


resourceTypes:
  readOnlyCollection:
    description: Collection of available <<resourcePathName>> in BookStore.
    get:
      description: Get a list of <<resourcePathName>>.
      responses:
        200:
          body:
            application/json:
              example: |

Summary
Endpoints
/books
/{bookID}
/file-content
/authors
/{Author}
/seriess
/seriess
/{BookID}
/books
```

*Figure 9.35: Result of Modified File names*

The source and file names modified specifications must look like above.

# Restructuring the project

Now we will restructure the project to match some of the RAML standards:

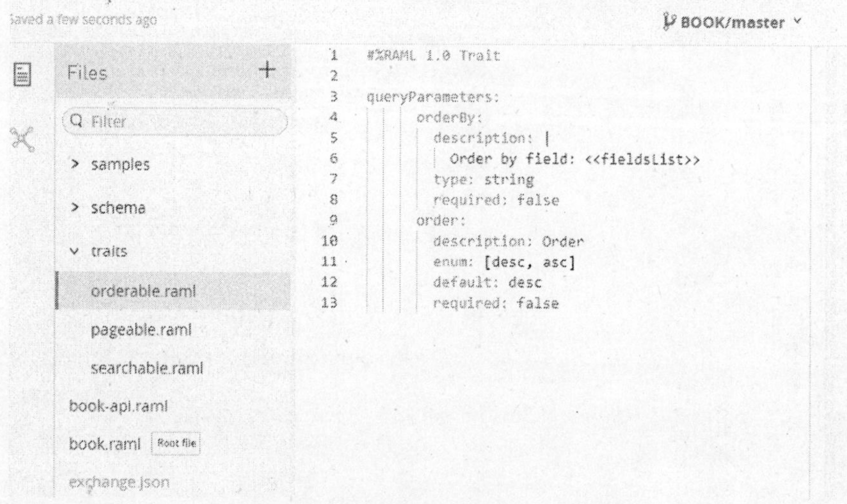


*Figure 9.36: Schema and Samples Folder*

We can have separate folders for schema, examples, resources, etc. The above screenshot shows the newly added folders and the `Orderable Trait` implementation:

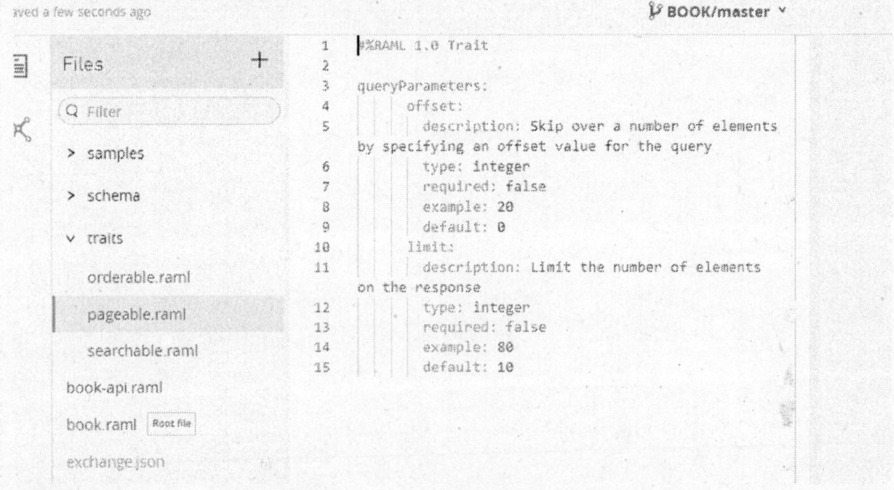


***Figure 9.37:** Traits folder - Pageable*

Implement the `pageable` trait as shown above:

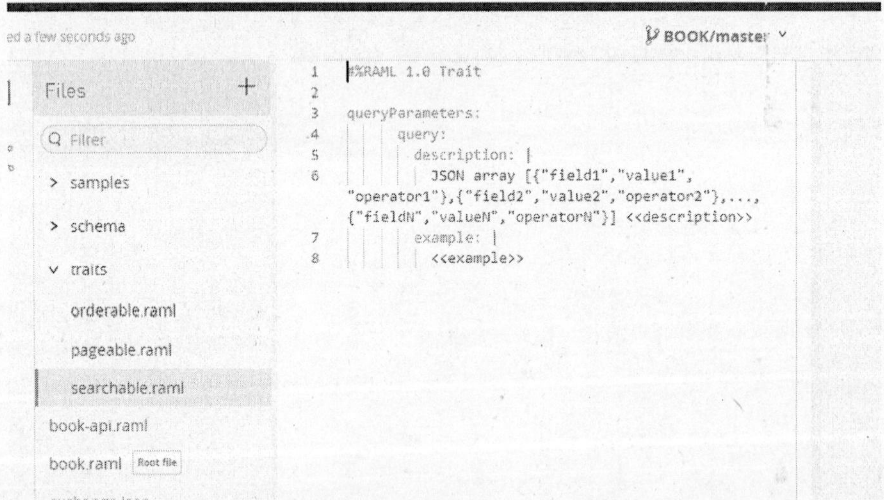


***Figure 9.38:** Traits folder - Searchable*

Implement the `Searchable` trait as shown above:

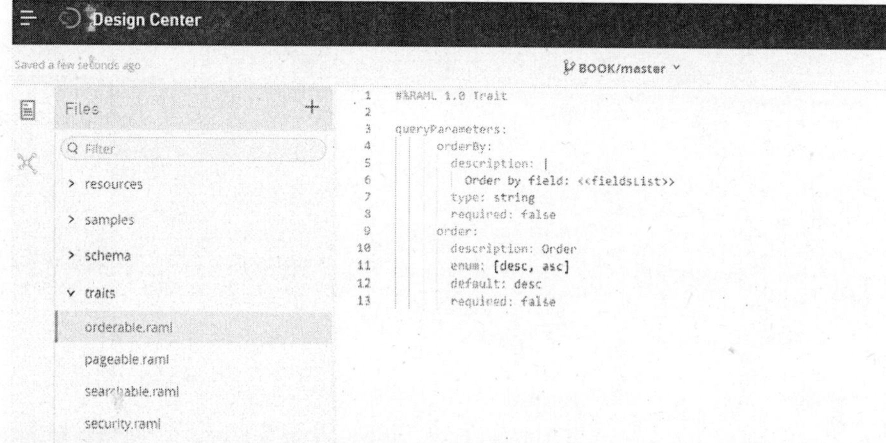


*Figure 9.39:* *Traits folder - Orderable*

Implement the `orderable` trait as shown above:

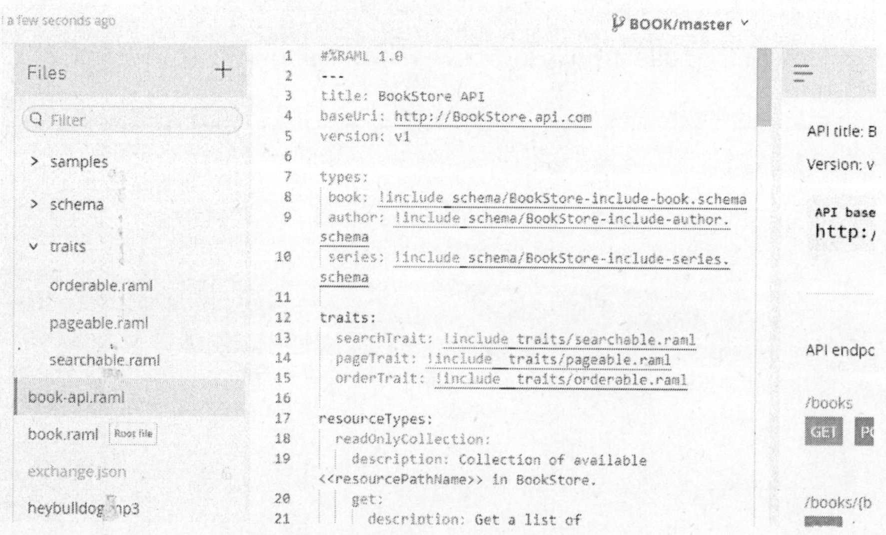


*Figure 9.40:* *BOOK API Traits Implemented*

After implementation the `BookAPI` must look like above:

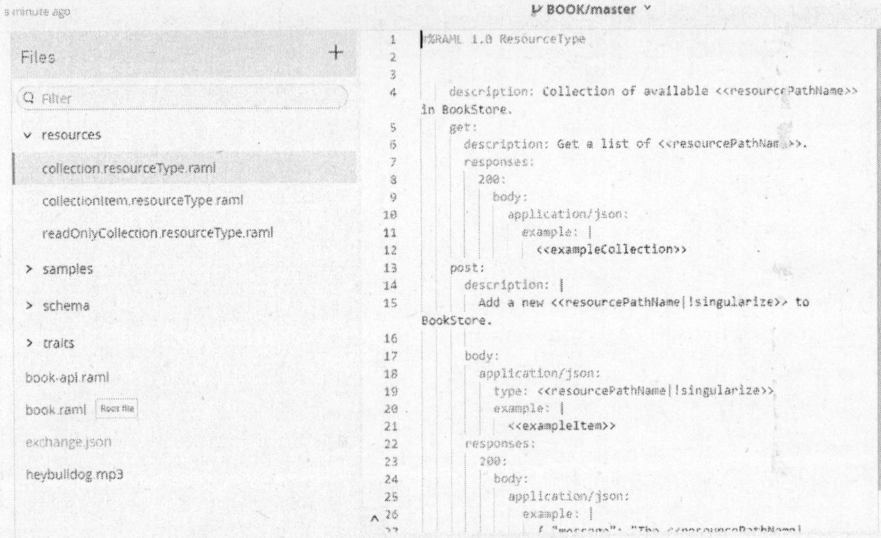

***Figure 9.41:*** *Resource Folder - Collection Resource*

Implement the collection resources as shown above in a new resources folder:

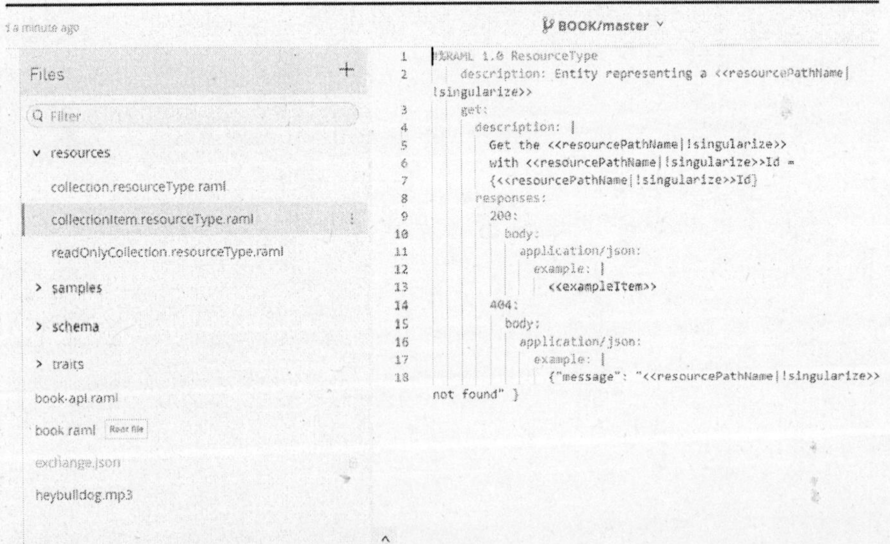

***Figure 9.42:*** *Resource Folder - CollectionItem Resource*

Implement the `collectionItem` resources as shown above:

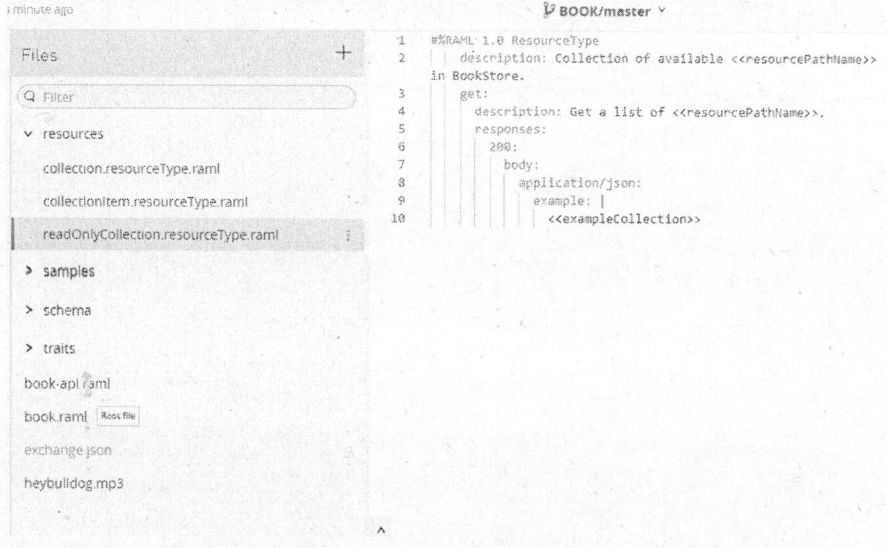


*Figure 9.43: Resource Folder - readOnlyCollection Resource*

Implement the `readOnlycollection` resources as shown above:

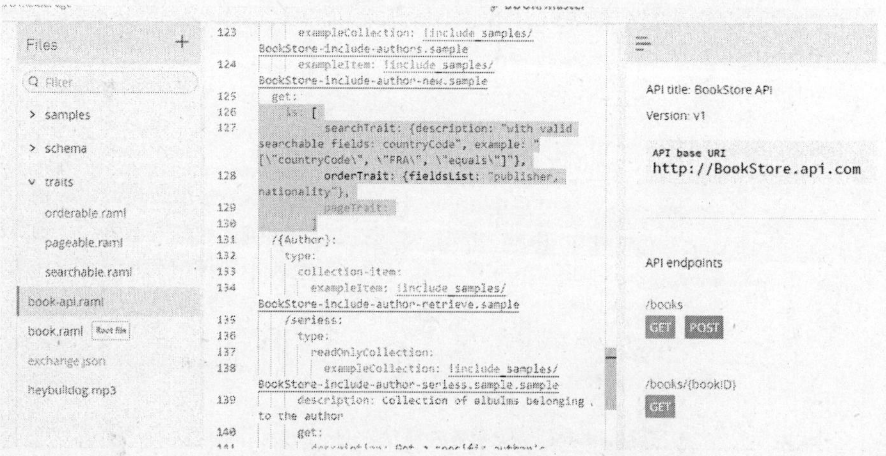


*Figure 9.44: Book API Resource Types Implemented*

After implementing all resources your API will be looking like this, have a look at get resource references and traits implementation:

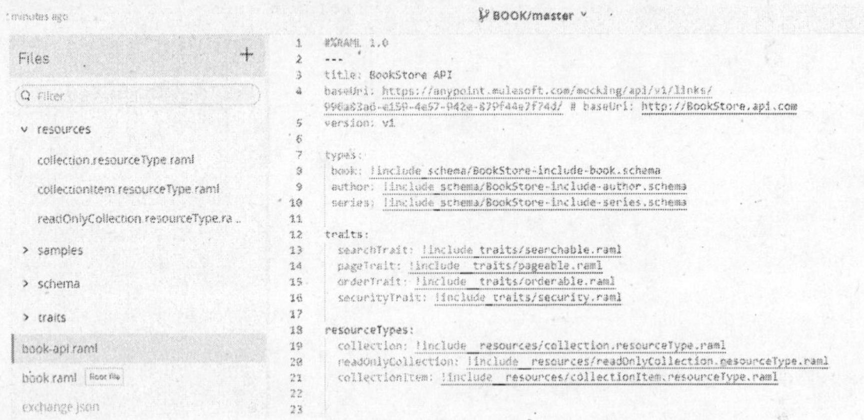

***Figure 9.45:*** *BookAPI RAML Final Look*

This is the final look of the new API specification created:

***Figure 9.46:*** *BookAPI RAML Final Execution*

Go ahead and execute the `BookAPI` RAML specification.

# Integrating with Anypoint Studio

Now we have to bring the API specifications inside the Anypoint Studio, this is mainly to check if the specifications are shared with a development team how this will look:

**Project Settings**
Create a Mule project in the workspace or in an external location.

Project Name: booktest

**Runtime**
Mule Server 4.3.0 EE

Install Runtimes

**API Implementation**
Add an API implementation to your project to automatically set up an APIkit router and create placeholder flows for each resource method

Import a published API | Import RAML from local file | Import from Design Center

Location:
https://anypoint.mulesoft.com/exchange/api/v1/organizations/f5993cfa-c12f-49d1-b71c-e93348c448ed/projects/76fcab99-b7d6-4628-afdd-4aa2c36ae47e/refs/master/

✓ You are importing the following API: BookStore API vv1 - base URI "https://anypoint.mulesoft.com/mocking/api/v1/links/996a83a6-e159-..."

⚠ You won't be able to stay in sync between Studio and Design Center. You can only manage your RAML files locally Learn how to stay in sync

☑ Scaffold flows from these API specifications

**Project location**
☑ Use default location

Finish | Cancel

*Figure 9.47: Import BOOKAPI into Anypoint Studio*

This is the dialogue after creating a new project and provide the credentials to access the Exchange then choosing our `BookAPI` RAML:

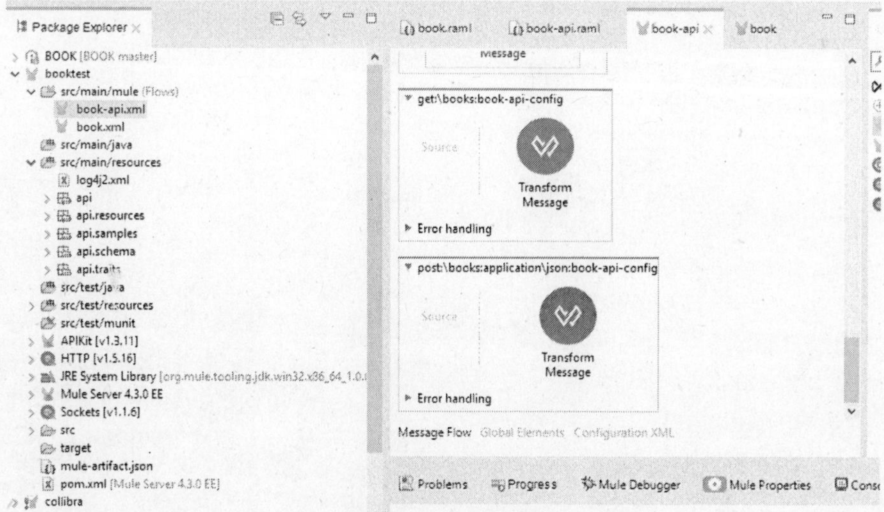


*Figure 9.48: Imported BOOKAPI*

The message flow and `APIKit` results after importing the API:

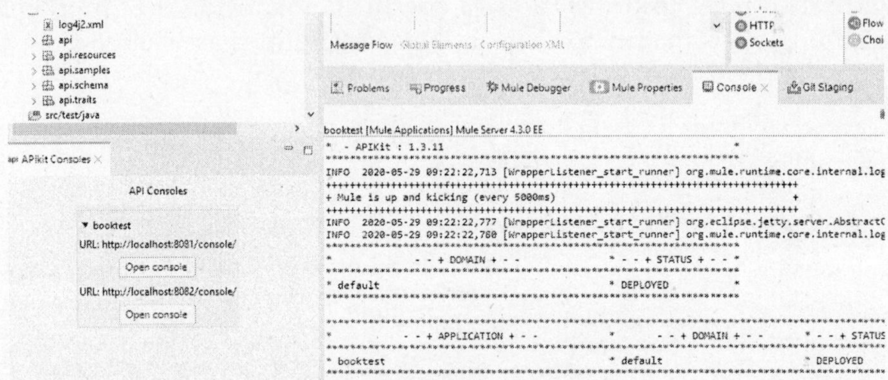


*Figure 9.49: BOOKAPI deployed*

Deploy the API and check the console output and `APIKit` console display:

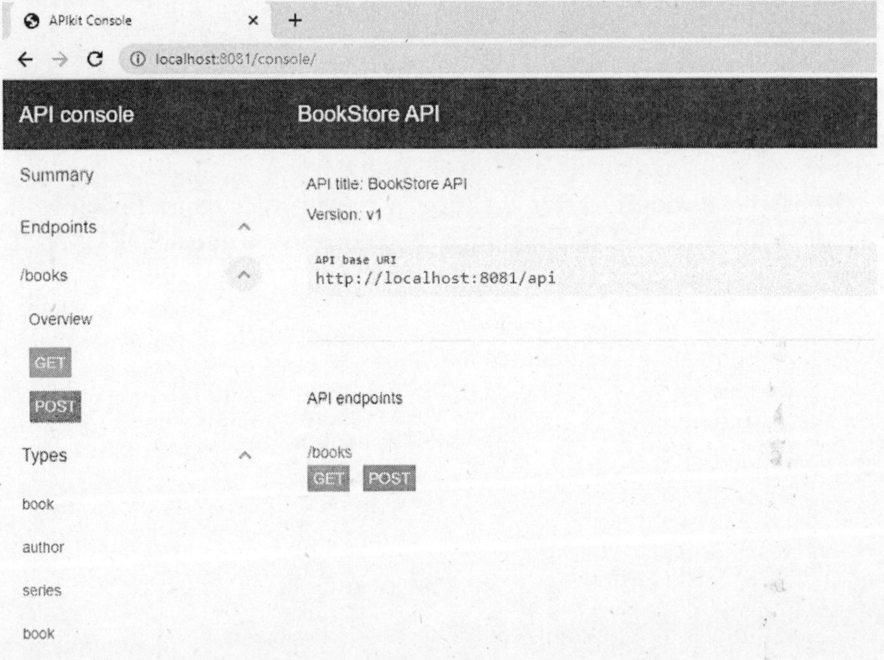


*Figure 9.50: BOOKAPI browser console*

Check the browser console as shown above:

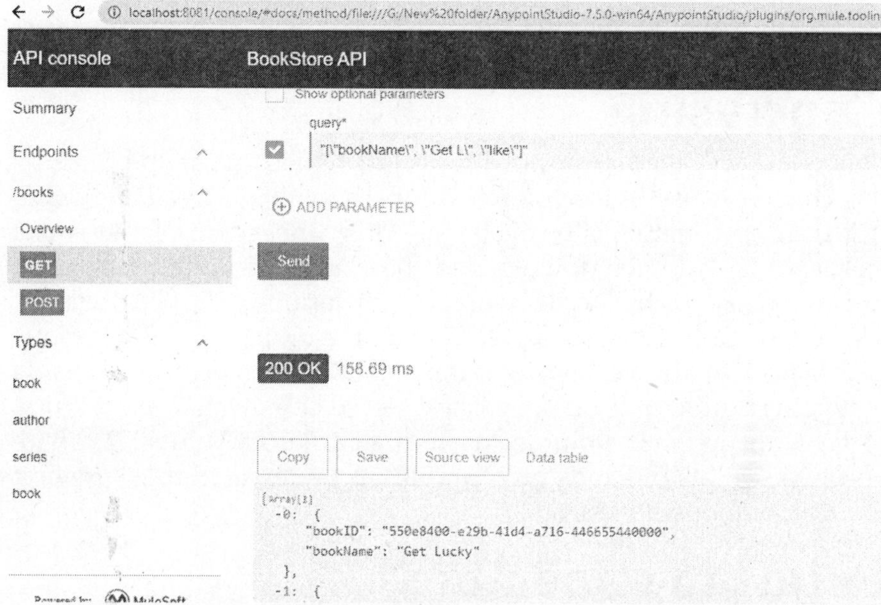


*Figure 9.51: BOOKAPI executed in the browser console*

Execute the endpoints:

*Figure 9.52: BOOKAPI executed in the browser console*

Execute the endpoints. This must be a logical endpoint for your RAML study and developing a RAML specification on your own by reusing the existing **raml.org** project codes.

# Conclusion

This is the last chapter of our Mastering Mulesoft Volume 1, Hope this chapter is useful for you to explore the publicly available demo REST APIs, commercially available APIs, and some of the social media APIs. We have downloaded the example bundle from raml.org and inspected the implementations of various API specifications. We understood how to reuse, restructure the project, and test various endpoints. Finally, we have integrated the RAML specification inside Anypoint Studio and deployed and tested it as well. We are good to go with our next volume Mastering Mulesoft Volume 2 where you will see lots of hands-on examples to understand the Anypoint Studio Components. Cheers.

# Points to remember

- This chapter does not require any technical prerequisites, anybody from any business domain can practice API designing using API designer, Anypoint Studio, and Console.
- This chapter demands you to focus more on Designing API Specifications rather than coding some implementations as an API designer.
- We also emphasize that as an API Designer you can take care of the entire ownership of API specifications and developers cannot modify the endpoint point specifications willingly or by mistake.

# Key terms to explore

- RAML
- CRUD/Transactions
- Roles
- Designer
- Exchange
- Studio
- Console
- Publish

# Index